THE
FREEDOM
SCALE

JAKE MORRETT

DEFIANCE PRESS
& PUBLISHING

The Freedom Scale

Copyright © 2024 by Jake Morrett
(Defiance Press & Publishing, LLC)

First Edition: 2024

Printed in the United States of America

10 9 8 7 6 5 4 3 2 1

All rights reserved. No part of this publication may be reproduced, distributed, or transmitted in any form or by any means, including photocopying, recording, or other electronic or mechanical methods, without the prior written permission of the publisher, except in the case of brief quotations embodied in critical reviews and certain other noncommercial uses permitted by copyright law.

This book is a work of non-fiction. The author has made every effort to ensure that the accuracy of the information in this book was correct at the time of the publication. Neither the author nor the publisher nor any other person(s) associated with this book may be held liable for any damages that may result from any of the ideas made by the author in this book.

DEFIANCE PRESS
& PUBLISHING

ISBN-13: 978-1-963102-57-4 (Paperback)
ISBN-13: 978-1-963102-56-7 (ebook)
ISBN-13: 978-1-963102-58-1 (Hardcover)

Published by Defiance Press & Publishing, LLC

Bulk orders of this book may be obtained by contacting Defiance Press & Publishing, LLC. www.defiancepress.com.

Public Relations Dept. – Defiance Press & Publishing, LLC
281-581-9300
pr@defiancepress.com

Defiance Press & Publishing, LLC
281-581-9300
info@defiancepress.com

Dedication

For my grandfather, James Albert Morrett Jr., a wise man from an earlier generation who taught me the value of freedom.

And

For my daughter, Adelia Eve, who will have to carry on the fight for freedom of future generations.

Contents

Introduction ... 5

I. Defining Freedom for Everyone

1. The Two Extremes ... 11
2. Building the Freedom Scale ... 17
3. Individual Requirements for Freedom ... 26
4. Societal Requirements for Freedom ... 37
5. Requirements for Retaining Freedom ... 56
6. Controlling Freedoms ... 68

II. Controlling the Tool that Allows Us to Trade: Money

7. Capitalism vs. Socialism ... 76
8. Income Taxes and Inflation ... 91
9. Business Regulations ... 108
10. Something for Nothing ... 119
11. Minimum Wage/ Living Wage ... 125
12. Unions ... 145
13. Afterthought on Taxes ... 151
14. Freedom in Retirement ... 158

III. The Keys to Controlling a Free Society

15. Speech and Expression ... 166
16. Elections ... 208
17. Gun Control ... 263
18. Healthcare ... 291
19. Education ... 310

IV. Deciding Where You Stand

20. Republicans or Democrats in Pursuit of Freedom? ... 336
21. ...Do You Support Real Freedom? ... 342
22. The Resolve for Freedom ... 351

Introduction

Hello good reader and thank you for your interest in my book. Just as an early heads up, know this will not read like your typical political book. I'm not big on bibliographies. I write in a way for people to be able to easily find online any facts I mention, if they choose to research what I said further. If I can find it, so can other people. I'm not a lawyer, an economist, or anyone involved professionally in politics. I'm your average, blue-collar guy, working an average blue-collar job. My degree is obviously not in writing or political science; I just want to live my life in peace with freedom.

I don't have time for B.S. I call it as I see it in the most upfront and honest way, I know in support of freedom for everyone, through common sense, logic, and most importantly by asking the questions many are afraid to ask these days. Religion doesn't play a factor when I discuss politics. I believe if religion is needed to make an argument, then that argument is already lost, as any religion is a matter of faith.

Sadly, politics these days is so highly partisan, freedom has almost become a hollow catchphrase in pursuit of what someone's political party wants. Too few people look at the impact of their party's actions on individual freedom for everyone, opting instead to focus on making sure their party wins.

I will tell you right now: I am a registered Republican, but like many in the party, I am not part of the religious right, and I hold a great many views that are considered Libertarian.

This means I don't share all the views traditionally associated with being Republican. I base my views through the lens of individual freedom instead of party politics, as I am sure many less vocal Independents and Republicans do. As such, I am able to maintain my skepticism of people from every political party.

With the exception of a few individuals, I am highly disappointed with the Republican Party in elected office as a whole in regard to promoting individual freedom. They are often too willing to compromise or be a part of increasing government power at the expense of individual freedom. Unfortunately, the Democrat Party is far worse in supporting individual freedom as I will explain.

I didn't arrive at my views overnight. They developed over many years, primarily after a conversation with my grandfather. The result was a unique and in-depth look at a wide variety of aspects regarding individual freedom for every American. This book is not based on any study, or any government or group standard I am aware of that measures freedom. It took years to look at and understand everything needed for freedom; how to define it for everyone; what allows the most individual freedom for everyone and to finally pinpoint the issues that most impact what I refer to as *controlling freedoms*.

I don't expect everyone to convert to my way of thinking about everything I wrote. It would be a very boring world if we agreed on everything, but I want to present a fresh perspective when we look at freedom.

I have three goals with this book. The first is to make you think; not just about the right questions to ask, but to look at what is *not* said. The second is to be an eye-opener for people reading this book, especially those that take their individual freedom for granted, and realize the danger freedom faces. Finally, it is my most sincere hope that you, the reader, will take an honest look at how you personally value freedom, not just for yourself, but for everyone else in the United States. Where you go from there is up to you.

I. Defining Freedom for Everyone

"For to be free is not merely to cast off one's own chains, but to live in a way that respects and enhances the freedom of others."
– Nelson Mandela

1. The Two Extremes

Freedom

1. the quality or state of being free: such as
a: the absence of necessity, coercion, or constraint in choice or action
b: liberation from slavery or restraint or from the power of another: INDEPENDENCE
c: the quality or state of being exempt or released usually from something onerous

2 a: political right

These are the main definitions of freedom according to Webster's online dictionary. It is argued that freedom is the single greatest principle the United States was founded on. It is why every member of our armed forces raises their right hand and swears to support and defend the Constitution with their life and without reservation. While there are some that merely do it for the benefits of being in the military, a large number do it because they believe in the freedom this country is supposed to truly represent.

How many of you have ever stopped and asked yourself, what does it truly mean to be free, and what does freedom mean to most people? In my experience, outside the military, many people on both sides have a narrow view of freedom. Those people only want freedom when it comes to issues that either they personally care about or their political party cares about. They also often mistake freedom with *free stuff* provided at taxpayer expense. Most of those people would gladly sacrifice the freedom of others if it benefited them, made them feel good, or is in line with their beliefs.

Around thirty years ago my grandfather explained freedom to me in the most basic sense. I had just gotten my first job and was excited to be getting a paycheck for the first time. His explanation focused on *my paycheck*, and the *taxes taken out*.

He included more than the basic talk we have heard about taxes. His talk included the two extremes as he referred to them. He did this by first asking me what the society we live in would be like if no taxes were taken out.

In theory, if there were no taxes, everyone would keep their entire paycheck. However, there would also be no government to ensure you were paid your agreed upon salary by your employer, or that you were even paid at all. Without any system of government in place to protect individual rights, people could be forced into slavery by those who are stronger. They could be extorted by those who are stronger to buy or produce certain goods or services. We would be a lawless society, where the strong prey upon the weak, taking by force what they want, when they want, and from whom they want in any manner they can get away with. The only place the strong would draw the line is at trying that on those who can more easily protect themselves and what they have. There is always someone bigger and stronger.

1. The Two Extremes

> *"Give me your shit, or I will kill you."*
> *– Neagan, The Walking Dead*

Anyone who has watched, The Walking Dead since the character Neagan was introduced, will instantly understand the quote above. For those unfamiliar; Neagan was the leader of a group of people called The Saviors in a zombie-ravaged world. They would extort through force and intimidation, food and supplies from other communities of survivors. They had the superior numbers and firepower to back up their threats. No Pop culture reference better describes anarchy, which is of course the first extreme my grandfather was talking about.

He then flipped the conversation around and asked me what kind of society we would have if the government took 100 percent of every paycheck we worked for and provided for everyone only what they felt everyone needed. We would have no say in this society. We would have no choice. In this extreme, the government knows what is best for everyone, and everyone must abide by their decisions. Those who do not will suffer the consequences for their disobedience. As I'm sure you have already guessed, the other extreme is slavery.

It can be argued that the less freedom you have, the more security you have. After all, prison inmates live in a secure environment; their meals, beds, and clothing, as well as all other necessities of life are provided for them. Yet they live as dictated by the penal system, with very few choices made by themselves. Now prison is far from a paradise or even safe, so I must ask: Would you give up your freedom and live as it is dictated without question by an outside force in order to live in a utopia with world peace, no world hunger, and no crime? Say for a moment it was possible to get all of that in exchange for every bit of individual freedom in the world; would you take that offer?

If your answer was yes, you are either a fool that wasn't paying attention, or you want to be a slave. I say this for two reasons. First, without freedom, what is offered may look more like a nightmare than paradise, depending on whether you are the master or the slave. The promise of security is only valid with strict compliance. Imagine what can be done for noncompliance to follow through on the promises of security in that utopia.

The second reason is that the security gained is only an illusion. It is an illusion, because everything is provided. You are not responsible for your life and thus must be provided for. The provider(s) in that utopia becomes the slave master(s). What a slave master can provide in security, he can also take away on a whim if it better suits his purpose. If it becomes more beneficial for the slave master to take away some of that security for whatever reason (like, say to gain compliance), what is to stop him from doing so? History has shown us time and again that those speaking out against such behavior usually face harsh consequences, when they are even mentioned, and not just erased from history.

To summarize, we have anarchy in a society when there is no government to make and enforce laws guarding against encroachment of liberty. Without such laws and the ability to enforce them, people could murder, rape, steal, or even enslave without fear of consequences from a governing authority and

1. The Two Extremes

would only have to concern themselves with the response from someone stronger that wants what they have. Slavery in society begins when a nation will not or cannot fight to preserve its freedom either from foreign powers who would take it by force or from domestic powers who would subvert it from within.

Do you see the main similarity between slavery and anarchy? The strong prey on the weak through force. Whether it is (A) a mob forcefully taking what they want from those who are weaker or (B) anyone with legal power usurping freedom for their own gains. It doesn't matter which it is. In both cases, people will be conquered by those who will do so for their own benefit by whatever means they feel they can get away with. The identity of the slave master is the only difference in the end result of each extreme on the scale. One is a government and the other is a group of strong, lawless tyrants.

My grandfather pointed out this irony in our conversation by saying that the only two things for certain in life are death and taxes. Even in a world without an official government, property is still taken from one group of people by the ruling authority. That saying about death and taxes would later hold more irony because my grandfather died many years ago on April 15 (Tax Day).

He and I concluded our conversation by discussing what the appropriate tax levels should be to provide the maximum amount of freedom to everyone. The question comes down to: Where does the happy median lie? We agreed that to attain the maximum amount of personal and economic freedom for everyone and to raise enough tax revenue to provide a functioning government, would be to follow the business model. This model is the same whether you are a business owner or a consumer. Get as much as you can for the lowest possible cost, which in this case would be taxing enough to collect the most revenue for basic government functions with the least amount of discouragement in investing or spending.

The Laffer curve, something created in the 1980s by John Laffer, during the Reagan administration, is the perfect example. If you tax people too much, they hoard their money and are reluctant to spend to expand their businesses or to start a new one. Tax too little, and the government doesn't collect enough revenue to pay for the most basic necessities. The key, like everything in life, is finding the proper balance.

This conversation with my grandfather also got me thinking about the bigger picture. The scale of freedom he described with the extremes being slavery and anarchy, applies to not only economic issues, but every political issue one could think of. This leads us to ask a big question about every political issue. How much freedom do you want not only for yourself, but for society? Before going further, we must build the Freedom Scale and apply it in a fair and equal manner for every individual. It must be applied on an individual level to ensure there are no abuses or favoritism.

Be advised: My analysis will only look at the rights of Americans and those living in this country *legally* when discussing the issues of the Freedom Scale. Sorry if this upsets anyone, but we need a universal standard for everyone included and citizenship or legal residency is one of those standards.

2. Building the Freedom Scale

Anyone doing an online search will find a number of graphs showing their interpretation of various political spectrums. Some are similar to mine. Some have even called it the Freedom Scale as well. Let me briefly discuss their take on this subject before going into my own.

On February 27, 2013, Glenn Beck created his own Freedom Scale on his show, which may be where I got the name for this book from, though I don't remember Freedom Scale being on his whiteboard when I watched it all those years ago. Maybe it stuck with me on a sub-conscience level, otherwise I probably would have picked a different name for this book. I remember watching that episode thinking back to that conversation with my grandfather so many years earlier. The extreme sides of Mr. Beck's Freedom Scale were anarchy and authoritarianism. He goes in depth with various politicians, political figures and news networks, trying to figure out where they belong on the scale, making a number of good points, but I think he over-complicated his Freedom Scale on his show trying to figure it out.

Anyone who wants to watch Mr. Beck's take on the Freedom Scale, can find it at the web address below.

https://archive.org/details/rth_25631957_1200K

In an article dated April 17, 2013, for *The Libertarian* written by Joe Bentley, titled 'The Freedom Scale: redefining left and right', we will see a take on the Freedom Scale similarly to Mr. Beck. His argument on economic and social slavery regarding Republicans and Democrats is fascinating, but is irrelevant to my argument.

Anyone who wants to read Mr. Bentley's article, can find it at the following web address.

https://www.the-libertarian.co.uk/the-freedom-scale-redefining-left-and-right/

Further discussion at the bottom of the web page containing Mr. Bentley's article suggests that this is something that has been discussed from various perspectives, including how the scale is presented.

Both Glenn Beck's show and Joe Bentley's article have elements you will find I have already discussed in this book. Mr. Beck discusses the need for minimal government being necessary for freedom. Mr. Bentley's article describes the same taxation litmus test I told you my grandfather explained to me decades earlier. I considered adding where different political ideologies would go on my scale, and making an in-depth argument about political parties specifically. Then I thought about how simple the concept of The Freedom Scale really is. There are two sides, and at each end, we have a horrible extreme that essentially goes to the same place. We have to decide on the proper balance of freedom between those extremes. While I will discuss political parties and ideologies in this book, there is no need for me to assign them a place on my Freedom Scale. Their actions and words make their place on the Freedom Scale obvious, as I will soon highlight.

2. Building the Freedom Scale

I have not heard of anyone else addressing or expanding on the idea of the Freedom Scale since these two examples from 2013. I am a bit disappointed, as this is an issue far more important than I think either Mr. Bently or Mr. Beck realized. Let me slow down before I get ahead of myself.

With my criteria for who is included established, it is time to show you the Freedom Scale in the simplest and most unbiased form. We have already established there are extremes on each side—slavery and anarchy. Maximum sustainable freedom is listed on the scale a few steps before anarchy and is as far as one can go before the scale slides into anarchy.

The middle ground one would think is for moderates. I consider the middle ground on the Freedom Scale to be for fence straddlers, rather than people who share both Republican and Democrat views. It is an area for people who want freedom in certain areas, but also want the government to take care of them and everyone else to a degree. It comes down to a question of how much you value liberty over largesse. The scale tips very easily, very quickly from one side to the other, so it is important to be mindful of what control and how much control you are willing to give the government. Nobody wants to find themselves in a place they can't come back from.

Everything on the slavery side will be referred to as oppression—referring to government or mob oppression. Everything on the freedom side will be referred to as liberty or freedom, as anarchy is only reached when the government is no longer able to protect its freedoms.

The Freedom Scale

Graph A.

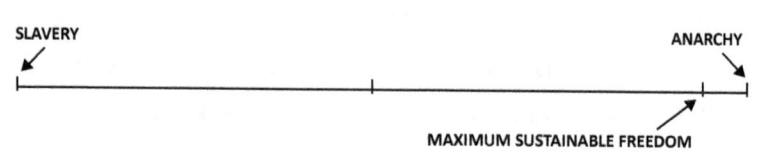

SLAVERY — ANARCHY

MAXIMUM SUSTAINABLE FREEDOM

Graph A. is the Freedom Scale from end to end in its simplest form. Moving from one end to the other in a straight line however, does not represent reality. Like love, freedom is not easy. It is something that takes effort, sacrifice and hard work to not only achieve, but to keep. Many claim to be supporters of freedom, but their actions can easily prove otherwise. Let's hit the Freedom Scale with a cold dose of reality, by looking at it as a journey from slavery to anarchy using Graph B.

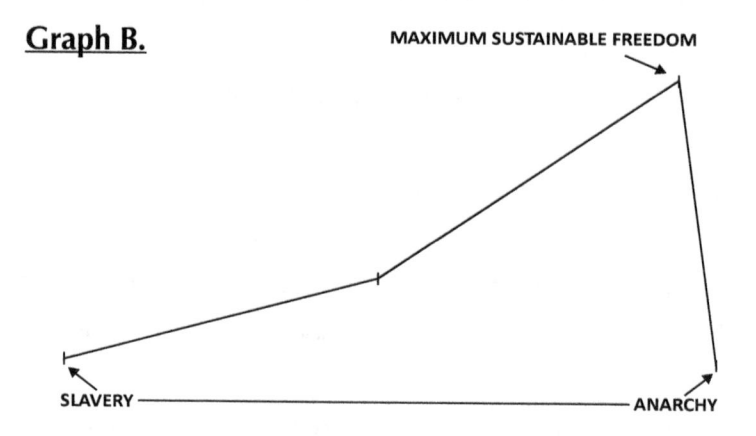

Graph B.

MAXIMUM SUSTAINABLE FREEDOM

SLAVERY ——— ANARCHY

Graph B. looks like a very good day on the stock or crypto market, followed by a bull run, and finally a crash. Unfortunately, taking human nature into account, balancing freedom is always slanted like this, rather than a straight line across. This is because so many politicians usually have their thumb on the scale by constantly trying to take as much power as they can. The more power and control citizens allow them to take, the less power and control those citizens have over their own lives, making the climb to maximum sustainable freedom all the more difficult. The ultimate goal for the most power-hungry politicians is to get to a point where the citizens have neither the ability nor the will to stop them, allowing them to create a society of slaves serving the government they represent. It can be said that would be the same goal for lawless tyrants under anarchy. This is why each extreme is shown on the same level in Graph B. The end result for each extreme is the same—a complete lack of freedom for society. The only thing keeping us from sliding all the way down to slavery is what citizens will tolerate politicians to do and their ability to remove such politicians.

This behavior has been the norm for much of human history. No country has gotten close to maximum sustainable freedom because power is what most concerns histories' rulers. The closest humans have ever gotten to maximum sustainable freedom is ironically that shining city on the hill that we call the United States.

The creation of the United States of America was the exception, placing a high value on individual freedom, and limited government which allows significant progress beyond the middle ground. Even though it wasn't a perfect system for everyone, it was a start. To be perfect for all doesn't mean tearing down the entire system and rebuilding it. That perfection involves the removal of hypocrisy, ensuring that what is written into law is practiced, and is applied to every individual in a manner that equally respects individual rights.

The Freedom Scale

This takes us to the next step in building the Freedom Scale. We need to clearly define aspects of what constitutes freedom for everyone, regardless of the issue. While the requirements for individual freedom are the main focus, the aspects of freedom in society and between two or more individuals must be addressed as well.

To qualify as freedom on an individual basis, the government and its laws cannot infringe on *any* individual's life, liberty, or property through force without due process of law, or by fraud. This includes deceit by and threat of force from the government, whether direct or implied. A person is free to do whatever they want so long as they do not cross this line with someone else.

Let's break that down a little further.

A main point of Frederic Bastiat's *"The Law"*, describes the role of the government and the laws it creates. The government and its laws must protect everyone's individual freedom by pursuing punishment against people that infringe on the life, liberty, and property of its individual citizens through force or fraud. In essence the role of the government in a free society is that of an impartial referee. Laws that protect people from rape and murder, for example, protect people from an infringement of their life, liberty, and property through the consequences of a conviction in a trial.

To qualify as freedom between two or more people, there must be mutual and informed consent of both parties. An example would be: You go to the store to buy a loaf of bread. You see the store's advertised price and agree to pay the store that amount in exchange for the loaf of bread. If you don't like the

2. Building the Freedom Scale

price, you go somewhere else.

Identifying what qualifies as freedom between two or more people is not just between private citizens. It must especially apply to government as government has the power of legal force behind it. In a purely free society, the government would only tax enough to provide for the most basic necessities in society, as well as to pass and enforce only enough laws to safeguard the individual freedom of its citizens—no more, no less. No such nation exists. Some politician is always trying to force what they feel is best on society regardless of how it impacts freedom, which is why we will look at the most important freedom topics allowing you to see how much you value freedom. That is in later chapters, though. One step at a time.

The next step is looking specifically at: What qualifies as an infringement of life, liberty, or property through force or fraud. Borrowing from the wording of the Nuremburg Code, for any arrangement or contract between two or more people to be on the liberty side, it must be a choice made between two or more informed, consenting adults without the intervention of any element of force, fraud, deceit, duress, or other ulterior form of constraint or coercion. This would cover a situation like the government twisting the arm of an employer with questionable mandates to ensure they get compliance from both the employer and employee. Non-compliance may mean loss of employment for the employee, and heavy fines, forced closure, or possible loss of the business for the employer in this situation.

What about laws governing various aspects of our lives such as public utilities? Isn't that a violation of our freedom?

The Freedom Scale

That is a good and interesting question. I remember a debate I once had where a person tried a 'gotcha' question on me to try to justify government control over various aspects of people's lives. She mentioned the written rules of the road including seat belt laws, speed limits, and insurance requirements. Keep in mind the roads throughout the country are built and maintained by the taxpayers. None of us owns a road except the roads on our private property.

As such the written rules of the road are written by our elected officials, and I would say most are written with our best interest in mind, at least in this case. As such, we must comply with the rules and conditions for driving on those roads, as nobody is forcing anyone else to drive. Take a bus, bum a ride from a friend, or ride a bike. There are plenty of other options if you are opposed to government issued driving requirements. It is no different than when you set foot on someone else's property. If you don't like the rules of their home, you leave.

Simple enough so far, but now we have to take a closer look at what is needed for freedom to exist. When it is stripped down to a pure product, what are the basic requirements needed for freedom to exist and be sustained? Think of freedom as a building with three parts: the foundation, the structure, and a roof.

The foundation of freedom starts with the smallest minority in the world—the individual. The individual must have three defining traits that are necessary and tightly intertwined. If one of the three is missing entirely, the foundation fails, and freedom cannot exist.

The structure built on the foundation of individual freedom

2. Building the Freedom Scale

is composed of four defining, tightly linked traits that make up what is needed for a free society. These four traits have a single purpose and unfortunately are not shared by every individual in society. That purpose ensures the same freedom for not merely a select group of people, but for every citizen in that society, even if the majority is against them. That is the focus of the structure. It requires both government practice and enforcement to protect the rights of every individual, as not every individual will think or act in the same way. The individual can be as mean and hateful as they want so long as they do not infringe on another person's individual liberty.

Finally, the roof, as you may have guessed, is needed by society to safeguard freedom from the storm of tyranny that is constantly trying to slowly but surely destroy both the structure and the foundation.

3. Individual Requirements for Freedom

Individual Choice

"You are not the victim of the world, but rather the master of your own destiny. It is your choices and decisions that determine your destiny."
– Roy T. Bennett

The first necessity for any individual to be free is *individual choice*. When you have a choice without either force or fraud, you have liberty. Individuals choose what field of work they wish to pursue, and which recreation they partake in. People choose how they proceed in living their own lives as liberty pertains to them. The choices we have in a free society are vast. When choice is taken away or severely hindered by a governing body, you have oppression as you must comply or face the consequences for your noncompliance. Plenty of people support such political action all the time for a variety of reasons. Those reasons vary from good intentions considering what they feel is right to bitter resentment as a result of individual choices they made that didn't work out well. Regardless of why, those reasons become the sugarcoated hook for politicians to sound virtuous.

    The decision for elected officials to interfere in our lives and take away our choices is often done by trying to highlight the

3. Individual Requirements for Freedom

noblest of reasons. Would you expect them to do otherwise and say they are looking to control you for their own selfish reasons? Of course not. Using that approach would be like trying to lure bees with vinegar instead of honey. What are some noble reasons we are given? Many involve arguing moral reasoning. During prohibition the moral argument to outlaw alcohol included reasons from reducing domestic violence, to reducing violence in society among other things. Who wouldn't want such results?

With prostitution in most parts of the U.S., a big moral argument is that it is degrading to women. As with so many other reasons, that conclusion is subjective. It depends on the individual. Some may see it as degrading, while others see it as empowering. Don't forget individual choice, even when it comes to bodily autonomy. Those seeking to make the choice for everyone think they know what is best for every individual, and they will impose it. They see it as the price for living in a civilized society. Another subjective viewpoint. It may be civilized in their view, but it comes at the expense of individual choice to choose for oneself.

Some will argue that we elect politicians to make choices that may take away individual choice for the benefit of society, so the informed consent is already there with the election to office of those representatives. I reply, "Not quite."

"An elected legislature can trample a man's rights as easily as a king can."
– Benjamin Martin, The Patriot

The Freedom Scale

No politician is elected unanimously, but by a majority, so they do not speak for everyone. Regardless of what most politicians say, most speak only for the majority that elected them, and that is *if they are honest*. The individual cannot assume that what this majority thinks 'best' is free from force or fraud.

This is one of the primary reasons why freedoms ultimately must reside with the individual.

A smart politician can find a way to justify any action they or their outspoken supporters want to take as a benefit to society no matter how much freedom it takes away. If they are really smart, they find a way to milk that support for all it is worth from those more outspoken constituents and get other constituents and colleagues to support it until they are in the majority. Looking at freedom on the individual level, it doesn't matter what the majority thinks, as it isn't a popularity contest. The popularity contest is democracy.

There is an old saying that describes democracy. It says democracy is two wolves and a sheep voting on what to have for dinner. Now that may be fine with you when it means you get what you want, but eventually everyone becomes the sheep in the scenario where freedom is trampled on and individual choice removed by the will of the majority. As individuals, sooner or later, everyone is in the minority.

Are there scenarios where the majority correctly and duly calls the shots without consent from every individual? Of course. Look at any group or organization that has numerous members. As individuals, we have different opinions. The larger the group, the greater the likelihood that not everyone will agree. So how do

3. Individual Requirements for Freedom

you resolve those problems acknowledging individual freedom in such group matters? The simple answer is individual choice.

In joining these groups, it is made known ahead of time that majority rules in deciding matters related to the group. If you find that unacceptable, you are free to not join or relinquish your membership. People may not like any of the choices available for whatever reason, but so long as there is no force or fraud, there is still a choice. Everyone must own their own choices as freedom requires that choice cannot come at the forced expense of someone else.

This leads us directly to the second requirement of individual freedom.

Personal Responsibility

"And the choices we make are ultimately our own responsibility."
– *Eleanor Roosevelt*

Hundreds of years ago the Declaration of Independence was presented to King George of England. It wasn't until years later at the end of the American Revolution, that Independence of the United States was recognized. But what did Independence mean? It meant that England no longer had a say in how the colonies were run. It also meant the colonies were then responsible for themselves. England would do nothing for them anymore; nor were they obligated. Independence is the first step in *personal responsibility*.

The Freedom Scale

Freedom requires the personal responsibility of every individual for the decisions and choices made in their own life, whether those choices are good or bad. Every individual is responsible for their own actions and—to a degree—the actions of their children who are not yet legally adults. This means you suffer the consequences when you make bad decisions and reap the benefits of making good decisions. It allows anyone, no matter who they are or where they came from, to be able to succeed beyond their wildest dreams based on the choices they make in their own life. Even if you fail miserably, you can always try again.

Various people don't choose freedom for one simple reason in this part of the foundation. They don't want the personal responsibility for their actions, choices, or lifestyle, especially the potential consequences of some individual choices. Facing some of those decisions may make some of those people feel bad. It is easier to blame someone else, or to blame racism, sexism or homophobia. Doing so allows those people to continue to feel good about themselves, and that is what becomes of primary importance to them. Thus, many of them develop the belief that it is someone else's responsibility to provide for everyone in situations where they may fail. If that weren't the case, they would have no problem deciding for themselves.

For those who believe in freedom, there is one alternative in line with the Freedom Scale to reject personally responsible. Convince someone else or a group of other people to agree of their own free will to take that responsibility for you. The children of weak parents, gold diggers, and others with an entitlement mentality successfully do it all the time.

3. Individual Requirements for Freedom

Most people looking to avoid responsibility don't see it that way. Many of them dance around the issues trying to justify their views as supporting liberty. Normally this is done in a lame, inconsistent, and often very hypocritical manner. They will say it is necessary for the greater good; it is the compassionate thing to do; it is the cost of living in a civilized society, or they give another reason—depending on the issue—to justify it. The problem is that once you start justifying such actions for those reasons, it is easy to justify encroachment of any freedom for the same reasons, as there is rarely consistency. This follows the same guidelines as politicians taking away choices from the public I mentioned earlier.

Speaking of the government being able to take things, there is nothing power-hungry politicians like more than infringing on the final individual necessity of freedom.

Privately Owned Property

"The system of private property is the most important guarantee of freedom, not only for those who own property, but scarcely less for those who do not."
– Freidrich Hayek, The Road to Serfdom

Please be aware there is a legal difference between personal property and private property. I, however, refuse to split hairs over the definition. Both personal and private property refer to what an individual owns. As such, both definitions will be interchangeable in this book, as both are equally essential to freedom.

The Freedom Scale

Why do people work? The answer is simple enough. You need to make money to survive; to pay for the necessities of life, as well as the things you want. Let's delve deeper into the answer though. The money you acquire under the rules of freedom belongs to you. No force or fraud is utilized to acquire it. Whether someone works for it, inherits it or makes it through the stock market, it doesn't matter. It is *their* private property, along with everything else they bought, were gifted, or inherited. When they spend it, they are trading value for value to supply someone else with what they want and need more than the money they worked for.

Say that someone else wants what you have. Are they free to take it? In a free society, not without your informed consent on terms agreeable to both you and the person who wants what you have. It then becomes a question of whether or not that someone else has the means and inclination to change your mind if you don't want to sell.

You may say, "But these are material things. They have no bearing on my freedom." Really? Do you see your paycheck belonging to you primarily or the government? Do you primarily own the fruits of your labor, or does the government? It is safe to say that those who believe the latter are the same ones who say any kind of tax breaks come at taxpayer expense. It can't come at taxpayer expense unless the money already belongs to the government first and foremost, and they are merely letting you keep what they feel you need.

Now try looking at it from the perspective of a slave. The slave master owns not only the slave, but everything used to feed

3. Individual Requirements for Freedom

the slave, clothe the slave, and shelter the slave. Because the slave master owns everything, he controls every aspect of the slave's life. What the slave master can give, he can just as easily take away on a whim to suit his needs.

"I am altering the deal, prey I don't alter it further."
– Darth Vader, The Empire Strikes Back

With private property you have primary control on how you choose to live. Whether you choose to spend more on luxuries or save your money instead is up to you. The same is true whether you choose to live well within your means or stretch yourself to your financial limit. The choice is yours when you own what you have, instead of someone else owning it.

This was put to the test in 2005, with the Supreme Court case Kelo vs. New London that argued against eminent domain. In this case the city of New London, Connecticut, was sued by some citizens when it was decided by elected officials that these citizens had to sell their property to a company because that company's business plans would create more tax revenue.

Before this case, if an individual or company wanted your property, they had to pay you what you wanted. They could not force you. If you refused to sell, they were out of luck. Remember real freedom requires mutually informed consent when two or more parties are involved.

This was the norm for the longest time as the Fifth Amendment of the United States Constitution states that private property shall not be taken for public use, without just compensation.

Public use was considered exactly what the term suggests. Public use. Creation of a park, road, courthouse, police station, or even a DMV. Something owned and operated by the government, which is used by the public where there is no profit to be made and no incentive to violate individual rights. A shopping mall for example, is used privately by the owners to make money for themselves by selling to the public. It also can be argued that "the public" use it to shop. This is true, but the owners can deny the entire public on a whim. It all depends on who owns the property after the sale and what they ultimately do with it.

The Supreme Court of the United States in a blow to freedom, ruled 5-4 (4 Democrat justices and 1 Republican justice against 4 Republican justices) that the government can use eminent domain to force Americans to sell to another private owner(s), so long as the government can make money off of it. Justice O'Conner in a dissenting opinion, I think, made the most valid point. She said that the decision by the majority eliminated any distinction between private and public use. How safe can the property of any individual be safe without such a distinction?

Where is the mutually informed consent? Without it there can be no agreed-upon price for what is fair, regardless of market value. Maybe the home or property in question has sentimental value, which is why they don't want to sell it. The value of the individual's home or property is far greater to them than the market value. Who decides what is a fair price in this case? Not you, the owner of the property. You are given what others consider to be a fair price. This isn't necessarily limited to either land or homes. Suppose some rich individual wants a rare antique that you own

3. Individual Requirements for Freedom

that has been in your family for generations, and it is not for sale at any price because of the sentimental value. What is to stop the buyer from getting the government to force you to sell because the government would receive a substantial tax revenue from the sale?

We finally get to the most important piece of property, and everybody has it—their own body. Every free individual owns their body. Free individuals make the choices of what and how much to eat and drink, what medicines to take, whether or not to exercise, whom to have sex with and countless other choices. With all those choices over your body comes the potential consequences of those choices: obesity, cholesterol levels, alcoholism, STDs. The possible list of resulting possibilities is endless when it comes to the result of our actions. We must take personal responsibility for everything we are dealt in life.

Now consider laws either past or present that infringe on bodily autonomy of the individual. Do such laws saying what we can and can't do with our own bodies without consequences imposed or coerced by the government, respect the freedom aspect of bodily autonomy?

You can now start to see the link between the three individual necessities of freedom. People need a right to possess privately owned property to have choice in life that isn't coerced or forced by someone else. The results of your choices are your personal responsibility and thus you must deal with the end result. These three parts of the foundation combined describe in detail what is needed for every individual to be free.

Now that we have touched on the individual necessities of

The Freedom Scale

freedom, the foundation, let us go into the four societal necessities for freedom that ensure equal freedom for every citizen in a society, (the structure on the foundation) no matter who they are. Individuals are free to disregard these societal necessities for others as long as they are not infringing on someone's individual liberties and so long as the law protects the individual freedom of everyone. Keep in mind though, if you are one of those people, consider what that says about you in regard to how you truly regard freedom, and the hypocrisy you show.

4. Societal Requirements for Freedom

Tolerance

"Tolerance implies no lack of commitment to one's own beliefs. Rather it condemns the oppression or persecution of others."
– John F. Kennedy

Let's face it; not everyone will be tolerant of other people and their differences, and many would argue that millions of people are intolerant. On an individual level, it is insignificant so long as there is enforcement of the law to protect everyone's liberty. The true intolerance that must concern a free society comes from two places.

The first comes from the mob pushing their views through force and physical intimidation, as it can lead to violence. The second comes from governing authorities on all levels, as government has the power to use force to push intolerance, which can encompass a wide variety of individual liberties based on any number of factors. Government can also use the implied threat of force to gain compliance through government agencies. Imagine a mob boss saying to a shop owner, "We strongly recommend you follow our guidelines" with two muscular henchmen behind him. Now imagine government officials or representatives saying to business owners, "We strongly recommend you follow our guidelines." Even though there is no law, the business owner knows any number of government agencies can be utilized against them, so why take the risk?

There is an important distinction regarding tolerance that most people overlook. It is the difference between tolerance and acceptance. You may not like someone else's beliefs, religion, sexual orientation, race, what they say or whatever else you can think of, but unless you try to forcibly change or suppress the individual liberty of a person or people with what you feel is right, you are neither tolerant, nor accepting. People are tolerant—if not accepting—merely speaking their beliefs to convince others without trying to involve government force. Those people are tolerant because despite disagreeing with you, they are not trying to force a change on you, suppress your individual rights in any way, or force their views on your children against your will. Those people can easily be ignored in those circumstances. If you are afraid they might convince people of their viewpoint, you are free to counter with your own words under the same guidelines.

What about areas where the lines are blurred? Such examples would be looking to have certain books removed from the libraries of public schools or starting a drag queen story time in public libraries. It is important to note the common factor in these two examples. Both are public places operated on tax dollars, and as such, the issues are determined by the will of the majority in the community. The books in question are not banned from public ownership; nor is having your own child read them if you as a

4. Societal Requirements for Freedom

parent disagree and feel they are appropriate. If a man wants to dress in drag, and host story time at his residence, he is free to do so, and other parents can decide if they feel it is appropriate to allow their children to attend.

What about speaking out in favor of something that infringes on an individual's life, liberty, or property, but has benefits for a person or a different group of people? Is that intolerance? No. It is a simple difference in opinion, so feel free to speak out all you want on either side. The definitions don't change or become an exception because someone believes it is for the 'greater good.' Otherwise, it becomes too easy to justify discrimination of free speech, thought, and expression when one side disagrees.

Yet intolerance for differing points of view is the biggest form of intolerance we face today in the United States. There is usually an attempt to silence those views, and the primary justification overall, is always for the greater good as they see it. We saw plenty of this with questioning details of a certain virus with the claim that people could die if we don't listen to specific experts. There was also plenty of this when questioning a number of aspects of a certain election, with claims of demanding answers to these questions, and doubting the result was an attempt at trying to overthrow a lawfully elected government in the most secure election in history.

One of my favorite attempts at such justification, comes from chants stating, "Hate speech does incite violence." Hurt feelings over what is said is not an infringement on liberty because what is considered hateful is subjective depending upon the individual, not society. Like the saying goes, "Opinions are like assholes, and everyone thinks everyone else's stinks." How you deal with it is your personal choice, and you bear the personal responsibility for any violent action you choose to engage in as a result. Ignoring some opinions would probably be the best choice in how to proceed.

At the time I write this, I am in my mid-forties. I don't care what others say or think about me or my beliefs. That is their individual right. I can easily ignore their words. I draw the line when those words become actions that suppress my liberties or the liberties of others.

Equal Standards Under the Law

"All too, will bear in mind this sacred principle, that though the will of the majority is in all cases to prevail, that will to be rightful, must be reasonable; that the minority possess their equal rights, which equal law must protect, and to violate would be oppression."
– Thomas Jefferson

Equal standards under the law runs parallel with tolerance but is still separate. Those who hold freedom in high regard and want a nation *"with liberty, and justice for all,"* do their best to apply the same standards to everyone regardless of their differences or similarities and whether or not they personally like them.

What does that mean more precisely "under the law"? It means that while people can be as intolerant, bigoted, sexist or homophobic as they want; no individual gets special consideration or treatment under the law because of their race, gender, sexual orientation, political affiliation, religion, etc. People deserve freedom of speech whether we agree with them or not and whether or not we like them. It means the politicians we like are not held to a lower standard than those we disagree with but are held to the exact same standard as those we disagree with if not higher. It means if you have a specific freedom that does not infringe on another individual's life, liberty, or property through force or fraud, that exact same freedom is not denied to others under the same guidelines. It means if you rape, murder, rob or in any other way infringe on someone else's freedom against their will, you don't walk because you are part of a special group or because the other party is in a marginalized group. The individual responsible for the offense must face the consequences.

What it does not mean is that individuals must apply equal standards to everyone in their personal and professional lives. It does not mean you have to associate with people you choose not to. It doesn't even mean you have to be polite to people if you don't want to. It does mean you can be a jerk and treat other people like dirt with no regard for their feelings, so long as you don't infringe on their freedoms.

As a result, some people have to work harder than others to attain the same goal depending on their skills, whom they know, the choices they have made in their life and how much money their family has. Our differences are why "under the law" is so valuable. While the road may be rockier for some, we no longer have "Jim Crow laws" to limit what one group of people can achieve by government force.

To force individuals to apply equal standards when dealing with others, infringes on freedom and defeats the purpose, however distasteful it may be at times. So long as the law does nothing to force discrimination and holds equal standards, freedom isn't violated.

What do we get when standards are not held equal for everyone 'under the law'? We get hypocrisy, favoritism, nepotism and political corruption. Certain people are vilified—not for the individual content of their character—but because of personal characteristics or beliefs for political gain. Doesn't paint a pretty picture on a large scale, does it? Such a path could easily lead to the destruction of personal liberty.

Charter of Negative Liberties

"The Constitution is a charter of negative liberties, says what the states can't do to you, says what the federal government can't do to you, but it doesn't say what the state or federal government must do on your behalf."
– Barrack Obama

What made the United States Constitution unique above all other governments and their Constitution is President Barrack Obama's description of the U.S. Constitution being a charter of negative liberties. That statement was from a 2001 radio interview. Regardless of what you think of Barrack Obama, he is exactly right in that quote.

While I'm sure President Obama was using this as a criticism of the United States Constitution, he neglects to mention that free-

4. Societal Requirements for Freedom

dom is easily swallowed up by any government without a written charter of negative liberties that is strictly enforced and holds freedom sacred above all other laws. Any Constitution that does not specifically lay out the limits of government power and what they cannot do, leaves the door open for power to quickly be abused by politicians that seek to impose what they feel is best.

Well sure it is understandable to have in place saying what the state and federal governments can't do to you, but why limit what the state or federal government can do to help people?

The primary goals for most elected officials involve achieving two main things while in office, and helping people is not one of them. Power and Money. Even if their goals are noble in the beginning, many appear unable to resist for long. Oftentimes the problems they claim to be fighting to eliminate are actually made worse. It can be argued that sometimes they are intentionally made worse for financial or political reasons. At best, they apply a Band-Aid by throwing money at the problem and leaving it for someone else to worry about later.

Numerous books have been written on this already, so I will only touch briefly on what is necessary and relevant to *The Freedom Scale*.

> **"Government, even in its best state, is but a necessary evil; in its worst state, an intolerable one."**
> **– Thomas Paine**

A necessary evil has never applied more to any institution than to government as it is needed to preserve freedom for all of its citizens, not only from foreign powers and criminals, but from within the halls of that government itself. Any representative government that is free, for the most part has only three basic and broadly encompassing duties to concern them. It has nothing else freedom lovers need or want besides: preserving/promoting the freedom of its citizens; ensuring that the operations of the country function smoothly; and protecting its citizens against invasion. In all three cases, they work for us.

To put it simply, the governments produce no services or goods that a person chooses to buy aside from stamps at the post office. They collect money from its citizens in a wide variety of ways, primarily taxes that are required to be paid (with coercion). Many supporters of big government parties immediately focus on improving roads, bridges, libraries, public schools, police departments, fire departments, etc. Such projects are considered to be making the country run smoothly. Specific infrastructure will be addressed later on. Regardless, no taxpayer voluntarily goes out to buy infrastructure.

A charter of negative liberties is of no use unless it is continually enforced. It is of no use if it is only enforced when:

- it is popular.
- people are convinced it is malleable to fit modern times.
- politicians know they can circumvent it for any number of reasons, at any time.

Seriously, how often do we see government enact programs or laws that go against the Constitution because they are made to sound good on paper?

4. Societal Requirements for Freedom

Many times, a new program where the government is the primary provider, will be explained as being good for everyone. The cost to society, however, is usually the loss of freedom in being able to choose. The main benefit is for the political class, as such measures give the political class more control over how society lives, and as a result creates increased dependency on the government by the population. Many in the population see the flaws but go straight to blaming those who opposed it for its failures when it doesn't work as promised. People who still support it afterwards often adopt the following mindset of: *It is better than nothing and where would we be without it?* This can easily be used to the advantage of smart politicians to get reelected by instilling fear that the program could disappear if they lose.

Other instances only provide feel-good measures at best to appease a certain group(s). Other times, the goal is simple pandering to gain support from specific groups later. Whatever the reasons, it is always best to be wary of politicians from all political parties.

Regrettably, today too many people are more interested in the new government benefits promised by the party's favored candidate, or how much they hate the opposing party's candidate, or even how much they hate the opposing party itself. Instead, we should ask how either candidate plans to protect or restore individual freedom for everyone. We see practically no serious mention of it in presidential debates. If you look closely, many things that politicians propose, go against individual freedom. One specific party will provide for everyone. They will enact mandates for the benefit of everyone. You will have no choice, but it will all be for your own good. During COVID-19, a good number of politicians focused on forcing compliance with what they felt was best, instead of convincing people on not only that issue, but a variety of issues. Many members of a certain party and the media avoided questioning the established narrative, and sometimes they went on the offensive against those who did question it.

> *"All tyrannies rule through fraud and force, but once the fraud is exposed, they must rely exclusively on force."*
> *– George Orwell*

This is the importance of a *charter of negative liberties*, and strictly enforcing it. It is why it is important to set the boundaries of what the political class can specifically do in regard to its citizens, and what it cannot do. As mentioned earlier, a smart politician can justify almost any action, even those that violate individual freedom, under the guise of it being for the 'public good.'

Policies are often primarily judged on the perceived intent of politicians, instead of the results. Adhering to the *charter of negative liberties* is usually ignored by politicians whenever they feel they can get away with it. Adhering strictly to the charter of negative liberties allows the idea to be vetted more to see if it is worthy of amending the Constitution. Since we don't see that today, it shows that far too many people take their freedom for granted. This leads us to the second necessity in a free representative government.

4. Societal Requirements for Freedom

Checks and Balances

***"The truth is that all men having power
ought to be mistrusted."
– James Madison***

The simple purpose of checks and balances is to keep one person or party from getting an unfair or undue advantage in their power over everyone else and thus to keep them from overstepping its bounds. This is the reason checks and balances were built into the United States Constitution with everyone's interests represented and the specific powers of the federal government specifically stated. The states' interests were to be represented by the Senate, hence the reason for two senators for each state regardless of size or population. The people's interests are represented by the House of Representatives, while the Executive Branch represents everyone's interests with the Supreme Court being the blind eye in settling disputes without bias.

The legislative branch makes the laws. They pass bills into laws only when there is enough of a majority to override a presidential veto. The executive branch passes and enforces the laws. The judicial branch rules on the constitutionality of the laws and can strike them down if found to be unconstitutional. However, the judicial branch cannot create or rewrite legislation in their rulings. If the courts could legally create or rewrite legislation presented to them so it is more in line with their beliefs, the checks and balances would be thrown out of kilter. To maintain checks and balances, unconstitutional legislation must be eliminated, advanced to a higher court for appeal, or sent back to a lower court, or to the legislature to be rewritten. Any judge that doesn't present rulings that they personally find distasteful at times is likely an activist judge, placing their self-interest over the rule of law.

The electoral college is a perfect example of how checks and balances work. Rather than the majority as a whole getting their way, each state has a voice dependent on their population, so the interests of rural states are not ignored in favor of states with the biggest cities with the biggest populations. It also reduces the likelihood of successful voter fraud, as power is not concentrated in a few select voices in highly populated areas but involves many voices across the country.

Another great example of checks and balances lies in how power works between the states and the federal government according to the Constitution. First look at the Tenth Amendment.

> **"The powers not delegated to the United States by the Constitution, nor prohibited by it to the states, are reserved to the states respectively, or to the people."**
> **– Amendment X, United States Constitution**

The powers of the federal government that override state laws come from powers specifically delegated to the federal government by the Constitution. If the states have a problem with federal laws, mandates, or any other kind of power that is not granted to the federal government by the Constitution, then the state laws must prevail, as they are reserved to the states respectively or to the people. A number of people will argue

4. Societal Requirements for Freedom

the supremacy clause (Article VI, Clause 2 of the United States Constitution) gives the federal government the power to override state laws. Many of those people think it can be used as a workaround at anytime for the federal government to get what they want. The Supremacy Clause does indeed override state law, but those people don't look at the condition of the Supremacy Clause to be used to override state law. That condition in the Supremacy Clause clearly states, *"This Constitution and the Laws of the United States which* shall *be made in Pursuance thereof."* In other words if federal laws or regulations step outside of the authority of the federal government granted by the Constitution, it becomes null and void in the face of state law under the Tenth Amendment. Doesn't get any clearer than that.

Other big government supporters will argue that the general welfare clause is the saving grace on the federal level. One quick question to ponder in response to that: If the Constitution were meant to be twisted to allow the federal government to do whatever they want in the name of "promoting the general welfare"—whether it is through a federal agency or any other kind of loophole—why is the Supremacy Clause even in the Constitution? There would also be no Tenth Amendment as we know it, and it certainly would not be a part of the Bill of Rights. Since when did the term "promoting" involve taking away individual choice, so the government can do what it wants?

As great as the Constitution is, I believe it doesn't go far enough in establishing checks and balances on the political class. I don't think the founders anticipated the degree party politics or corruption would play; nor did they anticipate the degree to which judicial activism would play a role in the politics of the future. The first step to adapting to these politicians is to understand how they operate.

Most politicians believe in four rules:

1. Get elected/re-elected.
2. Grab as much power as you can between elections.
3. Tow the party line.
4. Keep your political opponents out of the majority.

Getting voted out of office is the worst consequence most politicians face nowadays. Avoiding that consequence controls their decisions in governing. Many are career politicians, mastering what to say, when to say it, how to say it, and whom to say it to, so they don't worry as much about re-election until that time comes on their assigned year. They worry about it much less if they represent a constituency that is highly partisan to one political party.

Rules 2 and 3 are the primary focus of politicians when it is isn't election season. Come election season, many abandon rules 2 and 3 temporarily to focus on pandering, counting on their slick tongues and the short-term memory of voters. When focused on rules 2 and 3, their solutions are most often done in a manner granting them more power over the population at the expense of their freedom. Often, if they don't make things worse, they continue an endless cycle of the same solutions that ultimately fix nothing but are repeated every single time. It can be argued that this is the intent of elected officials to ensure they

4. Societal Requirements for Freedom

can continue to grab more power. Think about it. Why would these power-hungry men and women actually work to make things better when announcing their intent is often enough for many voters? Think along the same lines of a similar question. Why should we believe pharmaceutical companies are actually developing a cure for cancer when so much more money is made treating it instead? It is important to consider what is in the best interests of each.

Yes, I mentioned this before and, along with other things, I will mention repeatedly as needed. I don't do it for my health. Personally, I hate repeating myself. The reason for much of the repetition, is because in discussing politics and politicians, reasons often overlap with many things being interconnected. Other times it is the best way to hammer a point home.

Today too few politicians are held accountable for their private actions, but more importantly, they are not held responsible for the results of their policies. It has become the perfect feeding ground for the corrupt and power hungry to thrive. I think checks and balances need to be expanded to guarantee severe consequences for all politicians who not only violate the law, but for political proposals that become law, where the end results are not what was promised. Let their ability to run for reelection depend on such things—depending on the issues—rather than letting their promises alone allow them to run for office again and again.

The goal would be to create an environment where no corrupt or self-serving politician would dare set foot in. We have the Uniform Code of Military Justice holding our armed forces to a higher standard than civilians. Shouldn't a similar system be created and enforced to hold all of our elected officials to the highest standard of all?

We are holding Donald Trump accountable, so that is a start, right?

Maybe it is. However, it is blatantly one-sided in the worst ways. We see each side more than willing to tolerate corruption on their own side to varying degrees. That is only partisan politics, which people with political interests, can decide with a wink, wink, nudge, nudge. I'm talking about taking the partisanship out of the decision-making and requiring mandatory charges be filed where applicable, especially where ordinary people would have without question been charged and prosecuted. No special prosecutor would be able to say, "Yes, they broke the law, but because of this I have decided not to prosecute." as was the case with Hillary Clinton and Joe Biden.

In all honesty, such measures are needed in the immediate future to maintain checks and balances in this country, as we are getting closer to tyranny than most people realize. They don't know or don't care to see what is emerging on the national level. In one specific party it appears to be an attempt to do away with a two-party system on various levels in an underhanded manner. Look at the following examples:

- After the 2016 elections, there was talk of doing away with the electoral college in favor of the popular vote, after Hillary Clinton won the popular vote, but lost the electoral college to Donald Trump. Some states in an effort to create a work-around of the electoral college,

4. Societal Requirements for Freedom

created state laws to award their electoral college votes to the candidate who won the popular vote nationwide as opposed to the popular vote in that state.
- When Justice Amy Coney Barret was being nominated for the Supreme Court, there was widespread talk by the opposing party of both court packing and making Puerto Rico and the District of Columbia states. If either side were allowed to do either, where would the checks and balances be? One party could increase judge and justice majorities in their favor, that they know would rubber stamp any legislation passed if it were challenged in the courts. Creating new states whose population already overwhelmingly vote in one party's favor would prevent new judges and justices that disagree with them from being confirmed by the Senate.

These are just three noteworthy examples of how politicians look to undermine checks and balances. There must always be a system in place to prevent every side from going too far when they get power. If your party is losing support, the goal must be to figure out how to attract people to the proposals you are offering rather than to change the rules to give you the advantage and *force* proposals the people rejected.

You may dismiss this, if your preferred party is the one getting the extra power. But you need to ask what happens if and when they go too far? Who will stop them? They will just get voted out you say? The people living under authoritarian dictatorships that still have elections, have already thought of that. By the time it got to that point, it is was too late to be able to remove them from office.

There is another form of checks and balances power in the United States. It is the Civil Rights Act of 1964, and few people are aware of how much power they hold under it. It is a civil rights and labor law that makes discrimination based on race, religion, gender, or national origin illegal. Now you may be thinking that on the Freedom Scale, anyone can discriminate against whomever they want—such as an employer not wanting to hire women or someone of a certain faith. Technically that assumption would be correct, as that business owner would normally suffer the consequences of the outrage from the consumer population and likely go out of business. But what about the government?

We must ask ourselves what is to stop the government from forcing discrimination in one form or another? Jim Crow laws were a perfect example of the government forcing discrimination. A more recent example of such discrimination, would be those who chose not to take any of the vaccines available for COVID-19. In September of 2021, Joe Biden announced a presidential mandate of either being tested weekly for COVID-19 or taking the vaccine. Individuals that didn't comply would lose their jobs. Businesses that refused were threatened with heavy fines for each instance of non-compliance to ensure compliance with the mandate. Some businesses were also threatened that federal funds would be withheld from government programs such as Medicare and Medicaid.

The government had no authority to force individuals in this

4. Societal Requirements for Freedom

case, so they just applied pressure to the businesses to do the dirty work. It is a dangerous workaround that a government can employ to get what they want, which is why the Constitution and legislation like the Civil Rights Act of 1964 must be upheld, when the government oversteps its bounds in any situation.

Checks and balances don't stop with government. It is needed between two or more parties on a nongovernmental level. Take the relationship between employer and employee, for example. Each has an equal say in the relationship, and each can normally terminate that relationship at any time. The bargaining chip each has is that each brings to the table what the other needs. Neither gets to unilaterally change the rules of what is agreed upon, in the middle of the game to better suit their side, such as the employer refusing to pay the agreed-upon wage for the employee's work. There is mutual, informed consent where each is free to walk away and look elsewhere.

If there is a dispute, you need an impartial mediator, who is indifferent to whether you are rich or poor, black or white, male or female, or whatever, but will judge on the merits of the case alone, rather than personal bias. In a nutshell, checks and balances help keep everyone in line respecting the freedom of everyone else.

5. Requirements for Retaining Freedom

In a free society, it isn't hard finding people who will try to take freedom away, for money or personal power, or even out of patriotism to a foreign power. Foreign powers using military to fight is the obvious example. But domestic forces that constantly work to undermine freedom for money and/or power; attempts to undermine freedom by cloaking their attempts with good intentions. Ironically only two things are needed for a society to retain its freedom: skepticism and resolve.

Skepticism

"If a nation expects to be ignorant and free, in a state of civilization, it expects what never was and never will be."
– Thomas Jefferson

Do you believe everything you are told? Probably not because people usually have conflicting opinions. Odds are though that you or people you know readily believe what certain people tell you because you trust them. These people can be spiritual leaders, celebrities, teachers, family members, news anchors, politicians, or even certain political parties. People have a need to trust other people in their lives, at least in certain aspects. Blind trust, however, can be disastrous as there will usually be people from every walk of life looking to

5. Requirements for Retaining Freedom

take advantage of others for personal gain.

Do you think the majority of people in impoverished, tyrannical communist countries, supported a particular person because they wanted the way of life, they have now for themselves and their children? Most chose to remain ignorant, no matter how smart they were, or how much negative evidence was in front of them. Later on, many skeptics probably feared for their lives and remained silent as a result. They saw their best option as going along to get along. It is what happens when you choose to remain ignorant and simply accept what you are told without question.

I know what it is like to follow blindly. I allowed a narcissist member of my family to manipulate my feelings for most of my life. Allowing that manipulation instead of facing it, kept me from knowing a large part of my family until a few years ago. I saw this behavior long before that but kept ignoring it and making excuses for that family member. It is what it is. Just accept it. Eventually push came to shove after the birth of my daughter, and I couldn't ignore the narcissism anymore. I had to make a choice for her sake, if not my own. The choice I made taught me how important it is to embrace the truth and follow it, even though I hated doing it at the time.

Say your best friend tells you that your spouse is cheating on you. Do you call your friend a liar, or ask them to produce evidence, such as dates, times, places, people, etc.? Do you look at the evidence and judge for yourself or kick your best friend out of your house and out of your life without another word? One of these responses is governed by logic and reason. The other is governed by emotion. We have probably all known people in situations like this. Plenty make decisions that acts against their better judgment because of emotion.

Which do you think crooked politicians want their constituents governed by? Emotion or logic and reason? Before you say you support those who are all about logic and reason, because the other side is filled with hate, ask yourself a few things. Do you listen to and question both sides of the political aisle, or do you take the word of your preferred political party, elected official, or news outlet assuming the opposition is peddling lies, misinformation, and fake news? Do you look carefully at the context or take someone else's word for it? When your side says, "The science is settled," do you accept that they know what they are talking about and blindly trust those experts, or do you insist on hearing opposing arguments and seeing the data for yourself to draw your own conclusions? When scary statistics are brought up by politicians, do you question whether or not their solution will work and why, or do you blindly trust them because their words sound noble? Do you question flaws in the reasoning of the elected officials you support, or do you go along because you assume they mean well or know more than you do and have their reasons? Do you automatically assume those reasons are honorable? Do you automatically assume the accuracy of statements made from the other side of the political aisle?

Many people often travel the easy path in such situations because it is difficult to go against the grain. People want to fit in. They want to belong. They don't want to be the black sheep. Many authoritarian politicians and their allies in the media know

5. Requirements for Retaining Freedom

this and use it to their advantage as often as possible in a variety of measures.

It would be a good idea if those people who want to belong took a lesson from me about fitting in. I personally don't care if I fit in with the crowd or am disliked for my views. I don't even care if I am the only one with my viewpoints. I am courteous and respectful to everyone I come across and their views, but I won't be steamrolled or bullied to accept the B.S. of others. I also have no problem shattering their illusions.

> *"Talk to people. Ask questions. Learn the truth for yourself."*
> *– B'elanna Torres, Star Trek: Voyager*

Most people in this world have a self-serving agenda, especially those actively involved in politics. Many outlets push these agendas, such as schools and various media outlets. Being openly skeptical is the antidote to indoctrination. This can easily ostracize one from those who normally share similar views. Hence it is easier to stay quiet.

Since most of us don't have time to research everything in detail, I found the best way to tell whom to be most critical of is to look for these five things:

1. *Those who try on a regular basis to provoke emotion by name-calling or negative labeling.*
2. *Those who avoid debate insisting you trust what they say without providing evidence, specifics, or even a good reason.*

3. Those who avoid tough questioning from reporters or commentators who don't share their views.
4. Those who avoid answering direct questions they don't like; often they redirect the conversation instead without actually answering the question(s).
5. Those who see a difference of opinion as a personal attack, an act of intolerance, or misinformation. This allows them to go on the offensive against their opponent without explaining why what they said is wrong.

Do I question the motives and actions of the political candidates and the party I support? Absolutely. I won't condone, make excuses for, or ignore corruption or an abuse of power simply because they I support that political party. I won't blindly accept what some news agency presents as factual. I do my homework to look for any missing facts or context. Depending on what I find helps determine how I proceed.

Individuals rarely find a candidate they agree with everything on, and rarer still is the politician without some form of unwanted baggage. We each must decide what we can live with and what we can't. It isn't wise to only hold that light up to the opposing party, as that is an invitation for corruption. The longer that corruption continues, the more it is tolerated.

Corrupt behavior is encouraged by accepting politics as usual because you assume the guy from the other party is worse, or because you will be shunned by people in your party. Sometimes the other candidate is worse, and the best course of action is to hold your nose and vote to keep them out of office.

5. Requirements for Retaining Freedom

Sometimes shunning the behavior of the candidate from your own party means the other guy wins, which can suck. However, it helps keep your party more honest because it demonstrates to your elected party officials that actions have consequences and this type of behavior will not be tolerated. It is the primary reason why it is never a good practice to blindly vote down ballot for a single party.

Ask yourself a few things. What would your party or favored candidate have to do or say to officially lose your vote at the ballot box? When will what they say or do reach the point when you say to yourself, "Enough is enough"? It is practically unheard of to find a perfect politician, so it ultimately becomes a choice of how much will one tolerate, before they say I will not support this politician or this party anymore. I think most freedom loving people would agree the best time for that choice would be well before society is no longer in a position to stop the power-hungry politicians.

If you ignore skepticism of your party or any of their candidates to avoid being shunned, you must ask yourself a question: Is your silence serving your needs and those of your fellow party members, or is it serving the wants and needs of the party elite? Unless the goal is power over the opposition at any price, anyone answering honestly will clearly see it is the latter. If politicians are not held accountable for their actions in a consistent manner, nothing will stop them from pushing the boundaries to an unacceptable degree, just to see how far and for how long they can go before the people scream stop. We have had enough. Children do it all the time with their parents to get what they want.

Is it really so inconceivable to think that any politician from any party wouldn't push boundaries in the pursuit of power? So many people are blinded by their preconceived views of each party and certain politicians, by the time we reach that point, it may be too late to do anything.

Resolve

We already touched on this in discussing skepticism and choice. But retaining freedom is not just about being openly skeptical. It is about following through. The corrupt politicians won't roll over and give up their plans just because some of their constituents will stand up to them. Even if they are caught with their hand in the proverbial cookie jar, instead of just throwing up their hands and saying, "You got me," they will do everything to avoid taking responsibility. Few will resign without both overwhelming evidence against them, and the party elite turning their back on them.

Do not count on any media outlet to call out the corruption, or even assume Big Tech platforms will allow the information, especially when it comes to a specific political party. We will discuss later how biased they can be, but realize the heads of these companies, even if they don't agree with the politics of corrupt politicians, can still see what is going on. Why side with the corruption then? My guess is a combination of two answers. To begin with, they doubt the resolve of the American people. In addition to that, they see the resolve of a specific party that seeks to undermine freedom and grab as much power as possible.

5. Requirements for Retaining Freedom

They are fairly certain about how far that party will go and what they will likely achieve. Better to go along to get along, sharing in some of that power at the top, shaping peoples' lives, and be one of the last ones standing, instead of being ruined early on by going against what the rest have established as "mainstream."

What can you do against power and influence of that magnitude?

> *"I will not comply."*
> *– Seven of Nine, Star Trek: Voyager*

Numerous steps are involved showing resolve in the name of freedom. The place to start is peaceful non-compliance. It works. The main problem we see goes back to people not wanting to be the black sheep. It is easier to first look at what other people are doing. Why do it if there are consequences I don't like. In one word? Principles.

Consider the following examples. To begin with, think about the mandates for COVID-19. We had mask mandates, shot mandates, social distancing mandates. I avoided compliance as much as I saw fit because much of what was being said didn't add up. With the shot mandates, this was the most apparent. My wife and I were willing to lose our jobs over it. We stood tall with our non-compliance and won, as did many others.

Next, we look to the example of Governor Michelle Lujan Grisham of New Mexico in September of 2023. She looked to suspend firearm carry laws for private citizens in certain areas for thirty days. Percentage wise, more people in her state stood up to her, even in her own party. People openly defied and carried in those areas. Police and Sheriff departments refused to enforce her order from the beginning. Even an otherwise friendly news outlet to her party grilled her pretty hard in an interview on this. It was easy to stand against Governor Grisham, because she was primarily standing alone with little to no support in her methods. I would say imagine what could be done when many don't openly stand against such behavior, but it was already addressed with the COVID-19 example. In both examples, the people stood up to government overreach and won through noncompliance. That is the power of resolve through peaceful noncompliance.

It shouldn't matter what side the majority seems to be standing on in any case. Even if a group of politicians tell you that you need to do something, and it is reinforced by the media, academia, Hollywood, etc., with no law to back it up, the solution is simple. Peacefully refuse to comply if you feel it is wrong. Remind the politicians that they work for us. If they want us to comply with something that goes against our individual freedom, then they are obligated to provide a damn good reason, explaining it in excruciating detail, and answering every question to our satisfaction. Odds are they will not do so, or even try, and will instead resort to other tactics. They may resort to bullying. They may threaten in a variety of ways and to varying degrees. They may encourage others to do the dirty work for them, to make life difficult for those not blindly complying. Hold firm, but peacefully. Violence must be the absolute last resort, but the resolve of being willing to respond with force to preserve or regain freedom must always be there. While many find it easier to go along

5. Requirements for Retaining Freedom

with the mob mentality, Martin Luther King, Jr. proved in his civil rights marches that it is possible to achieve a major victory over tyranny through peaceful non-compliance.

> *"...with a firm reliance on the protection of divine Providence, we mutually pledge to each other our Lives, our Fortunes, and our sacred Honor."*
> *– The Declaration of Independence*

When all peaceful options at a resolution have failed, you must be willing to do what the founders of this country did. Resolve to hold tighter to freedom than those trying to take it from your grasp. The founding fathers were such men as demonstrated in their actions in the effort to be free from the tyranny of England. Signing the Declaration of Independence was widely acknowledged by those who signed it, that doing so would have most certainly meant a death sentence for treason to the crown if they were caught. After all, any number of shop keepers or other ordinary citizens could have easily turned them in.

These men were also shunned by mainstream English Society and viewed as dishonorable traitors to England and the King. They spit in the face of what English society saw as honorable to uphold the personal and sacred honor they held in their hearts for freedom.

Look closely at the lengths they went to in the service of achieving freedom for this country. Some of them were quite wealthy, and had much to lose. As stated in the Declaration of Independence, this included their lives, their fortunes, their sacred honor. They were willing to sacrifice everything, not on the

The Freedom Scale

guarantee of freedom, but for the chance to be free, with only their faith in God to sustain the belief that their resolve would be rewarded with victory.

Many knew the odds were stacked against them and the chance of victory might be slim at best, considering the strength of the British military at that time. They didn't care. The chance at gaining freedom and independence was worth the sacrifice of going to war. All other avenues had been exhausted. Still, this was the level of their resolve. Let us hope it never needs to reach that level again.

Finally, and most difficult of all in holding the resolve to maintain freedom, is how long it must be done. The saying *"Eternal vigilance is the price of liberty"* is often attributed to Thomas Jefferson, though it has never been found in any of his writings. Regardless, the quote is not wrong. Say we beat tyranny and corruption on one or even all levels of the government and drive them into the shadows and/or prison; it will not be the end. They and other like-minded individuals will always be waiting and watching for the right time to take advantage of the political climate and current events. They will be looking for the right angle to make themselves relevant in public life and to regain power to start the cycle again.

Before concluding this chapter, I have one more question. What do you value most in life from a political standpoint? Is it the partisan politics of your preferred party? Is it a sense of self-righteousness in your beliefs? How about largesse at the expense of taxpayers? Could it be as simple as individual freedom for every American?

5. Requirements for Retaining Freedom

All but the last one come from selfish desires and require no individual effort aside from voting for the politicians that support such measures. Remember that freedom costs; it takes immense effort from every individual because each is responsible for them self. You may not start life with the advantages others have, but you can achieve as much if not more than those people. You succeed and fail by your own decisions and your actions as a result of those decisions. Many people don't want to look in that mirror and see their own failure. It is easier to blame someone else instead of facing the reality of that failure. Let's ask the question another way.

How important is it to you for this country to be freer with more opportunities for not only your children and grandchildren but everyone else's when you leave this world compared to when you came in to it? Is it more important than the first selections I asked about? I know without hesitation what my answer is

I want them to have at least as much liberty in their life as I did in mine. Actually, I want all of them to have more. I want all the available opportunities not just for my daughter, but for all children of this great nation, no matter the color of their skin, sexual orientation or gender. Let our children and grandchildren succeed or fail on their own merit, and let us lead them by our own example.

How you answer the questions throughout this book, and how you choose to live your life afterward will indicate how much you value freedom for not only yourself, but for others and future generations.

6. Controlling Freedoms

"To enjoy freedom, we have to control ourselves."
– Virginia Woolf

Now that we have defined and identified the primary aspects freedom, and what they entail, we are going to address the things power hungry politicians look to control most. I call these things, the *controlling freedoms*.

Power hungry politicians go after controlling freedoms because they are in it for the long game, and the controlling freedoms have the biggest impact on the long game. Control over these areas by such politicians, allows easier control over every other possible freedom we have or can imagine. They are what must be controlled to undermine liberty from within and grant tyrants more power. They will be the main focus going forward.

More often than not, those politicians keep people focused on other less significant issues to distract them, or to spin the controlling freedoms addressed to gain support for allowing the politicians to do what they want.

We will focus on six main controlling freedoms although many more exist. To take the controlling freedoms lightly is a sure way to lose freedom from within by your own government. Enough people must first be convinced to give up their freedom willingly. Why would they do that? It starts by bringing into play

6. Controlling Freedoms

what George Orwell may have referred to as the 'Thought Police' in his book *1984*. It involves conditioning people to think and act a certain way. People don't easily give up their freedoms otherwise. Once that conditioning is accomplished in enough of the population, the next job of the tyrants is to create a legal way to retain power in spite of the fact that some people are already getting wise to what the tyrants are doing. This is where limiting the ability to choose comes into play. By the time enough people wake up to what is going on, the tyrants will already be in a position where the citizens won't be able to react either legally or forcefully.

Is losing control of one of the six *controlling* freedoms enough to lose freedom completely? I would say it is not only highly possible, but likely. With one area completely subverted by the government, we get the domino effect. When the politicians knock down one controlling freedom, they will aim to knock down another, and they will be able to do it easier than they did the first one. Over time they will try to do that to all of them.

Why would people willingly submit to such measures? Are the controlling freedoms that hard to understand? In all honesty, they are easy to understand, but people can easily be manipulated, especially if it is what they want to hear. Good politicians are the best at telling their constituents *what* they want to hear, *when* they want to hear it, and *how* they want to hear it. This approach allows them to sell what they are doing as being for the greater good.

This conditioning of people in question is an aspect that has been around much longer than I have been alive, and will likely

The Freedom Scale

always be around. The problem for the politicians is many people aren't buying the snake oil from a particular party anymore, making it possible to thwart their plans for controlling freedom. It is part of what made Donald Trump so popular. He didn't give the same sales pitch so many other politicians do, and he even challenged them and their enablers.

Let's look at a few examples of controlling freedoms, before going onto the six that I list. Food, water, clothing, and housing are examples of what people need to live. Maintaining access to them requires either complying with those controlling the access or going without, which can easily mean death. Most would choose compliance in order to live.

While total control over any of these four by the government would create a tremendous increase in control over the population, it would cause too much of an uproar in this country at this point in history. Done too quickly such a move could easily create a second American Civil War. If you look at what has happened in communist and third world countries that went after those things, you saw a lot of civil unrest among the population, quelled by the force of government. Doing such a thing in the United States would not be a smart move because a large number of its citizens own firearms and value their freedom.

Of course, some people will be upset about corporations or landlords controlling access. In those areas there is free market competition to help keep prices down. With the government, it is possible to use legal authority to get rid of the competition.

Despite everything I have said so far, it would be okay with some people for the government to be one of the main or the

6. Controlling Freedoms

only provider of goods and services to the general public. Very well. Let's explain it another way for those people.

We already looked at the functions of the different branches of government, in regards to laws. Now look at the different branches of government primarily act as officials making the rules and the referees calling the plays in sports. They are meant to be impartial and neutral to the players in the game. No special benefits are provided by the government for either team regardless of who is on either team.

Now imagine a ballgame where the opposing team is made up of the friends and family of the referees and game officials. What if those same referees and officials decide to actively join their family and friends' team and have the ability to change the rules as the game progresses because it benefits them. Would you voluntarily play? Nobody would play the opposing team as they would constantly make the calls and change the rules to benefit themselves. There is no way you would be able to win.

Life isn't a game though, and yet we are forced to play under the rules laid down by two major sides whose officials are vying to control the government. The intentions of both sides are not entirely impartial or innocent, especially when it comes to the Constitution. Anyone who thinks otherwise is a brainwashed fool.

There are reasons why allowing the government to have excess power regardless of political affiliation is *foolish*. Government are the only ones that have the exclusive advantage of being able to change the rules, enforce those rules on everyone, make exceptions, and most importantly pick winners and losers.

The Freedom Scale

They can tax and/or regulate the competition out of business, and subsidize some or all of what they are selling. The perfect example is the Post Office. It is constantly subsidized by the government because there is not enough income to keep that agency going through postage and delivery sales. Think UPS or FedEx could do the same and stay in business?

It isn't so farfetched to assume the ultimate goal of tyrants is for government to have a monopoly on providing a specific good or service if they play the game with controlling freedom. Mail service is not even close to being a controlling freedom, especially in the digital age. With controlling freedoms, not only would the government have the ultimate say; people would be dependent on the government for that good or service. Assuming this is their ultimate goal: What *choice* will you have other than the government option, other than going without if that is even an option? Remember, I mentioned mandates earlier? Mandates can be applied on the consumers. Saying you will just go without is pointless, assuming going without is even an option to survive. The government gets what they want through tax dollars, even if people decide to go without, so it is no skin off their back.

Any government that gains enough control of any kind of good or service, gets to decide who gets what, how much, and how often, which they can then leverage over the population taking control over the population in that aspect. Sounds like a master controlling their slaves, making abuse of controlling freedoms in their hands especially dangerous.

While our state and federal governments have their claws in each controlling freedom, they have not gained absolute control

6. Controlling Freedoms

over any single one. Yet! But they are close, and it is on more than one front.

Given that my inspiration for writing this book started when I talked with my grandfather about taxes and economics; it seems fitting we tackle the first controlling freedom in this book, which is money or more specifically, the fruits of our labor. This area is extensive. There are a number of sub-categories to this section, and we will discuss various aspects. Keep in mind that I discuss only *some* of the absolute basics to make the point on the Freedom Scale—when it comes to taxes and economics as it is a vast subject, and I am not an economist. The remaining controlling freedoms will be addressed in Section III.

II. Controlling the Tool that Allows Us to Trade: Money

"You must gain control over your money, or the lack of it will forever control you."
– Dave Ramsey

7. Capitalism vs. Socialism

In American society today, capitalism is degraded, and socialism is praised by one wing of the political spectrum as well as supported by a large number of millennials and Gen Z. Why? The simple answer is it promotes a vision of what they and other socialists see as a just and fair in society. It would be hard to get agreement on the claim that socialism is *just* and *fair* from others who don't share that ideology. A better question would be, which system promotes individual freedom in society regarding the fruits of one's labor?

Let's start by looking at a pure and simple definition of capitalism. What is it exactly? It is an economic system where private entities and individuals own the fruits of their labor and use that ownership to freely control a country's economy. To paraphrase Ayn Rand in *Atlas Shrugged,* It is a system where—regardless of personal wealth—individuals from one party voluntarily trade value for value with another party. The first party trades with the second party money, goods or services that the first party finds to be more valuable.

Let me paraphrase Rand one last time in explaining what is money. It is a tool that allows us to trade. Your goods for mine; your efforts for mine. A person earns money by producing value and as a result, offers the value of their hard work (money) to someone in exchange for products or services they are selling.

7. Capitalism vs. Socialism

It is a relationship where both parties get something they want.

In its most basic form, capitalism applies every aspect of freedom for everyone—not just the rich as anti-capitalists would have you believe—and makes everyone's life both better and easier in the process.

- With both parties there must be *mutually informed consent* in the buying and selling of products or goods.
- There are numerous *choices* of products and services, and numerous providers for people to choose from. Your choices are only limited to the providers who supply what you want and what you can afford.
- Capitalism respects the individual rights of every participant. If one party doesn't want to participate, that is their right, and there is no transaction.
- Engaging in capitalism allows one to make the most out of their life, providing for themselves and their family based on personal decisions and drive to succeed.

The entrepreneur is the main driver in capitalism bringing their goods and services to market. They have the drive to be better than the other guy in serving the public. Their drive is what many socialists consider to be selfish, as much of their motivation is profit for themselves. So long as they don't infringe on people through force, or fraud, so what? They are the ones who make available products and services that are cheaper, better, and faster with their entrepreneurial spirit.

Sometimes entrepreneurs work together to create new products with that spirit. Look at everything that has been both created and made accessible to everyone by a wide variety of entrepreneurs in a wide variety of fields over the last 150 years. Automobiles, refrigerators, cookies, and even candy bars are just a drop in the bucket, and all have improved over time thanks to creative thinking and the competition afforded by capitalism. Life continues to change with each passing generation in terms of quality of life, as new items and technology become available and more affordable to everyone because of the entrepreneur. Today we enjoy streaming services, smart phones, and the internet; things that didn't exist when I was a child. I can only imagine what capitalism and entrepreneurs will bring when today's children are my age, assuming it is allowed to flourish and not stagnate by any form of crony capitalism.

Capitalism is not an easy road for most; nor should it be. You own your successes, but you also own your failures. Bailouts for businesses are not part of capitalism, but a form of crony capitalism. Yet, despite any failure one may suffer, they can learn from their mistakes and still succeed beyond their wildest dreams under this system. Henry Heinz and Clarence Birdseye are perfect examples. Both at one time lost everything in business before making it big. The government didn't bail them out. In fact, government bailouts are very anti-capitalist allowing people to skirt their failure at the expense of the taxpayer.

When looking at capitalism among everyday people, there are plenty of rags to riches stories. The same cannot be said about those living under socialism unless you examine the political class and those who benefit most from the best interest of those politicians.

7. Capitalism vs. Socialism

The story of socialism is indeed quite different and takes on a variety of forms. All of them share the characteristics of subverting freedom among the population, which in turn gives power and control to the political class by creating dependence on the government to be provided through tax dollars. All people are required to comply with the decisions the socialists feel are best for everyone. It doesn't matter that it infringes on individual liberty.

With the different types of socialism and the resulting massive failures that each form of socialism has produced, we must ask why anyone still wants to enact it. People like Bernie Sanders and his supporters tell us that isn't real socialism. Many of them argue that real socialism hasn't been tried yet. What they advocate for is what they call, "Democratic Socialism". It is often accompanied by arguments that capitalism should be considered "Corporate Socialism."

In fairness to the socialists, we will be examining three forms of socialism as described by a meme that appears to come from a group that supports Democratic Socialism and Bernie Sanders called Women for Justice. This meme is entitled 'Socialism 101'. If you are interested in seeing it online here is the link.

https://www.pinterest.com/pin/bernie-sanders--106256872446860094/

After we look at each description from the apparent socialist perspective, we will examine it to see how much spin there is and to see if the descriptions of each maintain freedom.

What is socialism as defined by Socialism 101?

Socialism: *"The government owns most major industries.*

A single party or dictator rules the government. The system allows for little personal freedom, and is closely aligned with Authoritarianism."

That description sounds pretty accurate to me. Government of a singular mindset owns and controls aspects of most if not all businesses as well as most everything else, leaving no room for descent. Sounds very much like the form of modern-day slavery discussed earlier. Moving on.

Corporate Socialism: *"The Government mostly benefits wealthy corporations. Most major industries are privately owned, but still receive substantial tax cuts, bailouts and other benefits at the expense of the taxpayer. It is driven by the corporations' ability to influence laws with large amounts of $$$ to pay for legislation that favors corporations' ability to make even more $$$. With corporate socialism, the wealthy become even wealthier at the expense of lower classes. This system is essentially a Plutocracy = rule by the wealthy."*

This description is the practice of crony capitalism that I was talking about. The only self-identifying capitalists who support this are those in the wealthy corporations that benefit most. Why wouldn't they? It is easier and probably cheaper to lobby politicians to give certain benefits to your company instead of having to keep on your toes and stay one up on your competition in the free market. It is easier to get government bailouts than having to be fully responsible for the success or failure of your business.

7. Capitalism vs. Socialism

Unfortunately, our capitalist system is tainted with *crony capitalism*. It could be politicians thinking they know what is best for us and using corporations to push through what they want. It could be corporations, who are paying off politicians to ensure their competition doesn't become a threat or ensuring that they get cushy government contracts. Personally, I think it is likely a combination of the two. No group of people has cornered the market on corruption.

We have seen heavy interaction between corporations and politicians that definitely raised a few eyebrows. The issue of mandates regarding the COVID-19 vaccines come to mind. Another is the government's trying to pick winners using tax dollars to promote electric cars. In both of these instances, the corporations make a fortune off of taxpayer dollars. Then we hear complaints that this is why capitalism has failed, and we need *Democratic Socialism*. It is like seeing that poison was added to medicine, and rather than addressing the poison and filtering it out, it is decided to instead to filter out the medicine and try to rework the poison.

True capitalists don't believe in bailouts, or lopsided rules and regulations through lobbyists giving an unfair edge, or any other kind of crony capitalism. The only way a bailout would be justified on the Freedom Scale is if the government forced a business to close their doors through no fault of the business itself. The COVID-19 pandemic would certainly qualify.

The true capitalist wants equal treatment under the law to give them an opportunity to climb as high as possible by their own merits, with no backroom deals between politicians and those at the top of the business world. They don't want politicians to pick the winners or losers but to stay neutral. I and many other true capitalists would love to see the lobbyists put out of business. True capitalists want the poison taken out of the medicine.

Do the wealthy become wealthier at the expense of lower classes under the current rules? In a sense, yes, but not in the way you might think. While the upcoming entrepreneur is limited in starting off, depending on their assets, it is their responsibility to overcome. That is not the expense I am talking about though. The playing field of opportunity is not leveled because of lobbying to give the big corporations a legal advantage. For it to be level, the government must remain neutral. Until they are neutral, there is an unfair advantage. This is the only way the wealthy become wealthier at the expense of the lower classes. It can be argued doing this is a form of both force and fraud.

I call some serious B.S. on the line about tax breaks for the wealthy at the expense of tax payers. This infers that the money earned by people isn't really theirs but the governments. This is true for individuals; there is nothing wrong with businesses being able to keep more of the money they make as well, if you believe in freedom. It goes straight to the question: Is the money you work for primarily your property or the property of the government?

Based on the analysis of Corporate Socialism, that makes two out of the three forms of socialism incompatible with freedom. Before we go into "Democratic Socialism," be aware I will also look at the specific policies and proposals of Senator Bernie

7. Capitalism vs. Socialism

Sanders for better clarification on the tax and spending policies.

Democratic Socialism: *"The government mostly benefits the citizens. Major industries can be privately owned (Capitalism), but do not receive handouts from the government at the taxpayers' expense. The tax burden is shared equitably, with wealthy corporations and individuals paying their fair share to help fund public services like education, healthcare, police, firefighters, roads, libraries, etc. With this system, the middle class thrives and poverty decreases. This system most closely aligns with Democracy = rule by the people".*

A much nicer tone in describing Democratic Socialism, isn't it? Let's see if it holds up to scrutiny. *Mostly benefits the citizens?* Sounds good so far. What are the details? *Major industries can be publicly owned (Capitalism)?* Pump the breaks a second. In capitalism, major industries *are* privately owned (whether by individuals or by shareholders), not "can be owned." Ownership can only be public or private, with public being government owned. Very often, government-owned businesses don't work out too well in a free society. Remember the referee analogy? What stops the government from abusing their power as a business owner?

The tax burden is shared equitably, with wealthy corporations and individuals paying their fair share. Define fair share and equitable. Roughly the same percentage as middle class and the poor? Not according to Senator Sanders who becomes very vague on what their fair share is when asked. He is equally

83

vague on who and what constitutes being wealthy. Also, keep in mind corporations don't pay taxes in much the same way that the government doesn't pay for anything. Taxpayers pay. The only source of revenue for corporations is from the people who buy their products and services, unless corporate socialism is present. If they have to pay corporate taxes, it comes out of the money they get from what they are selling. This means fewer and smaller raises for employees, higher cost of their products, and slower growth of the company. Bottom line: It is just another way for Uncle Sam to double dip into your pocket. . . . *to help fund public services.*

Public services are much more broadly defined than roads, police, and fire departments, etc. under Democratic Socialism. In a free society, public service is tightly defined as something average people cannot do for themselves. In all of the above examples, the infrastructure is neutral, with no specific business interest. This keeps freedom for all secure.

The problem with a broad definition of public services, is that an argument can be made for deeming anything a *public service.* Where is the line drawn? Democratic Socialism already looks to expand the definition of public services to include things like college education and universal healthcare among other things, according to their advocates. These are things people are shown to be able to provide for themselves.

Undisputed public services, such as police and fire departments, respond to all emergencies and don't delay or fail to provide service because of a business rival. The same is true for roads. Roads must be built and maintained for all and not

7. Capitalism vs. Socialism

ignored in certain areas because it helps a business rival. This is why public services cannot be run privately and without the consideration of profit. A person may not drive, but he still buys the goods brought to market through the roads his taxes help pay for. His house may never burn down or be burglarized, but the fire and police department are always there to respond, regardless of who the person is.

Senator Sanders proposes changes that would force the taxpayer to pay for things most people already provide for themselves. This responsibility would fall primarily (though not entirely) on the wealthy to pay for through tax hikes, according to Sanders. However, the combined wealth of every billionaire in the country would barely scratch the surface of Mr. Sander's spending plans. Most importantly, Senator Sanders plans to expand these public services without the public being offered the choice to say, "Thanks, but no thanks. You pay for it if you want it out of your own pocket."

You must comply at least with the money you make (your property) to help fund it for the wants of the Democratic Socialists and Sanders vision for the United States or suffer the consequences, even if you choose not to use them. But with competition gone with the rise of the government monopoly, there is no other choice to acquire what you need.

That is a dangerous aspect. Few if any of those considering socialism go so far as to support this brand. People will be stuck with what the government provides. People will get only what the government *feels* they need. Cue the slave master and slave analogy again.

People think that what is being provided by the government isn't good enough? "Oh, that is someone else's fault" is likely what the politicians will say. After all, when was the last time any of us heard any politician admit they were wrong or the effects of a policy they supported was disastrous?

Businesses may be privately owned, but the federal government under Bernie's vision, can tell you what price you have to sell your goods or services for; what you and everyone else working for the company must be paid for your work; who you can sell to; how you produce your products; who gets priority in receiving goods or serves, etc. The list goes on and on. If you can imagine it, they can regulate it in that way.

Plainly speaking it violates all three necessities for individual freedom.

But this means the middle class thrives and poverty decreases according to many Democratic Socialists. Nordic countries are often pointed to as the shining example of how Democratic Socialism works. Yet few people look to scratch beneath the surface in looking at those countries.

Senator Sanders said we should look to countries like Denmark or Sweden as examples for Democratic Socialism in the 2020 Democrat primaries. However, I doubt it is Senator Sanders' goal to be like them, especially since Denmark's prime minister, Lars Lokke Rasmussen while speaking at Harvard's Kennedy School of Government, is quoted as saying "Denmark is far from a socialist planned economy. Denmark is a market economy."

I question Sander's claim to make us like one of these Nordic countries for one simple reason. Sanders is not trying to do exactly what they have done in these Nordic countries to make them economically successful. In numerous instances he proposes doing the exact opposite of what they did. Sweden drastically reduced government spending, regulation, and privatized many government services. Let me clarify the last part. The Swedish government doesn't have a monopoly on services Democratic Socialists in the U.S. want on our businesses or the degree of regulation they have.

In Sweden everyone is taxed an outrageous amount of their income, especially the poor. Yet the main narrative heard from Sanders and his supporters is tax the rich to pay for all this. We don't hear Bernie or any of his followers say tax all of us the necessary amount to fund all this. We don't hear from Sanders about following Sweden's model of deregulation.

You can't build a Ferrari using the parts and instructions of a Gremlin and claim you are modeling it after a Ferrari. It may have four wheels, two seats, an engine, transmission, etc., but it won't look anything like or operate anywhere nearly as efficiently as a Ferrari. That is what Bernie is trying to sell you in his vision of Democratic Socialism—a Gremlin made to sound like a Ferrari. You need to follow the Ferrari blueprint to get the Ferrari.

I learned a lot of this watching a PBS documentary called *Sweden Lessons For America* hosted by a Swedish man by the name of Jonah Norberg. Now be my guest in trying to cherry pick it apart, but I guarantee none of Sanders proposals follow closely with what Sweden did. The point is if you want a country like Sweden, you follow the model as close as possible instead of cherry picking what you would like to incorporate. Otherwise, something crucial may be missing.

The system most closely aligned with Democracy = rule by the people. This statement is partially correct, but still misleading. Democracy in its purest form is mob rule. The majority gets what they want even if it is at the expense of the minority. This was addressed earlier in mentioning two wolves and one sheep voting on what is for dinner. The mob gets what it wants, and when it doesn't, there is often violence to coerce compliance from those not going along. Freedom lost because of the will of the majority is no different than freedom lost because of the will of an authoritarian dictator.

Nowhere in talking about any form of socialism, do you hear talk of personal responsibility? An individual's primary responsibility is to provide for others and to the state first and foremost as the state sees fit. Allowing individual choice can run contrary to this responsibility, to the state's interests, and to the desires of the Democratic Socialists; therefore, everyone must be forced to comply for the 'greater good.' In this regard Democratic Socialism is no different than any other form of socialism. Individual freedom is severely curtailed for what is seen as the greater good by certain individuals.

Think that is inaccurate or blown out of proportion? Answer the following questions then. What aspects of individual freedom does any form of socialism support on an economic level? Does it leave the decision between the consumer and the supplier to come to freely reach a conclusion in a transaction that is mutually beneficial to both? Does it allow you to keep the fruits

7. Capitalism vs. Socialism

of your labor providing for you and your family first? Does it leave people with as many choices on how to live as capitalism provides? Does it give people as many opportunities to escape poverty as capitalism? Does it leave you to freely pursue your own life, liberty and happiness without interference?

The answer to all of the above is *no*. Put bluntly, socialism takes property, choices, and personal responsibility away from the individual and gives it to certain people to provide for 'everyone.' as they see fit. In all examples of socialism, two things are a constant. Politicians live 'high on the hog' and the average citizen lives with what those politicians decide they need and what they decide is fair.

We have heard from Democratic Socialists that their model of socialism is taken from Nordic countries and that countries like Cuba and Venezuela are not real examples of socialism. I believe the Democratic Socialists believe it when the say it, and we hear this from them often. Yet never have I ever heard from them what will prevent their version of socialism from becoming corrupted as every other version has become corrupted. No safeguards against that corruption are ever mentioned. Most important: When was the last time anyone can recall that freedom was directly addressed by those supporting socialism. The most we hear is how with X, Y or Z paid for by the government, people will have the freedom to pursue A, B or C. It still violates the entire foundation of individual freedom as it takes from one group to give to another. Then it becomes a mad rush for people to take more out of socialist benefits than they put in.

> *"The essential notion of a capitalist society... is voluntary cooperation, voluntary exchange. The essential notion of a socialist society is force."*
> *– Milton Friedman*

The plain fact of the matter is that all forms of self-identifying socialism run contrary to freedom as force is required to gain compliance. Choice, property, and personal responsibility are forcibly taken away from everyone, and people are forced to work and be responsible to provide for the good of others as defined by the dictates of a select few, and their supporters, instead of providing only for themselves and their family.

What is the word for that again? Oh, that's right. Slavery.

8. Income Taxes and Inflation: Controlling the Fruits of Your Labor

"Collecting more taxes than is absolutely necessary is legalized robbery."
– Calvin Coolidge

To begin the discussion of taxes on the Freedom scale, you must first ask yourself a few questions.

1. <u>Do you believe the money you work for should belong to you first and foremost, and then you pay your share in taxes, or do you believe that the money you work for belongs to the government first and foremost and you are entitled to whatever they decide to let you have?</u>

In one scenario, you work primarily to support yourself and your family. In the other scenario, the government takes priority, and you work to support them and the programs they feel are needed for you and the rest of the people. Now if you believe the latter is just and are OK with it, that is your choice. It is, however, dangerous for politicians see it that way (and most likely do) because unless you are rich or have influence, they will see you as nothing more than another name working for them and their interests.

Take the Trump tax cuts from late 2017. Democrats voted against them along party lines. House Minority leader Nancy

Pelosi even went so far as to say, "This GOP tax scam is simply theft, monumental, brazen theft from the American middle-class and from every person who aspires to reach it." Let that sink in for a minute. How can a tax cut for everyone (including the middle class) be theft from the middle class, unless you believe that the money people work for does not belong to the individual taxpayer first and foremost, but instead to the government to redistribute as it sees fit? I don't know about you, but my main reason for getting up every morning and going to work is to support myself and my family, not politicians and what they and their constituents feel is best for us.

2. <u>Do you believe you are entitled to a higher or lesser percentage of the money you work for (taking all available deductions into consideration) than other people?</u>

To be truly fair to every American, everyone should pay the same percentage under all forms of taxation, and get the exact same deductions, under the same rules whether they are rich, poor, or middle class. Under an income tax system, if you force someone to pay a different tax rate or exclude them from being able to make a deduction that someone else can under the same criteria other than income, it doesn't hold everyone to the same standard, and it infringes on the property of the person paying a higher percentage.

Most people don't start off their working life in the middle upper classes. They have to further their education; they have to gain experience and some work longer hours each week to get further ahead. There are also those that sacrifice luxuries when

8. Income Taxes and Inflation

they are younger to achieve a better life for them and their families, later on. I certainly did.

Does that mean people who make say $30,000 a year should pay the same percentage of income taxes as someone making $2 million a year? Looking at it technically, yes. However, if there are no taxes paid on the first $30,000 of income for everyone, the argument could be made that the same standard is being applied to everyone and giving people the best opportunity to climb out of poverty.

Also consider that the government already takes taxes out of every paycheck for workers who are not freelance. Even if a person gets back all the tax money, they paid the previous year, they don't get interest back on the money taken out of their paycheck. This makes the question of who is paying the proper amount in taxes more questionable than it already is.

The biggest problem is an overly complicated tax code that average blue collar workers don't fully understand; nor do they have the time to properly understand it. Rich people have tax attorneys to save them as much money as possible, and the tax code is complicated for *those* attorneys.

Just adding new taxes on top or only raising the tax rate on the wealthy will do little if the areas the tax lawyers exploit for their clients are not tied up. The best remedy is to wipe out much of the current tax code and start again. Keep it as simple as possible, so everyone can follow it and clearly see who pays their fair share and who does not.

I can imagine that many power-hungry politicians do not want this. If the issue of taxes were simplified so everyone could easily understand it, the argument would likely turn from, "They are not paying their fair share," to "Quit wasting my tax dollars on ridiculous political pursuits." It would also prevent politicians from being bought by the wealthy through campaign contributions, political fundraisers, or whatever.

3. <u>Do the rich in this country owe us more than we already get from them?</u>

It has been hammered repeatedly into people that being rich is bad. Making a large profit is bad. Is it really though? They provide millions of jobs and billions in revenue. They keep the heart of our economy beating. I would say that is a good thing.

Do they owe us a higher percentage of their wealth through taxes? Looking at it from a freedom standpoint, I would say *no*. Everyone is equally entitled to their privately owned property no matter how rich or poor they are. Let the same rules apply to everyone equally, and let those rules be simplified, so everyone can see it clearly.

A number of vague arguments are made in an attempt to justify taking more from the rich and thereby often complicating the issue. These arguments range from being misleading to outright lying. Continuing in the pursuit of being fair, let's go over the most repeated arguments with the biggest reason centered around paying their fair share.

But be warned I will be asking the tough questions that will force a mirror on the wealth envy crowd. Some of you may not like what you see, if you are honest with yourself.

<u>The rich get richer and the poor get poorer.</u>

8. Income Taxes and Inflation

To a certain degree, people are correct when they say this, but most often not for the reason those who are not rich will easily admit to. The rich get richer by continuing to do what made them rich in the first place. Normally, the 'rich getting richer' by working hard, sacrificing, and responsible decision-making—not at the expense of the poor or their employees.

And the poor get poorer by doing and continuing to do what made them poor in the first place. That 'process' primarily consists of working the bare minimum, if working at all; self-indulgence for the sake of the moment, and poor decision-making in lifestyle choices.

This brings us back to one of the three basic requirements of freedom—choice. The choices you make can take you as far as you want in a free country. In pursuing a medical degree to become a doctor, that individual likely sacrifices years of any meaningful social life, to get a college degree; even more years to get a medical degree; and more years still in residency to become an M.D. or D.O. If that specialty is in high demand, they make more money as a result. Most who go to medical school make these sacrifices and put in the hard work to help ensure a prosperous future for themselves and their family. They know if they go out and party too much and get failing grades as a result, get a girl pregnant or get in trouble with the law, it is likely the end of their dream of becoming a doctor.

Success and failure start with the individual and their choices.

<u>The rich pay lower taxes than regular folk. We only want them to pay their fair share.</u>

The claim of only wanting the rich to pay their fair share is an interesting one to me, as the people saying this never clearly define what a rich person's fair share is. Some people claim the rich pay less in income taxes than the average blue-collar person. Let's examine that as well as a distinction rarely looked at.

Some rich people, such as CEOs, have stocks among other things as part of their compensation for doing their job. After receiving the stock, they take a loan out at a bank with the stock as collateral. It is debt on a loan, not a paycheck, and thus cannot be taxed as income. My guess is they pay less on the interest of the loan than they would in taxes, and bet on the appreciation of the stock to keep out of pocket costs to a minimum. Such an approach wouldn't be practical for the blue-collar taxpayer who lives from paycheck to paycheck.

The average person also does not hire a tax attorney or accountant to do their taxes to save money. A rich person does, because of the amount they can save. The average person can in many cases take advantage of the same breaks, but doesn't know where to find the breaks, and they don't hire someone because of the cost. Even if the average person hires a tax service, I'd be willing to bet they hire someone less knowledgeable, and the benefit is minimal. That is not to say there are breaks that would only apply to the rich person, but those would need to be looked at on an individual basis. It goes back to the tax code being overly complicated.

Going deeper, it is important to look at the distinction between wealth and income. Wealth is what someone is worth at any one point in time. Someone who owns millions of dollars in stock A on any given day, can find the stock becomes worth-

8. Income Taxes and Inflation

less in the future. Yet while it is worth millions many say to tax him on it. To pay that tax, that stock has to be liquidated, as no actual money is made until that happens. This clearly shows how having millions of dollars in the bank and being worth millions of dollars are two very different things. A person may be money poor, but asset rich. My grandfather, was such a man. He had a diverse portfolio of investments from stocks to precious metals, but lived on a budget, liquefying those assets as little as possible. Is it right to tax a person on something before they have cashed out any of the value on it? After all that asset may be worth nothing by the time they cash it out.

In continuing our distinction between wealth and income, look specifically at the income tax, and ask a few questions. Are they paying taxes that the average person is not paying? Suppose the salary is low, but part of the compensation is housing, utilities and a car. I would imagine those would be taxed under a separate category as they are still benefits of a job, but can't be liquidated.

Now suppose the rich person takes a year off and lives off of what they have in their safe at home. During that time their stocks grow in value by millions of dollars, but they don't cash out at all. What is their fair share to pay in taxes? They made no income from a job. Their stocks have not put a single dollar in their pocket. What is their "fair share" to pay in taxes?

If a number of other than zero is thrown out to apply to this circumstance, it isn't about paying a fair share, but about wealth envy. The same rules for taxable income apply to the blue collar and the white-collar person. The same goes for paying taxes on assets such as stocks. When the rich crowd is taxed their fair share, rarely does that mean they pay the same *percentage* as the blue-collar worker; they pay a higher percentage as you are about to see. They don't like the fact there are loopholes in the tax code that are more practical for the rich as opposed to everyone else—that is assuming they understand this rather than simply parroting what others say.

<u>The rich can afford to pay more; so, they should.</u>

Here we have an open admission against freedom. The people who support this, are essentially saying they believe the wealthy are entitled to less of their property and thus less freedom than others who make less. Just because someone can *afford* to pay more in taxes, does not mean it is less of an infringement than having them pay a higher percentage. Those people want the extra government goodies, but they want someone else to pay for them. How is that not outright theft? I guess it is OK with them because the thief is 'sharing.'

Remember what I told you about the conversation with my grandfather at the start of this book? If 100 percent of your paycheck was taken in taxes, you would be a slave and there would be no incentive to work any harder than you have to, other than fear. There is no getting around that. Some of these rich people already pay well over half the money they make in taxes, and it is still not enough for the class warfare crowd. They are always insisting that the rich pay more and more in taxes; yet we never hear about any of the class warfare crowd who are wealthy, or the politicians who support them, putting their money where

8. Income Taxes and Inflation

their mouth is, and voluntarily paying more in taxes.

There are those in the class warfare crowd who say, "Tax the rich at 90 percent" and blatantly don't want the same percentage applied to themselves. Those who believe this way and are not politicians forget one simple thing. If the government can take 90+ percent of the paycheck of one class of people, they can do it to any class of people if they do it over time. The trick for the politicians is to keep enough people dependent on them to ensure their reelection. If taxing the middle class at 90 percent will eventually ensure their reelection because 70 percent of the country is poor and depends on government programs, most politicians would probably do it without hesitation because it is the easiest path to reelection and continued power, using the same argument they currently use on the rich.

Such an attitude of the freeloaders not only hurts the well-off, but those who are up and coming entrepreneurs. Take the owner of a popular restaurant for example. Did he start off this way? Most likely not. He most likely started off as a busboy, waiter, or even a cook and worked his way up to management. Over the course of that time, he probably went to school to gain further education on the restaurant industry, whether as a chef, hotel/restaurant management or some other type of degree to help him open his own restaurant. Going to school and working at the same time, this man probably lived on a tight budget. Even after getting his college degree, he most likely stayed employed in the restaurant industry to save money for his own business and pay off student loans. Then he has to go through the entire process of opening a restaurant: save start-up money, secure loans, scout possible locations, create a menu, hire staff. It is a long and costly process. Now say that restaurant becomes successful and turns a huge profit. Does the owner live as lavishly as possible? Sometimes they do. Other times they decide to use those profits to open a second branch, but they rarely do it right away, unsure how well their business will do. Sometimes, they opt for sacrificing more personal luxury now for more potential luxury later. Most often they opt for a balance between their personal luxury, and investing in the future. If they continue to be successful, they may go nationwide or become a Michelin Star restaurant.

Now if you tax that restaurant owner more because he can afford to pay more at the time, he will be much more cautious before expanding or remodeling; he will weigh the consequences more carefully on whether it is worth all the time and effort to open another store only to pay a higher percentage in taxes. The raises and bonuses for his employees will also be less because of the higher tax rate.

The Trump tax cuts have caught flack as being primarily benefiting the rich, with the $1,000 bonuses being just crumbs, even though many of the companies increased their minimum wage voluntarily under the tax cuts. We even had more factories come back to the U.S. This helps prove my point. The rich will reinvest their money to *make* more money. As you can see it is not only the rich that benefit.

<u>Inflation is just the rich raising the cost of everything for the record profits they are making while avoiding paying their fair share.</u>

This is the most recent go to argument for going after the rich

8. Income Taxes and Inflation

from multiple angles. The situation for inflation starting in 2021 is far more complicated than price gouging for record profits. Not only are the details and context important, a lot of it goes back to supply and demand. I am no economist, and there's far more to the situation than I will write, but what I have to say and the questions raised will show there is more to inflation than the perceived price gouging we hear about.

We kept hearing about record profits across the board for so many companies, with numerous people speculating that many companies entered an agreement to raise prices. That is neither sustainable or realistic, especially if you are a big believer in corporate greed. That greed would be exactly why such a thing is unlikely. Getting a leg up on your competition is what makes money for businesses. Should we honestly believe so many stopped being competitive when being competitive could make them much more money? Let us not forget that all the small business mom and pop stores would have had to be in on it to. Their prices went up with all the big-name stores.

Something else we have seen besides record profits is more empty shelves at stores and higher prices, leading us back to supply and demand. The government response to COVID-19 slowed down trade and shipping, primarily at the ports, so goods couldn't get to market as fast. We started seeing empty shelves, and people started buying in quantity figuring they won't be able to get the products they want later. Demand increased on a supply that became limited, and it took time to catch up. As a result, prices went up. Prices went up not just for consumers but businesses as well. When demand gets too high on a limited supply, businesses will pay more to ensure they have available goods and services for their customers. This extra cost has to be paid for, so it is passed on to the consumer.

If supply and demand was ignored and the cost didn't go up, what do you think would happen? Shelves would be completely barren as people would likely panic and buy whenever new items arrive at the store. Don't believe me? We saw that happen with toilet paper and hand sanitizer at the start of COVID-19. That is just one part of inflation. What about something more recent?

The big gripe we hear about record profits for companies, especially during the largest period of inflation in forty years, is people feeling they are being cheated and those record profits are being made at the expense of the consumer. But are they really being cheated or are businesses just trying to survive? Some cheating is probably going on, but how widespread is it?

To answer both questions, we have to look at the pie chart of expenses for the companies. First, look at all of the operating costs. Are those costs higher than previous years? Are the percentages approximately still the same? Are there new expenses the companies have to pay that may account for increased prices at the store? If the percentage is roughly the same but the dollar amount, they take in has skyrocketed, the business is just trying to survive. Prices generally go up when operating costs go up so the business doesn't go under. If there are discrepancies, be sure to remember to look at the supply and demand aspect, to look for a plausible explanation before jumping to conclusions.

This brings us to the profit margin and what exactly it is. The

8. Income Taxes and Inflation

profit margin is the percentage of what is pocketed by the company after all of the bills are paid. Has that part of the pie graph increased? If it has, note how much, and go back to looking at operating costs. Does the business have enough staff? Are there bonuses being offered to recruit staff? The percentage set aside for payroll doesn't change, which is why the employees that stay don't automatically get the big pay bump or retention bonuses for sticking around when staffing is dire. Any extra percentage saved from payroll may be counted towards the profit margin, although that money isn't exactly going into the pockets of the CEOs. Most likely it is being set aside to pay for new hires when they do come in, and any bonuses offered. The business didn't raise their profit margin, but had lower expenses that they were able to meet through their increased profit margin. Hospitals are the perfect example. Most were incredibly short-staffed during the COVID-19 pandemic, and offering ridiculous bonuses to keep up.

The final big issue to consider in discussing inflation is the amount of money in circulation. More money is printed by a nation, because the government wants to spend more, to supposedly solve problems that nation is facing. Yet, no nation has ever solved it's problems by printing more money. All that does is create a new problem. In this case, the new problem is the decrease in the value of their currency.

With more money in circulation, there are more dollars chasing the same amount of consumer goods and services, increasing consumer demand. Sometimes demand increases faster than the rate of production. This is a major reason for the forty-year-high inflation rate during Biden's first years in office. Printing more money was the only way keep up with all of that COVID-19 spending.

It was not hard to imagine such a scenario, especially in combination with all of the covid restrictions we saw in place. I mentioned earlier how some think this inflation is a case of businesses being greedy and has nothing to do with printing more money or the result of other government action. What made me so sure early on? Life.

Let me tell you of an experience my family had during this inflation. In early 2022 my wife had to replace the SUV she'd had for a year when it was totaled in an accident. Buying something comparable would cost about $9000 more. This is hardly 'chump change' for most people, but finding something comparable was not easy, even with the significant price increase in those vehicles. People were still out in force buying. Even though she had gap insurance and only had the vehicle for a year she was paying mostly interest in that time, our insurance company cut her a check for around $8,500, after paying off the vehicle to cover the increased value of the vehicle that was totaled. Hardly corporate greed at work if she was cut such a substantial check.

Even with such examples existing everywhere, some people still ardently defended Biden. They held steadfast in their belief that it was just the greed of the corporations. I have laid out more than enough information to prove otherwise, but let's take it a step further, do some critical thinking, and ask the important questions.

If simply printing more money doesn't cause inflation,

8. Income Taxes and Inflation

why does this country have a national debt? Why not just print enough to cover federal spending? Keeping that train of thought going, why bother taxing anyone to raise federal revenue? If the big corporations are just jacking up prices out of greed why not have government cut checks to people to make up the difference? Why not also have the government cut even more checks to the people to ensure a "fair and livable wage"? Why not print more money to solve all financial problems? The simple reason is printing more money doesn't work: If it did work, there would be no third world countries, and the old Soviet Union would never have collapsed. One of the best examples showing the result of simply printing more money comes from Germany's Weimar Republic after World War I. Between the beginning of 1918 to the beginning of 1922, the value of 1 German paper mark (the currency at the time) went from being worth just over 1 gold mark to 1 gold mark being as valuable as around 100 paper marks. At the end of 1922, the value of the paper mark dropped significantly more, needing 10,000 paper marks to equal 1 gold mark. By the end of 1923, one gold mark was equal to about 1 trillion paper marks. Such desperation by the population allowed Hitler to come to power, and we all know what happened then.

So why does the government keep putting more money in circulation if it leads to inflation? It is quite simple. The debt accumulated by a nation is not tied to the value of its currency. So, politicians essentially keep lessening the value of the fruits of our labor so they can continue recklessly spending our tax dollars. They stave off having to pay the piper for another day. This becomes an attack on our liberty by devaluing our property,

The Freedom Scale

i.e., the money we make. Then they have the nerve to tell us we should be mad at those making more than us or sellers charging higher prices for their goods and services. Sadly, plenty of people buy into it, hook, line and sinker for a variety of reasons.

Not liking the high price of a good or service does not mean the business is cheating the people. That good or service is only as valuable as what someone else is willing to pay for it. If you don't like the price, go somewhere else. If it isn't available cheaper elsewhere, one of three things will happen.

1. *The product or service will be discontinued due to its costing more than enough people are willing to pay.*
2. *People will accept the new cost of the service or product, and this cost will become the new normal.*
3. *An entrepreneur will figure out a way to make it better and/or cheaper, keeping the price low. That is true unless unnecessary detrimental restrictions such as price controls have been put in place.*

Despite what some may think, the free market adapts for the betterment of the consumer and businesses even during inflation. It is not in any company's interest to price-gouge the consumer. Put a price too high even on an essential good or service, and people buy only the bare minimum to get by if there is no competition. As a rule of thumb, companies want people buying what they are selling as much as possible, as often as possible, even if they don't need it. That way if new competition comes

8. Income Taxes and Inflation

along, they aren't immediately put out of business from upsetting their consumer base by gouging them. Competition becomes the best assurance against price gouging.

9. Business Regulations

"I don't want to have anything to do with the government. And yet if we don't have any regulations, there goes civilization, there goes security, and there goes protecting you against what people are going to sell you."
- Charles Grodin

Much like taxes, regulation in the business world is a necessary evil, and as with taxes, too much regulation runs contrary to freedom. Why are regulations needed to protect freedom? Before regulations started popping up, there were many claims on many products that could not be backed up. As you can guess, this can be considered fraud, and is a violation of mutually informed consent.

For this chapter, we will focus primarily on the food and beverage industry as our main example because it is easiest to explain. In the late nineteenth century, the food industry was much different than it is today. Preserving food was more difficult with no freezers or refrigerators, and the condition of food sold was more questionable than it is today. Proper sanitation and quality were not required, and in a number of situations could not even be produced.

Take the creation of tomato ketchup. Henry Heinz originally created it to mask the foul taste of spoiling or rotted food. He

9. Business Regulations

made his product under more sanitary conditions than most other food businesses at that time. It wasn't long before many other copycats started making their own brand of tomato ketchup using fillers and preservatives—some of which were dangerous—to undercut costs. In response Heinz had his son lobbied the U.S. government for passage of the Pure Food and Drug Act, which included laws requiring standards of purity, consistency and quality. The passage of this act put many of Heinz's competitors out of business. Eventually the Food and Drug Administration was created to oversee such issues, and many other government agencies were created to handle and oversee laws and regulations in other areas.

Now, it is reasonable to think that regulations created by the Pure Food and Drug Act required standards that go against freedom to a certain degree. After all people would only need to read the side of the bottle of Heinz Ketchup to see the ingredients. Whether people read them or not, it is still informed consent if they buy it of their own free will. This is a valid argument. The other side can also reasonably argue, since food is a perishable item, without certain standards of quality, consistency and purity regarding the process, informed consent of the possible consequences of ingestion, become much more difficult to determine in many circumstances. People can still let meat sit out and spoil before eating it if they choose, so having quality control in the meat we buy could be acceptable under the Freedom Scale.

How about adopting a compromise to ensure safety and informed consent, without infringing on freedom? Stores either sell under FDA guidelines of quality, purity, and consistency on everything, or nothing is guaranteed. Stores that accept the guidelines are inspected and certified by the FDA and get documentation proving they are compliant and are open to continuous inspection to prove compliance. Those that don't, must advertise this and have customers sign a waiver showing informed consent. The same would apply to restaurants.

The guidelines clarify issues under today's laws and regulations that make it a felony to sell unpasteurized milk which has more bacteria and can be harmful, but there are people who prefer to drink unpasteurized milk. So long as it is labeled unpasteurized and follows the above compromise, what is the problem since that is all it would take to ensure freedom? What about children, you may ask. Hold the parent(s) or guardian(s) fully liable for any negative effects the children suffer from such food or drinks. There is room for compromise, but the main question is simple and to the point. How much control do you want to give the government in deciding what you are allowed to put in your body?

One thing the Pure Food and Drug Act got right on the side of freedom: It required manufacturers be able to back up their claims about the product. Many sodas early on were marketed as wonder tonics able to cure a variety of ailments. C.W. Post made similar claims about *Grape Nuts* when he first brought it to market. Requiring manufacturers to back up their claims prevents fraud. Whether or not the manufacturer believed it cured an ailment is beside the point. They had to be able to prove it. No question the requirement is due to mutually informed consent.

Surely, we must have standards for cleanliness, sanitation and

9. Business Regulations

quality control for everyone, right? To varying degrees depending on the business, yes. Working in surgery, I know how important sterility is in preventing post operative infections. There should be universal guidelines everyone can agree on for the safety of patients and staff in all medical settings.

While minimal cleanliness, sanitary standards, and quality control should be required of all businesses, most of them would comply without being required to maintain good public relations. In fact, it was businesses that encouraged the government to establish such standards. The Coca Cola Company led by example in promoting those standards. In 1923, they tried bottling for the first time to expand into the European market. The European bottling companies that were hired were not sanitary, spilled syrup was everywhere along with bug and rodent excrement that could easily contaminate the product throughout the factories. The result in Europe was a disaster as many got sick from drinking the product because of the bottling conditions.

Afterwards, Robert Woodruff came to power in the Coca Cola company and wanted to try bottling again. Woodruff then ordered samples from various bottling companies, which he found disgusting. Rather than abandon the idea, he incentivized the bottling companies by offering them perks to adhere to his cleanliness standards. Those that refused to go along, intentionally had things made harder for them, such as shipments being delayed. This resulted in lost revenue for those bottling companies and an increase in the quality of the bottled drink overall. Would every company take such initiative on their own?

The Freedom Scale

It is highly doubtful. There will always be people looking to take shortcuts to save a buck.

There is a possible alternative for those who disagree with me on this point and think minimal measures are not needed to ensure the safety of consumers against those who would take the shortcuts. Go back to the compromise mentioned earlier and adopt the same methods. Free choice is given, and in nearly every circumstance, there would be compliance with FDA regulations for one simple reason: Peace of mind. People pay more for something primarily for convenience and for peace of mind, and I think peace of mind would outweigh cost, especially when it comes to quality of food and drink.

In continuing with the example of Coca Cola, look at the rise of their biggest rival, Pepsi. Initially sold at Loft's soda fountains, a number of soda jerks there would serve Pepsi when they were asked for Coke. They said nothing because Coke was no longer available at Loft's locations. Something referred to as 'good substitution' is still fraud. The customer expects what they ask for. This is why when you go to a restaurant, and ask for a Coke, they sometimes ask you if Pepsi is OK. If you say *yes*, that is 'informed consent' that the substitute for what you ordered is acceptable.

Now, we have seen the benefits of regulation. Let us look at the downside of regulation, which comes when regulations are excessive or politicians favor certain businesses. During the Great Depression, Pepsi started bottling their product in 12-ounce bottles, using the bottles that beer was bottled in before Prohibition. Coke bottled in 6-ounce bottles. To give them an edge and stay in business, Pepsi sold their 12-ounce bottles

9. Business Regulations

for the same price as a 6-ounce bottle of Coke. Now imagine if the response was passing regulations at the "request" of Coca Cola, saying, "all soda has to be sold in 6-ounce bottles to be legal." Pepsi would likely not be in business today.

Yet today Washington DC is filled with lobbyists representing a variety of large companies, lobbying the federal government for rules and regulations to give their company an edge. There is so much regulation, it is hard to keep track of it all. More regulation is added all the time, enforced by a wide variety of government agencies with a number of the regulations that are either redundant or obsolete, and compliance costs businesses a great deal of money. This isn't as big a problem for large businesses, who can afford the lobbying efforts and the added cost of regulations. Some of them I am sure actually prefer it, as they don't want any 'little guy' catching up with them and becoming a threat. It is easier for the big businesses to lobby to help keep the competition down instead of innovating to make their product better to stay ahead. This success is coming at the forced expense of others, which is primarily small businesses and consumers.

These regulations were added by our elected officials because they believed those regulations would help the American people—or could there be a more selfish reason? Is it possible there is a *quid pro quo* among certain politicians and businesses in this regard? I wouldn't be surprised if we learned for certain that there was. Makes one more great argument for keeping regulations to a minimum.

One of the best reasons for minimal regulation is illustrated by a story my grandfather told me when I was a young boy about

The Freedom Scale

how much government regulations can hurt society. He told me he was friends with the man who created the first automated car wash, and that this man in the early 1970s, I think, successfully built and tested a car that got seventy highway miles per gallon of gas. He did this for less than the cost of a new car at that time. Why was it never put into production? This man built the vehicle privately ignoring government regulations. He wanted to learn what the minimum amount needed to make a car was. As it turned out, the cost of complying with government regulations on the production of automobiles, made his car unaffordable for the consumer and unprofitable for any salesperson.

Is this a tall tale or fact? I don't know. With my grandfather long gone, I cannot verify it; nor do I have more information on this matter, not even a name.

Imagine though for a moment that a car manufacturer was given the task of creating a car with only three requirements, and suppose he ignored all other regulations.

The Three Requirements:

- Not infringe on safety. (with airbag requirements being the exception)
- Get 70 highway miles on a gallon of gasoline (with regulations on gasoline standards ignored if they choose).
- Cost to be less or no more than the cheapest new car.

I am sure it could be done. The logical way to go about it

9. Business Regulations

would be to look at what regulations are necessary, remove the ones that are not, and then build the vehicle. Leave a way for regulations to be easily reversed. If it can only be applied to this specific product for this specific reason, give it a thorough vetting and make the decision from there with full transparency to the public. Individuals then decide for themselves, and freedom is restored.

My grandfather's story took place around half a century ago. More recently X-Prize offered a $10 million prize to the winner of such a challenge. The challenge was to produce a car that could get 100 miles per gallon. To win, the competitors were judged in a variety of other categories, such as appearance and safety. The car the winning team produced got 102 miles per gallon. Imagine how much more affordable and available such cars would be without excessive regulations.

While far from perfect in regulation reduction, Donald Trump was successful to a degree removing five regulations for every new one passed, although he exaggerated it to be more than it was. Being a businessman, before he was President, he would know. This could help explain why the economy was so good under him before COVID-19. His successor to the White House, Joe Biden has shown no sign I can see of trying to do something similar in reducing excessive regulations.

Having an excess of laws and regulations in place unfortunately allows politicians to play an aspect of fascism to their advantage. Unlike any form of socialism where businesses are owned by the government or certain people, this aspect of fascism says the businesses are privately owned but directed by the government through laws and regulations. When prices go up if say through inflation, the politicians just scream price gouging by the private business, and those consumed with wealth envy go along and are willing to accept new regulations.

Look at how much the cost of gasoline went up the first few years of Biden's presidency. Many of his supporters kept claiming he had no control over the cost of gas, and it was just price gouging by the evil oil companies. His supporters did not look at what he may have been doing that would lead to a price increase, such as denying drilling leases for oil companies. Then, when prices slowly started going down, they gave Biden credit. One question more than others in determining whether or not price gouging was in effect—they never asked. If corporate greed was the reason for price increases at the pump, why did gas prices go down at all, unless other factors played a role?

As I have shown, regulations to a degree, can be a very good thing, when they apply reasonable standards of quality and consistency and make sure businesses can back up their claims. Regulation clearly goes too far when it infringes on others to give one group a competitive edge, or when government has too much power. The writers of regulations must be impartial referees when it comes to what is enacted. If that means a big donor doesn't get a competitive edge because certain regulations are not passed, so be it.

Here is one final thing worth mentioning: There is a point where regulation and taxes merge in a most unsettling manner, and that is excise taxes. These taxes are on specific items and can be a way of targeting certain companies for a variety of reasons.

9. Business Regulations

These taxes can either be directly on the consumer or hidden in the price passed on to the consumer by the retailer. Such examples include buying a pack of cigarettes, a gallon of gasoline (or diesel), or even a bottle of alcohol among others.

What makes excise taxes so unsettling? As I said, it singles out specific products. Don't want people smoking? Implement and keep increasing the excise tax on cigarettes and cigars. Want more people to drive electric cars? Impose an excise tax on all internal combustion engine vehicles, gas, car parts, etc. and keep increasing it. Don't want people drinking sodas because of the sugar content? Implement and keep increasing an excise tax on all of those beverages. You get the picture. This may not be the reason for every politician voting for excise taxes, but it still is a means to accomplishing the same authoritarian ends.

Excise taxes picks winners and losers and allows politicians to move you in the direction that they want and feel is best. It becomes a manner of control over American consumers and producers, as well as a possible way for politicians to make some extra money on the side. Consider the possibility of a politician voting in favor of an excise tax because those on the receiving end of that tax don't make political contributions. Or another real possibility: Organizations or individuals including big campaign contributors to those politicians would benefit financially.

Nothing would be safe. Just move the excise tax in the same manner as the Overton Window. Start out with a small excise tax, and slowly increase it over a period of time to avoid being noticed. By the time anyone takes notice, the new price has already been common place for a while. That would be how something popular like coffee would be attacked. After all, caffeine is addictive and not exactly healthy.

But the Overton Window approach wouldn't always be the approach for utilizing an excise tax. It can possibly be used as a back door to circumventing individual liberty more directly in the short term. Say you want to restrict future firearms ownership on law abiding citizens, but the Second Amendment prevents that, despite what the outspoken advocates want. By passing a massive excise tax on guns and/or ammunition that most people cannot afford, the same goal is largely accomplished without a ban. The majority of politicians won't be voted out of office if most of their constituents support it, and they still largely do an end run around freedom.

Whether or not you support the measure on guns is not the point. The point is that if politicians can circumvent this freedom with an excise tax, how many other freedoms can be circumvented? Perhaps one or two will affect issues that do matter to you. How about a large excise tax on all abortions? Would that become the convincing argument to get rid of excise taxes completely or would the issues important to you be the hypocritical exceptions to the rule?

A solution will be addressed in a few chapters. Keep reading.

10. Something for Nothing: Government Entitlement Programs

"When a portion of wealth is transferred from the person who has acquired it, without his consent and without compensation, to someone who has not created it, whether this is by force or by – to anyone who does not own it, then I say there has been a violation of property rights and there has been an act of plunder."
– Frederic Bastiat, The Law

We have all heard of government programs designed to help the "less fortunate" in our society. The biggest examples are welfare, government housing, Medicaid and food stamps. Now that we have established that private property is essential to freedom, and that the money we work for is our private property, we must ask about our money being forcibly taken to subsidize the "less fortunate."

Some will argue that under freedom, all help for these people should be voluntary, and they would be correct. Opponents will say that voluntary charity would not cover the needed expenses. Maybe it will, maybe it won't, but it is our money, and we have a right to see our money spent in a way we see fit. If our money is spent in a reckless manner by a charity, we don't donate to that charity anymore. Why should government get a pass?

The Freedom Scale

I have no problem with my tax dollars helping those in financial distress, people who have fallen on hard times and need help. The main problem every freedom loving American has with entitlement programs is how they are enacted and run, as no great incentive is offered for people to get off of these programs and no choice is given to us in withholding our tax dollars for them. While there are those who only use the benefits until they get back on their feet, others abuse the system to get a free ride at our expense for as long as they can and become dependent on the system. When a person becomes dependent on others to provide for them, the person becomes a slave to the provider's will.

The solution, if our society chooses to keep such programs, must be to remove the incentives—as much as possible—to be a part of these systems, so they are only used by people for a short period of time and only under dire circumstances.

What are some ways to do that? We can start with limiting the timeframe for receiving such benefits. Also, create a minimum timeframe between the times a person is living on their own until they can reapply for these handouts. Let's look at specific programs going forward.

I remember when I first joined the working class, there was a single mom at the restaurant where I worked. She left shortly after she started the job, making the comment that she made more on welfare than working at the restaurant. Having welfare payments greater than the minimum wage is a large part of the problem. More concerning is the ability to get even more money when having additional children while on welfare. Start off by

10. Something for Nothing

slashing welfare payments, so people only receive the working minimum wage. Allow an exemption to the payment slash for those going to school for an in-demand trade that will provide them more money. Next, stop increasing welfare for people who have children while collecting welfare.

With food stamps, only allow certain foods to be bought. Stop allowing people to use food stamps to purchase steaks, chips, sodas, junk food, preprocessed frozen food, alcohol, or any kind of high-end food. Also disallow food stamps be converted into cash. Limit the foods to be bought to include lunch meat, cheese, rice, beans, fresh fruit and vegetables among some others. In other words, allow only 'poor people' food and food of a high nutritional value. Anyone who wants to buy junk food or anything I listed above, can buy it when they have a job and are using their earnings to buy these things.

How about Medicaid benefits? Recipients must abide by specific health criteria during that timeframe. Ban consumption and use of alcohol, drugs, and nicotine products. Require weekly screenings to ensure compliance. If we the taxpayers are going to be paying their medical bills, then we should have a say in what substances they can indulge in that can create costly medical issues.

Finally, we get to government housing. Often times the housing is beat up and run down as the tenants abuse it. After all they have no personal stake in it, so why care about maintaining it? Speaking from personal experience, the solution is to apply the same rules of on base barracks housing for single service members in the military. Have surprise weekly inspections of

The Freedom Scale

the living environment. Any property not authorized cannot be present such as certain luxury items. Having a 60' 4K plasma tv, demonstrates a luxury someone needing this government assistance cannot afford, and thus is not authorized. Such luxury items present would be confiscated and sold to help reimburse the taxpayers. All private property coming into the housing would be inventoried for such reasons. As such, the recipients of government housing will also take responsibility for everything owned by the taxpayers in such housing.Cleanliness must be maintained at all times with no damage to the housing facility the recipients reside in. Any violation would result in removal from the government housing, along with violating any other rules as a condition set forth.

Something I have been saying for years, which would apply to recipients of any of the handouts above is removal of the ability to legally vote in elections. A person or family would have to be off of welfare for 6 months prior to an election to be eligible to vote and is ineligible for any of these benefits for a minimum of six months after they vote in an election. At the very least, it would cut out wasteful spending and start discouraging dependence on such programs.

Don't think such measures are fair? Think they violate the rights or dignity of the people dependent on those handouts? Many parents have said to their children, "While you live under my house, you will live by my rules." This is no different. Allowing the ability of people on any of these programs to vote in elections for example, creates a conflict of interest. The people receiving taxpayer funded benefits will be most inclined to vote

10. Something for Nothing

for the people and measures that will give them the most benefits with the least restrictions, as their lifestyle depends it. There is an old saying. "Those robbing Peter to pay Paul, can always count on Paul's support." In this case, Peter is the taxpayer, and Paul is the recipient of these social programs. Why do you think you never hear of slashing any of these programs when it comes to government spending, but you hear about how spending cuts will hurt those on Social Security? Politicians know what their supporters will turn on them for. Cuts to government handouts isn't a universal scare tactic for most taxpayers, but a surefire way to lose a specific voting bloc, if you already support generous handouts and suddenly want to reign them in.

To bottom line my feelings on how the recipients of these handouts feel about such rules and requirements for receiving taxpayer funded support is simple. I don't care what their feelings are about it. If someone is living off of the fruits of my labor, I want strict rules to help ensure I am not being taken advantage of since I don't have a choice in my tax dollars paying for them. As taxpayers we are entitled to that. The recipients are not entitled to any such consideration. Beggars can't be choosers.

It all comes back to the foundation of freedom. Applying for these handouts is an individual choice. If the rules and requirements are too much, then don't get them. If the personal responsibility to follow through with the rules and requirements of these programs is too much, then don't choose to apply for them. Plenty of people choose to be homeless instead of accept the rules of others. The people looking for the benefits of these programs may not like what they have to agree to, but

The Freedom Scale

why should that matter? They are only supposed to be temporary measures to help people get back on their feet. Those who have the most problems with it, I imagine are those looking to exploit these programs. Why else should anyone be outraged over temporary measures?

11. Minimum Wage/ Living Wage

Minimum wage requires that employers be forced to pay a set minimum amount of money for the work that they provide. A living wage requires that employers be forced to pay what others determine is needed to live on. Pretty straight forward in both descriptions. This issue will be dissected from multiple angles, often sounding repetitive, but it is important to best gauge the full spectrum. There are questions to be asked and considered that some people may not have even thought about before. To start this discussion, we first have to go back to basics.

Seven Factors determining pay

Before deciding if raising the minimum wage, or even creating a living wage for everyone is better, we have to look at the main things employers look at in deciding the compensation for a job they are offering. What currently determines wages for any job is primarily narrowed down to any combination of seven things.

Experience: The more experience a person has in a particular skill set, the less training they need for a particular job and the more efficiently they perform that job, thus deserving higher pay. These are normally the people who do the best work and train new hires about how to best perform their job for a specific company.

The Freedom Scale

Education: Some jobs require various degrees of education. It could be as little as a high school diploma to a master's degree or doctorate, and could extend to requiring certification or licensing. The jobs requiring additional education outside of high school normally require years of extra education at minimum. Thus, people need to be paid more who have acquired the specific skill set with their education for a particular job; otherwise, nobody would bother getting that education.

Supply and Demand: Experience and education will only take you so far. There must be a demand for your field of work. A college degree does not automatically create a great deal of demand. Numerous fields of work pay well without requiring a college degree. Trash collectors, for example, do a job that most people are capable of but don't want because of everything it entails. Without a doubt we need people willing to do this work, but extra incentive is needed for people to choose this employment. Aside from the smell and handling the disgust most people have with garbage on a daily basis, there is also the factor of getting up early in the morning as well as having to do the job in unfavorable weather conditions. How many people are willing to tolerate such conditions day in and day out?

Now look at someone with a degree whose job is in high demand like a registered nurse. There are education requirements of an associate's degree to a bachelor's degree. Licensing in each state is also required. Now the limited number of people with an RN degree and license, for example, already limits the number of people qualified for this job. Now if colleges turned out far

11. Minimum Wage/ Living Wage

more RNs than there was a demand for, their nice salaries would stagnate, because there is a much larger group of potential employees for employers to choose from.

Also pay may vary amongst RNs with the different RN positions available. Many may not want to work in the emergency department or the graveyard shift, so those nurses may be offered more than the standard RN. The most ideal positions may offer less compensation, as those positions often draw more applicants. With more applicants, the odds are better there will be a desirable candidate in a better price range for the employer.

Danger level: The hazard level of a job can be the least determining factor in determining the pay of a job but is still pretty significant. Various jobs are always present from those requiring a significant amount of education to those requiring little education. Take a corrections officer (CO). While it can be very hazardous, it requires little training compared to other jobs, and is not very high paying starting out, but the amount of pay depends on where they work. A CO at a maximum-security prison for example, gets paid far more than someone at a standard prison, because the danger is significantly higher when housing convicted rapists and murderers as opposed to counterfeiters and petty thieves; Corrections officers need to be incentivized to take the more dangerous positions. After all, if the pay were the same across the board for all COs, nobody would volunteer to work in maximum-security prisons.

Skill level: This requirement relies most on the individual's natural abilities and experience. It is a question of where do the individual's talents reside, more than how high is their IQ.

The Freedom Scale

Take a realtor for example. A college degree may be desired but not required. If you look at the example of a realtor, you know that while they need to be proficient in the paperwork aspect of realty, being a good salesman helps more than anything else, something that can be gained with prior experience.

A doctor can be the most skilled surgeon in the world, but it doesn't automatically mean he would ever be a good salesman no matter how hard he tries, how smart he is, or how good his bedside manner is. Plenty of surgeons don't have to sell their skills to their patients, the same way realtors do. This is especially true if the patients are either dying or in pain and want that pain to go away first and foremost. It's a different story when people can shop around.

Value produced: The amount of money someone earns in a job also reflects how much money is made by a company as a result of the individual's contribution. The realtor who sells a house for $200,000 does not pocket $300,000 for himself, let alone make anything for the realty company he works for. The value isn't there for anyone to make $300,000 off of that sale. The commission my realtor got when I sold my house was 6 percent. My realtor did not pocket that entire amount. He like many others, worked for a large realty group, and that group has lots of expenses.

Insisting that everyone who works deserves a living wage, doesn't necessarily make every worker worth that wage. It only become worth it when someone sees the value produced as being worth it and has the desire and means to pay for it.

11. Minimum Wage/ Living Wage

Responsibility: Many people rail against the CEOs and owners of big companies, but don't look at the big picture. It is their responsibility to make sure the company they represent makes as much money as possible. If a burger flipper doesn't do their job properly, a few customers may be lost and the flipper loses his job. If an owner or CEO doesn't do their job properly, stores close, sometimes the entire business, costing many more jobs, not to mention livelihoods. When the main Kellogg factory burned down in 1907, Will Kellogg had to secure the loans to rebuild. His neck was on the line to repay those loans, not the employees of the factory.

There lies the difference in responsibility. A CEO normally has years of leadership and managerial experience in the field, and years of education. Those best qualified are in short supply. If you want the people best qualified to do the jobs where responsibility and good decision-making is the main focus, you have to pay for it. Put it this way, would you as a shareholder of a fortune 500 company where your retirement is invested, want the person making the decisions to have the best track record of making money for a company? Or do want some guy who only seems to have the most basic skills? The more money involved in the company, the more incentive is needed to recruit the best and the brightest to run the day-to-day operation and make sure they don't lose ground to the competition.

Let's look at something more basic in responsibility, like the Captain of a Naval vessel. He is paid far more than everyone under his command, but he is also the one ultimately responsible for the proper operation of his ship and the lives of his crew. If his ship runs aground, he is still responsible and will likely be relieved of command, even if he was asleep in his quarters at the time; he is ultimately responsible for making sure that everyone under his command is properly trained can do their job efficiently.

Uncomfortable Questions on the Issues

Who are the people on minimum wage, and who are those *demanding* a living wage? The vast majority are kids in high school; kids working their way through college, and people with little to no ambition to advance beyond their current station in the working world. Most lack marketable job skills elsewhere as a result of that lack of ambition. There are also a number of retirees and people between jobs working for minimum wage until they find something better.

I admit for a number of years after I got out of high school, I was one of those people with no real ambition. After getting out of the Navy, I worked in corrections, which paid only a little better than minimum wage at the facilities and department I worked in. I then moved to private security and contract security. While contract security work paid well, jobs were few and far between and very competitive when there wasn't demand for a lot of people or requirements for applicants were too much of a hurdle. Being married at that time, and looking to have children with my wife, I had a choice to make. Do I continue my schooling and get a degree or keep scrounging for good security jobs that would likely take me away from home for long stretches at a time?

11. Minimum Wage/ Living Wage

I chose the former and used my GI bill to get my associate's degree and certification in surgical technology. This is a job always in demand, so much so travel positions are available all over the country that pay more than standard surgical technologist positions. I make a pretty good living where I am at now, and the demand is only increasing in many parts of the country.

I was told once that whatever job a person has is a conditional gift from an employer that can be taken back at any time by that employer, even if you do your job very well. To a large degree this is true in a free society. Say you are applying to be a restaurant cook. Before you get the job, a number of factors must be considered (positive and negative) including the factors listed earlier. You tell the boss interviewing you what you want to make and looking over your resume, he decides whether or not to pay you what you are asking, or to negotiate, or to decline your application. Say he decides to hire you. You agree to do this work, during these hours, on these specific days for this amount of pay and benefits for however long the employer decides they need your services. He reserves the right to send you home early if the restaurant isn't too busy, or he may later say he doesn't require your services any longer and fires you. You, on the other hand, reserve the right to leave that job at any time for any reason.

Here you have a mutually informed decision between the employer and you, the new employee. Both of you have freely come to an agreement in the terms without the use of force. He pays you the mutually agreed upon value of your work, and you do the work agreed upon. You both win.

Say you like working for this employer and are good at your

The Freedom Scale

job and want to earn more doing it. You have the opportunity for advancement. You could become the kitchen manager, general manager or even end up owning that restaurant or several like it. That, however, will depend on the choices you make. It's a great start to do more than is expected of you, do your job better than expected, and agree to help out on shifts when you are needed when nobody else is willing or available. Going to school for culinary arts or hotel/ restaurant management would be a huge boost and help you advance to such a goal.

Let's look at the main arguments for increasing the minimum wage and mandating a living wage, and then see where it stands on the Freedom Scale.

<u>The wealthy get rich at the expense of their employees who make minimum wage plus tips the customers leave them, while the owners make millions.</u>

Let me address that by talking about one of my favorite television shows, *Bar Rescue*. The show opens by saying that "every year, hundreds of failing bars will close their doors for good." Many times, the bars were successful at one time.

Most episodes go the same way; a bar in debt will go out of business soon unless bar expert, John Taffer helps them. Normally the audience of the show is treated to outrageous behavior from the staff and owners. There is yelling back and forth, and then John steps in adding to that behavior to wake up the owners and the staff to reality before helping the bar. A key thing on the show is often the laziness of many employees. Everyone in the working world has seen similar behavior from fellow employees, perhaps even engaged in that behavior themselves. That can be

11. Minimum Wage/ Living Wage

seen as the worker getting richer at the expense of their employer.

However, one specific element in nearly every case must be considered. The owners are mismanaging their bar and losing money. If the bar goes under, the owners lose everything. The bar, their home, their life savings, and a horrible credit rating is what they are left with as they struggle to rebuild their life. What did the employees lose? At most their job. They didn't put their livelihood on the line like the owner, so why should a regular employee make a large amount of money like the owner of the company?

Now the owner of any business will normally not pay their employee more than they feel the employee's skills are worth. If the employee feels they are not being paid enough, there are normally two options. They can ask for a raise or quit and look for a job that will pay what they believe they are worth. Unless they have a contract, nobody is forcing them to work there if they don't want to. Of course, where a contract was signed, both parties made a mutually informed and consensual choice. Nobody forced them to take that job in the first place. The decision for the employee to have a job is a decision reached by mutual, informed, consent between the employer and employee without force or fraud.

<u>People can't survive on minimum wage, let alone support a family on minimum wage; thus, it needs to be increased a living wage.</u>

In demanding a living wage, the people who support it don't ever seem to elaborate on the specific details of everything it entails when making this claim. What kind of housing would the living wage provide? What kind of transportation? How about the food budget, job benefits, or even the size of the family? The most important questions though are how a living wage is decided, and who makes the decisions surrounding everything a living wage entails?

I imagine the reason we don't hear the details is because each person wanting a living wage has their own definition or required changes to meet their needs. The person with a family of three to support would need far more in every aspect than a single person living in a studio apartment.

Is it fair to pay the man with a family the living wage to support his family and then pay the single man only enough to support himself for the same work and the same hours at the same facility? Should far more money be given to the man with the family for the sole reason that he needs it more? After all, a man with a wife and kids can't support his family on the single man's living wage. A number of other scenarios might be considered. What if the single person living in the studio apartment is in walking distance to work and the grocery store. Should he really be paid to afford a car when he doesn't need it?

Taking all of this into consideration in discussing a living wage, sounds eerily similar to the thinking of one of the chief architects of communism. He was in no way a friend or champion of freedom.

> *"From each according to his ability, to each according to his needs."*
> *– Karl Marx*

Luckily, actual freedom loving people do not embrace this

11. Minimum Wage/ Living Wage

Marxist line of thinking, looking to force employers to pay what the entitled feel is just. This is because they realize one important thing. It is about personal responsibility. Having a family is a choice. The actions leading to people having children is a choice. If you don't have enough marketable job skills to make more than minimum wage, you shouldn't be engaging in the actions that result in pregnancy without taking adequate precautions.

Supporting yourself is your personal responsibility. Your choices will be limited, based on your income, but it is possible. You may need to get one or more roommates. You may not be able to afford to live in the type of place you want or the neighborhood you want. You may need to get more than one job. You may be eating ramen noodles a few nights a week and have no money to go out or have the desired luxuries, but you can make it. 'Wanting more' encourages people to advance their position in life, so they can get more. Others are so lazy; they would prefer to have politicians force their employer to pay them more. It is easier to push for politicians to do it for them, and with enough lazy people, many politicians are more than willing to accommodate them. The result is a group of people with an overblown sense of entitlement.

<u>Without the employees the business can't make nearly as much money. Without a living wage workers are paid slave wages to make their employer rich. The employees operate the stores and sell the products, and as such are having the fruits of their labor stolen by their employers.</u>

This is the primary argument I hear for a living wage. It is an argument that is not rooted in reality, as it cannot stand up under scrutiny. It is approached from an entitled standpoint of trying to have your cake and eat it too. Let me elaborate.

Like most individuals, every business, big or small has a budget, and staying in business is a constant balancing act. Usually, a percentage of every dollar that a business makes has a designated purpose in their budget, usually represented in a pie chart. That money has to be used first for necessities including the building, utilities, insurance, cleaning supplies, equipment such as cash registers, computers, uniforms, etc. Probably the biggest expense is their employees. Employee pay and benefits usually amounts to approximately 1/3 of a company's budget. After all financial obligations are met, the profit is calculated, and the owners get paid from that. If the business is doing poorly, should the employees still get their living wage from the business? The owners don't. Their living wage comes from the profits of the business. If the company doesn't make money, the owners don't make money, but the employees still get paid for their hours worked. Are employees willing to forgo a guaranteed payday if sales are down or the business is losing money? If business is good, are employees willing to share the burden of business expenses, and pay a portion of their living wage for repairs, updates, taxes and other expenses of their employer's business?

Here is a better perspective to consider for those demanding a living wage and believing the fruits of their labor are stolen to make their bosses rich. Do the employees own the means of production for the products being sold? How about the business, or even the cash register/POS system to process the transactions?

11. Minimum Wage/ Living Wage

Do employees even own the products they are selling or making? Is their name even on the lease to the building? No. The owners own or are responsible for paying for all of that allowing the employees the opportunity to earn a living doing their job. Would it be right for the owners to charge employees a fee for use of their resources to make or sell the product? After all someone's labor had to pay for the operating costs. Couldn't using all those resources the employer owns and the employee uses free of charge be considered stealing the fruits of the owner's labor if they are not paid a fee for the employees using it?

No employee would work under such conditions. So why would anyone expect a prospective business owner to take such a huge risk in opening a business for such little reward—even if successful—by being forced to pay employees so much more than the market dictates they are worth? There is of course a solution for those who insist on a living wage for everyone.

Let them start their own company, selling whatever they want. Let the focus of their advertising be that they pay a living wage, instead of focusing on quality or value, and see how successful they are and for how long. I imagine they would not be very successful as no business regardless of politics has ever done that to my knowledge. That is likely because it moves from someone else's money being on the line, to their money being on the line. As politicians are well aware, it is easy to be generous with someone else's money. Yes, employees are important in producing, but the money has to come from the consumer. The wants and needs of the consumer come first.

Looking on the surface, focusing on large businesses and

The Freedom Scale

ignoring small businesses, it is easy to say the big CEOs make several million dollars a year so they can afford to pay a living wage. Assume for a moment that it is as simple as that with no adverse consequences for big corporations. Competition decreases for those big corporations because many small business owners are not millionaires and sometimes cannot afford to offer what advocates consider a living wage. What company is hurt more financially by living wage requirements more? It certainly doesn't hurt the CEO and his multibillion-dollar company near as much as the small business. That CEO can also go a different route as he can afford lobbyists to push new rules that his startup competition cannot afford. Just look at the exemption to a minimum wage law in California that Governor Newsom gave to the multi-billion-dollar restaurant chain, Panera Bread.

The question of workers or CEOs often makes the assumptions CEOs do nothing and get everything while the average employee slaves away and gets next to nothing. Big CEOs, however, rarely if ever sit back in their corner office watching the money flow in. They often answer to a board of directors who want a much bigger return on the investment of that CEO's lush compensation package. CEOs constantly have to make the decisions that keep the business in business, as no big corporation is immune to failure. Circuit City, Toys R' Us, and Blockbuster Video, were all once nationwide businesses. Now, each is either out of business or it is a shell of their former successful model, at best. Several thousand jobs are gone because of the poor leadership that led those companies to ruin. This shows that good CEOs and good owners running a company are far more valuable than an aver-

11. Minimum Wage/ Living Wage

age employee demanding a living wage. Those CEOs can choose to retire whenever they want. They won't be hurt if companies are forced to give in. They can chill on a tropical beach and enjoy retirement. Let it be a headache for the next guy. How much would it hurt the employees of that corporation though, if they were forced to hire a CEO not up to the task of that position, who then led the company to its downfall because they were forced to provide the living wage that the advocates want? The downfall would be because of a sense entitlement and wealth envy.

<u>Billionaires are hoarding the wealth, leaving little for everyone else, especially their employees. It isn't right, especially with so many people starving.</u>

This is actually an argument that can and has been used for taxing the rich more. This is one of my favorites because scratching the surface makes the entire argument collapse. It would have you believe that all rich people live like Scrooge McDuck, with a huge money bin holding all of their money so that they can swim in the gold coins. That would be a perfect example of hoarding the money, and what I always think of whenever I hear this argument.

While I have no doubt, most billionaires have considerable wealth that they could liquidate easily; I am fairly certain that is not where the majority of their wealth lies. In reality most of the wealth of billionaires is tied up in banks, stocks, bonds, and other investments to bring in more money. The money is going out into the world. It is paying salaries; it is giving banks enough money to offer loans. Bottom line, the money isn't sitting idle. It is fueling our economy.

Even if money is being hoarded by a rich individual who earned it, so what? It is their business and their money. People in the U.S. have been rising out of debt and becoming successful for hundreds of years in this country; even when they were the underdog, they didn't have to resort to theft or vote for thieves to act on their behalf.

An Endless Cycle

"One of the great mistakes is to judge policies and programs by their intentions rather than their results."
–Milton Friedman

We have gone over the reasons primarily in this chapter, but haven't really addressed the freedom aspect as much yet. Sometimes more practical reasoning is needed before applying the freedom aspect, as politicians can make answers that go against freedom sound appealing. With that said, requiring either a minimum wage or a living wage runs contrary to individual freedom, as both infringe on it in numerous ways.

Both force the requirement that one of the two parties involved must pay at least X amount, which in some cases is more than it would be otherwise. This creates a negative and endless cycle offering no lasting solution. Let us look at the minimum wage first.

- Entertaining raising minimum wage encourages people with minimal marketable job skills to avoid taking **personal responsibility** for their decisions, and as a result

11. Minimum Wage/ Living Wage

forces the rest of society to subsidize them in their profession. They want to have their cake and eat it too. They want the money in order to live more comfortably, and feel entitled to that money without having to work harder for it.

- This in turn decreases purchasing power for everyone regardless of salary, as prices will go up to help offset the new minimum wage. The amount of money made by people in higher paying positions doesn't automatically go up. You just have to hope an annual cost of living increase at your job makes up the difference. Eventually you get back to point where people are screaming for another increase in the minimum wage, because they are right back where they started.

Now look at mandating a living wage. This would likely affect far more people than the small percentage of the population living on minimum wage, so we would easily see more drastic effects, especially depending on what that new living wage would entail. One of the direct consequences of mandating a living wage is it would easily create a greater shortage in professions with higher demand.

Assume for a moment that a minimum living wage was passed and was comparable to a licensed practical nurse which is a step below an RN, but still has a significant demand. Nobody would pay for the education to become an LPN, much less the licensing fees as well as the work and expense to acquire and maintain that license if they were not well compensated. If someone flipping burgers would be making approximately the same amount of money with far less hassle, why would people such as the LPNs bother to keep up with their licensing let alone the responsibility of patient care when they can move to a different job for the same pay with less responsibility? Odds are LPNs and people making similar pay would replace the burger flipper, for a variety of reasons. How does that help the original burger flippers? How would that help patients that need an LPN for home health, hospice, or even nursing home care when all of them left for an easier job that pays the same?

`What is the incentive for anyone to be an LPN when they can work in a less stressful job flipping burgers, or working a cash register? LPNs after all have already shown commitment in both their job and educations, making them more ideal for a business owner to hire than the average burger flipper. Seriously; for roughly the same daily compensation, would you rather be wiping an 80-year-old man's ass in hospice or asking would you like fries with your burger? So, to keep the incentive to become or stay an LPN, incentives above that new minimum living wage have to be created for them. Now look at all the other jobs whose compensation and requirements are similar to LPNs and factor them in as well. What do you think that will lead to? You guessed it. Higher wages all around that creep all the way up the wage ladder over time, before the demand for a new living wage comes up once again, starting the entire cycle all over.

11. Minimum Wage/ Living Wage

Lists of Threes

What is the best course of action to help individuals avoid poverty if not a mandated living wage? The answer lies in the freedom aspect of personal responsibility. According to the Brookings Institution and their research, there are three common denominators an individual needs to get out of poverty. Their research shows it applies to 98 percent of the U.S. population who do these things.

1. *Have a full-time job.*
2. *Graduate High School.*
3. *Don't get married and have children until you are at least twenty-one years old.*

I outlined my work history earlier. My only child was not born until I was thirty-seven years old and had been married approximately ten years. I wanted to be able to give my daughter everything I could, so my wife and I struggled for years to get where we wanted in life *before* having a child. We did this so we wouldn't have to struggle and fight over money once we became parents. This meant getting my degree, securing a good job, and buying a house before having a child. It was many years of hard work and sacrifice. I can only imagine how much harder everything would have been otherwise, if we didn't take personal responsibility for our lives in our plans for the future.

One final thought on this topic. Columnist Walter Williams, once asked probably the most important question regarding the minimum wage. If the minimum wage works so well in lifting

The Freedom Scale

people out of poverty, why are we sending billions of tax dollars in foreign aid and relief to numerous other countries, instead of telling these countries to raise their minimum wage? After all, if it worked, we could save billions of taxpayer dollars and help these countries in one fell swoop. Kill two birds with one stone. Yet we never hear this question brought up to our elected officials. I wonder why.

12. Unions

Unions started off as a way to get businesses concerned about their employees. In all honesty, I agree unions were crucial in dealing with the abuse of employees by their employers. Unfortunately, the pendulum of good they have done has swung the other direction into something completely different. When you look at it honestly, unions have become more insignificant in today's world with the creation of the internet and social media and companies wanting good public relations.

First let us define unions and explain what they do. Put simply, unions are part of a collective group of employees within a company. The group uses the collective bargaining power of its members to negotiate what they want from the employer. A single union may represent many different employees, working in many different companies depending on how big they are. If the union strikes, every member of that union stops working where the strike occurred, requiring the owners to negotiate.

Today the fight on the Union front is primarily on the state level, between union states and right-to-work states. In Union states, a unionized workforce requires their members (the workers) to pay dues to support the unions. In return, the unions collectively bargain with the employer for various pay and benefits. The individual cannot opt out. If someone wants to work for a specific company that is unionized, they must join the union and pay the dues.

Does this fall under freedom? Of course, it does. It is one of those situations, where the majority must rule. Union members can be separated by job title at a specific company, but it is the choice of the majority. If someone doesn't like it, they are free to look elsewhere for employment.

In my own experience, I have worked at a medical facility that was largely union, but the position I was hired for was non-union at the time. This was established by other workers in my field who worked at the facility and voted not to join a union before I was hired. I was made aware early on of this fact and still chose to accept the job when it was offered. Overall, I was treated very poorly. I was told by others with the same job title as I, that was the norm there because we were not union. I was fired approximately two months later very suddenly and without warning, being told my work was not up to their expectations, despite my orientation officer telling me otherwise the entire time before my dismissal.

Was I treated unfairly? I certainly believed so. Were they well within their rights to get rid of me? Absolutely. As mentioned earlier, in a free society, an employer can terminate any employee at any time for any reason, just as the employee can choose to quit working for that employer at any time for any reason. To meet the standards of freedom, a union must be freely accepted by the employer. Fear of the negative consequences such as picket lines that do not impede workers from going to work; bad public relations, etc. still count as free will since

12. Unions

force was not used to get compliance.

Business owners will do whatever they feel is in their company's best interest. If it is better for the company to accept unions where the company is located, they will do so.

> *"The biggest myth about labor unions is that unions are for the workers. Unions are for unions, just as corporations are for corporations, and politicians are for politicians."*
> *– Thomas Sowell*

So why the big argument between right to work states and union states? To sum it up in one word: power. The more union members, the more dues paid, the more power the unions and their leaders have. This wouldn't be such a big deal, if unions were not so political and highly partisan in those politics. Many don't want to be part of a union for this reason. The best way to resolve this would be to get unions out of politics. No more union fundraisers for politicians, no more type of financial support for any politician or political party from any union.

In the same manner, partial or unionized companies at the least would need the same restrictions. What is good for one is good for all. But like with so many other things when it comes to politics, rarely do things follow the path of a simple solution.

What would be the next best option? I would say those individuals who don't want their union membership dues going to support a politician or a political party, should have their membership dues cut by the percentage the union spends to support politicians. For example, if a union spends 30 percent of the money it collects from their members' dues on supporting or

The Freedom Scale

promoting politics, refund 30 percent of union dues to union members who don't personally support the union's political affiliations. Seems reasonable, don't you think?

Unions however in general oppose any right to work measure including the one I just mentioned. They argue that all people in a unionized workforce must pay their dues, or it decreases the union's effectiveness—because even the non-unionized members get the benefits—and thus must pay union dues. Why? Do the union officials really care about the non-union workforce? Looking from my experience, the answer is an emphatic "no." They care about union dues. They care about power. Fewer political palms can be greased if there are fewer union members. After all, why work for an important cause when you can rely on political favors to get what you want.

As far as the union's effectiveness being negatively affected, I say, "That is their problem." Too many unions nowadays go the route of political expediency to address their issues. Maybe that is part of the problem. It begs the question: "Why do you need the unions and the union leaders—who normally make an outrageous amount of money for running the union—if they can't do the job on their own?"

If union membership is declining because many members at various companies have decided to do away with the union, then the fault is with the union and its leadership. It is up to the union leadership to improve the numbers by finding ways to appeal to workers they wish to represent.

Before leaving the issue of unions, there is one more aspect to address. Unions in government jobs. Because unions are so

12. Unions

highly political, it is undeniable that a portion of taxpayer dollars for government union employees is funneled directly back to political parties and candidates. Politicians normally run up huge debts in the areas unions represent. The more companies give to union employees, the more dues are required and the more politicians get from the union support. Here it is doubtful the pro-union politicians would cut any benefit for government employees or support any right to work legislation that could diminish the amount of union dues taken in.

Some unions aren't even trying to hide pushing the agenda of some pro-union politicians. Look at the Los Angeles Teachers' Union in the summer of 2020. They were very reluctant to go back to teaching public school in the fall because of COVID-19 and to some people understandably so. Yet they made a list of demands that had nothing to do with COVID-19, that they wanted implemented before returning to work in the fall.

Such measures unrelated to the virus included:

1. *Implementation of a moratorium on charter schools. Nothing like using politicians you support to openly hurt your closest competition.*
2. *Defunding the police.*
3. *A tax on the wealthy.*
4. *Implementing Universal Healthcare on the U.S.*

How could we reel in abuses of union government employees with politicians? Quite simply actually. Limit the negotiating power of elected officials, and give it only to non-union voters at the ballot box. If the union doesn't agree to what the taxpayers feel is fair, then individual union workers would be able to choose whether to work as non-union workers or to look elsewhere for employment. Politicians would get nothing from supporting unions as unions would have nothing to offer in return, other than kind words. How efficient do you think the Post Office or the DMV would become if the salaries of the employees working there suddenly depended on customer satisfaction?

It all comes back to power. Everyone wants an edge on everyone else, but checks and balances must be maintained on all sides. I don't care if it is a company greasing political palms or a union. Any time one side is given too much of a political advantage over the other side, the pendulum swings too far resulting in disaster. The only ones constantly winning in such situations are the politicians and the union bosses.

13. Afterthought on Taxes

"Where there is an income tax, the just man will pay more and the unjust less on the same income."
– Plato, The Republic

This was a puzzle to me: the issue of collecting necessary tax revenue, without violating the three necessities of freedom's foundation. The current method of taxation after all is not voluntary, but a form of extortion. Pay up, or we haul you off to jail. The answer on the federal level, lies in a little-known proposal called The FairTax Act, which was first introduced in 2005.

The FairTax is a one-time, 23 percent inclusive sales tax on all new goods and services. That means a used item is not taxed, whether it is an antique, a car, or even a house. Renting something is considered a service, and thus would be taxed under the FairTax.

You are probably thinking it's another way for the government to take our money. Here is the dirty secret on the FairTax and part of the reason you likely have not heard of it. The FairTax involves the permanent and complete removal of every form of federal taxation (repeal of the Sixteenth Amendment to the United States Constitution would also be needed, which made an income tax Constitutional) and have them replaced with a **one-time** tax on all new goods and services at a 23 percent inclusive rate.

Those against the FairTax prefer to say the tax rate is 30 percent. Which is true? In proper context only the 23 percent is true, so let me explain where the 30 percent claim comes from and how that can be true. The 23 percent rate is inclusive and the 30 percent rate is exclusive. What is the difference? Say you go to the convenience store and buy a cup of coffee for the advertised price of $1.00. We all know we have to pay a little more at the register for state sales tax, so you make sure you have a dollar and some change at the register. That state sales tax is tax exclusive. The same principle applies here. If the FairTax were exclusive, you would need an extra 30 cents for that cup of coffee to pay the advertised price. Being an inclusive tax, however, the FairTax is already included in the advertised price, so the government is sent 23 cents on the cup of coffee. Now take away 23 percent of that dollar for that cup of coffee, and you are left with 77 cents. Adding 23 percent of 77 cents won't bring you back to a dollar. Thirty percent must be added to 77 cents to reach $1.00, and that is where the 30 percent claim comes from. This is why the FairTax being written and described as *inclusive* is so important.

Think that would create more expensive products and services at the store? Not exactly. Remember, all forms of Federal Tax are eliminated under the FairTax and the current tax system; we already pay about 22 percent of every dollar we spend to the federal government in embedded taxes. The payroll tax is one such example we will expand upon. So, the lumber company, the furniture manufacturer, and every other middleman business involved in creating your furniture would no longer pay payroll

13. Afterthought on Taxes

taxes. The FairTax is only collected on the final product sold to the consumer. What is to stop those middleman companies from pocketing all that money saved? Competition. If these middleman companies won't cut a better deal for the retailers, the retailers will go elsewhere, and those middlemen will end up going out of business. Factoring this in, the cost of new goods and services would stay approximately the same.

Now think about how much money that puts in your pocket. No federal taxes when you buy or sell a used home or car. No federal taxes of any kind taken out of your paycheck. No inheritance taxes on your children when you die. No taxing your savings accounts or your investments. No more worries about properly filling out and processing your federal income tax forms or hiring an accountant to do it. It becomes the responsibility of the businesses to pay taxes to the government under this system, not the consumer.

The FairTax also makes it easier for ordinary people to start their own business, but in doing so, it also creates a highly competitive marketplace. Businesses headquartered overseas would look to move to or back to the United States as under the FairTax, the United States would become the biggest tax haven for businesses in the world because all other taxes have been removed. The biggest upside is that big businesses cannot get advantages such as special tax breaks that are the result of lobbying politicians. This helps level the playing field for smaller businesses.

It gets better though. Every citizen would also be credited with a monthly prebate check. The amount of the check will depend on the cost of living for the area where someone lives and the size of the family. This check would allow everyone to live tax free up to the poverty level and would be sent out to every American citizen and foreign citizens working in this country legally regardless of how much money they make. People would finally be able to ensure the well-being of their family with the money they earn before Uncle Sam claims it. The amount of tax people would pay for the bare necessities would be gone. Every individual would get to choose how much they pay in taxes by how much they choose to spend on certain items and services.

The 23 percent inclusive rate is designed to be revenue neutral for the government. This means it is designed to bring approximately the same amount in tax revenue to the government as the current system does. Since the biggest difference under this system is people would have a choice in what they pay in taxes by their spending, the amount of tax revenue collected is not a sure-fire guarantee.

While advocates of the FairTax say it would abolish the IRS, it probably would not be abolished, but reduced and revamped because all taxes would be collected exclusively from businesses by the state governments, minus a collection fee, with the rest then passed on to the federal government. Some type of organization needs to oversee the collection of taxes from the states to ensure that there are no shenanigans on the state level. The states after all are run by politicians who love to spend as much taxpayer money as possible. With no oversight, they could grab even more.

It seems like this would be something everyone, both socialists and capitalists alike could get behind. Unfortunately, only

13. Afterthought on Taxes

a portion of one political party supports it. Care to guess which one? There are many reasons given, but the most likely reason in most cases, once again comes back to *power*. Politicians would no longer be able to pit rich vs. poor vs. middle class, as all business owners would be paying taxes to the government based on what they sold you. The argument of class warfare goes out the window, and the political class loses power over the citizens as a result. There would likely be more focus on wasteful government spending as a result, and many politicians won't want that. Big corporations would no longer have tax advantages over smaller businesses, and no amount of political lobbying would change that.

I found it amusing to discuss the FairTax recently with some opponents who are not elected officials, but still think it is a big benefit for the rich, allowing them to take advantage of the poor and middle class. Yet none of them could clearly say *how* because citizens choose how much they pay in federal taxes through their spending habits. Don't want to pay federal taxes under the FairTax? Then live at the poverty level.

The rich people who want the fancy new cars, exotic vacations and every other big luxury will personally pay heavily in taxes. People who make money under the table and through illegal means will no longer be able to hide that money unless they live below the poverty level because taxes under this system will be paid exclusively on what is bought and not on a person's income.

Do I think the FairTax is perfect? No, I do not. The flaws I see in it, are not concerning how it would work, but involve the lack of measures in place to prevent politicians and certain others from manipulating it for their own gain: political or otherwise. I informed the group who represents the FairTax and advocates for it, Americans for Fair Taxation, of my concerns and how they could remedy such problems, but there was no continued conversation after that. Oh well. That is their problem.

Judging from the last paragraph, you have probably already guessed that I am not a representative of Americans for Fair Taxation; nor was I approached to promote the FairTax. But taxes have always been the exception to the rule in freedom as they primarily require government force to collect. The FairTax breaks that exception allowing the most freedom.

I am not going to discuss the arguments and counter arguments for and against the FairTax. I explained the most basic information on the FairTax, and I did not answer a wide range of questions such a proposal brings up. If you want to read in detail the arguments and counter-arguments on the FairTax, most are available in the FairTax books written by both former radio talk show host, Neal Boortz, and former Congressman John Linder, as well as directly from Americans for Fair Taxation. Other proposals for reforming the tax system such as a flat tax lean more towards freedom. Having read both FairTax books multiple times looking for flaws, I can find none in how it would work. Because of the choice in paying taxes and respect for private property promoted to the American people under the FairTax, I believe it is the best option for funding the federal government based on freedom for everyone.

I highly advise everyone to do their own research because I

13. Afterthought on Taxes

don't want anyone blindly taking my word or anyone else's word on it. Look at all the arguments on the FairTax, from both those that support it and those that are against it and decide for yourself which side has the better argument. If you get only the pros and cons on something from one side, often key information is ignored or misconstrued. FairTax proponents already address the arguments against it.

14. Freedom in Retirement

The older we get, the more we want to retire from working life in comfort. Achieving financial security in retirement is something that can be obtained easily enough in a free country for those who carefully weigh their decisions on the issue and take responsibility for it with proper planning.

Social Security, a part of the New Deal, was created during the Great Depression as a form of insurance for the elderly at a time when more than half of senior citizens lived in poverty. It became the first federal act to advocate federal assistance for senior citizens. Over the years it has morphed from a form of insurance providing benefits for the elderly into a mandatory retirement system most every American must pay into. There are little known exemptions such as a religious clause, but every way out involves a lot of hoops to jump through and there is no guarantee you will be successful in opting out. Until there is a clear and definitive way out with everyone being openly given that choice, I will continue to refer to it as mandatory.

Today it has become what is known as a Ponzi scheme, where the money is collected by tomorrow's recipients pay for the benefits of today's beneficiaries. Ponzi schemes are illegal for any private business to engage in, but seems perfectly acceptable for the United States government to not only engage in, but ensure enrollment in for its citizens from the time they start working.

14. Freedom in Retirement

The entire argument of Social Security is about as straight forward as they come, so this will probably be one of the shorter chapters to this book.

You often hear various arguments on the subject of Social Security, about how it is unsustainable and will collapse in X number of years. That is true. As with most Ponzi schemes, the only focus is on the short-term gains. Those responsible plan to deal with the problems at a later time, or even better, have others deal with them at a later time, preferably long after those responsible are dead and buried. One argument in favor of Social Security, is that a retirement fund is needed for senior citizens to help them in their old age. This is also true, but politicians as a natural rule seem to generally put helping themselves above helping anyone else as the money set aside for Social Security was already spent a long time ago. Hence the likely reason, why the individual choice in participating is made obscure and personal responsibility is taken away from the individual.

It can be argued that some individuals must be forced to save for retirement; otherwise, they will have nothing. Such an idea goes against the Freedom Scale, but is there room for compromise? Even if it is just a little room? I believe there is, though it can be open for debate.

Mandatory withholdings for retirement would come out of your paycheck with a twist. The government cannot touch it. It leaves your paycheck, and is immediately deposited into a form of savings bank account in your name, or an IRA, a 401K, 403B, the stock market, or any other number of choices in numerous combinations. Regardless of what is decided, it would be your

The Freedom Scale

choice. Here is the catch though. You cannot touch that money until you reach retirement age, or become disabled or experience some other qualifying factor. You can move the money or portions of it around within that time frame, but no spending. As investors would say, you can diversify your portfolio. If you die before you can collect, everything in that retirement can be passed on to a beneficiary of your choice. It could even be deposited into someone else's retirement account—your choice—rather than the recipient receiving a menial sum from Social Security when death occurs, especially if you paid a fortune into Social Security and never got to enjoy retirement. Over a few generations, many of our grandchildren and great grandchildren could retire quite nicely or even earlier than expected. This would be just what you pay into Social Security. Imagine putting more into such an account with a retirement package your employer may offer.

The main thing that causes apprehension under this system is that you the individual, would be responsible for the decisions with this money in your retirement account. What if you made bad decisions? The consequences of those decisions would be yours as well. There would be no government bailout or safety net if you make poor decisions that cost you everything. You could always hire an investing firm to minimize the risk. Some investors only get paid with positive results. But what do I know?

The main argument made against openly privatizing Social Security is the uncertainty of the stock market. What if we have another Great Depression and people lose everything? First of all, if I can easily choose to get out of Social Security, that is my business. If I lose everything, that is also my business. I will not

14. Freedom in Retirement

demand others take care of me. But I will humor this argument for a moment, as such fears are greatly exaggerated.

"I swear by my life and my love of it, I will never live for the sake of another man, nor ask another man to live for mine."
– John Gault, Atlas Shrugged

Have you ever heard of the Depression of 1920? Neither had I until several years ago. I believe I first heard about it on the Glenn Beck program when it was still on Fox News. When we hear about the 1920s, we think of the term, 'the roaring 20s,' which was a time of great prosperity until the stock market crashed on October 29, 1929 and led to the Great Depression.

But another depression had occurred nearly 10 years earlier under President Warren G. Harding. At this point following World War I, the Gross National Product had declined 17 percent, and unemployment had gone from 4 percent to almost 12 percent. What did President Harding do? Quite the opposite of what FDR did in response to the Great Depression. Instead of massive expansion of government programs and spending, Harding cut the national budget by nearly half between 1920 and 1922, as well as slashing tax rates for all income groups. By 1922, unemployment was down to 6.7 percent, and down to 2.4 percent the following year, leading into the roaring 20s. Compare that with FDR's response to the Great Depression—massive government expansion in the form of taxes, regulations and entitlement programs, which showed little to no promise until the start of WWII over a decade later. The point here is that left to its own devices, the market will recover on its own without interference from the government.

To continue with the matter of the risk of investing in retirement, I point to my last employer. There we had a retirement package in the form of a 403B, where my employer matched up to 4 percent depending on what I invested. Some of my coworkers, (mainly the younger ones) put the bare minimum into their 403B, preferring to spend and enjoy as much as they could right then. That was my line of thinking as well until a few years ago. I was working at the hospital when I finally decided to start planning for the long term and looked more closely at my 403B and everything it entailed.

In my 403B there are options such as: How much do I want taken out of my check to contribute to the 403B? Another key option is: What kind of stock am I looking to invest in? The choices range in combinations of high risk, potentially high reward to safe bets with less reward.

Under such a system more people could potentially retire sooner. But what about those who like Social Security run by the government and don't want to see it go anywhere? Well, there is an option for those people as well. Let them stay on it if they want to, but the safety net of the government printing more money to keep it afloat needs to end. One option is to follow Switzerland's lead. Their state retirement is tied to their country's economy. When their economy thrives, so do retirement benefits. It kind of forces an incentive for politicians to work in the best interests of their country's economy rather than their own political self-interests, wouldn't you say? That would

14. Freedom in Retirement

make it easier those who want to exit Social Security and stop paying into it to do so. It may require giving up all the money you put into it up to that point, but tell me truthfully: Is it a deal you would take? The answer is different for everyone. Personally, I would and I'm forty-seven years old as I write this. Why would some people be forced to take such a loss? For so many people to withdraw suddenly and take the money with them, the system would likely collapse immediately, especially with so many baby boomers now getting Social Security. If it had been optional from the beginning, it would never have been an issue.

The point is, people are not given an open choice in deciding whether or not to participate in Social Security. This fact alone shows what a colossal failure Social Security is. After all, if it were a good deal, there would be no need for our children and grandchildren to be forced to pay for our retirement. There would be no need for anyone to be forced to be a part of it. Like I asked with income taxes: Does the money you work for belong to you first and foremost, or the government?

I have always looked at both my successes and failures as my own. I want my daughter's successes and failures to be *her* own. I do not want her forced to be responsible for my retirement, just as I do not look to be held accountable for her decisions when she becomes an adult. If she wants to take care of me when I get old, that will be her choice. The choice needs to be hers and not those in government who feel *they* know what is best for us.

III. The Keys to Controlling a Free Society

"To exercise some sort of control over others is the secret motive of every selfish person."
– Wallace D. Wattles

15. Speech and Expression: Silencing Dissent

"Free speech is meant to protect unpopular speech. Popular speech, by definition, needs no protection."
– Neal Boortz

Free Speech vs. Hate Speech

One of the biggest necessities in a free society, is the right to freely express your views and opinions. More importantly, it is the right to challenge what is popular or the accepted narrative. People are imprisoned or killed in other countries for speaking out in such a manner. This is why freedom of speech is part of the First Amendment in the United States Constitution. In a free society, nobody can control what an individual thinks or says. To do so, infringes on the rights of the individual.

Now bear in mind, freedom of speech and expression means freedom from government taking action against you, not private entities. You cannot force a private newspaper to print your opinion piece, if it isn't your newspaper. Nor can you walk into your boss's office and tell him what you really think of him because of 'freedom of speech.' There are consequences. Your boss has that same freedom of speech to say, "You're fired," and the freedom of expression to carry it out.

In recent years, however, freedom of speech has become divided, primarily along party lines. Many Democrats do not share

15. Speech and Expression

the view of Mr. Boortz about the need to protect an unpopular viewpoint. Minnesota Governor, Tim Walz is quoted as saying in a 2022 interview "There's no guarantee to free speech on misinformation or hate speech, and especially around our democracy." It is hard to believe this quote is taken out-of-context, as it is pretty damning and straight forward. In every context, free speech of every individual is protected against government retaliation even if the speech is completely false or there are those that consider it hateful. So, who's freedom of speech was he specifically referring to exactly in that quote?

Unfortunately, attacks against free speech in one form or another are not isolated incidents in this day and age. In many instances, the views expressed must be in line with the views on the left; otherwise, they label it 'hate speech,' and that can incite violence in their opinion. Such instances include labeling those with dissenting views. We'll get into some of those labels momentarily.

Now should there be consequences for speech likely to create civil unrest and potentially harm people? Absolutely. You cannot yell "fire" in a crowded movie theatre for the same reason you cannot yell "bomb" on an airplane. Such actions create panic and hysteria for people looking to save themselves. Inciting a riot or panic is deliberately and blatantly pushing for violence or reckless action from a group of people. Often there is little room for interpretation.

"Hate speech" as defined primarily by Democrats and their supporters, however, is not speech creating immediate life-threatening panic or specifically pushing violence. Not respecting someone's preferred pronouns for example, is not a direct or strongly hinted call to violence. It is simply saying something the other person doesn't like if that is the extent of it. With that kind of 'hate speech,' every individual can choose how to respond. People are free to walk away and not listen. They are free to let it go. No matter how much someone may feel threatened by being misgendered, it comes back to the old saying, "Actions speak louder than words."

Wait just one minute. There is no actual push to make laws restricting freedom of speech, so how can Democrats or anyone else be attempting to silence dissent? A very good question! They don't need a law silencing dissent. They just need to control the narrative and condition people to believe and act a certain way without question. This can range from bully tactics to repeating something over and over until it is believed. Both were observed in Nazi Germany with the Brownshirts and the propaganda machine.

In the past, many big colleges and universities invited guest speakers with known conservative views. Many times, students that support Democrats imitate Brownshirts and hold massive protests to keep the conservative speaker from being heard on campus. Sometimes as a result the speaker is disinvited because of threats of violence or drowned out by the protests. Why do this? If you are on the right side of the argument, what do you have to fear from a different perspective? If the opposing viewpoint is so bad, it should be easy to tear that opposing viewpoint to shreds with dispassionate facts. Allowing the opposing viewpoint to talk would expose how horrible that

15. Speech and Expression

viewpoint is from their own mouths.

There is a saying in my profession. *Res Ipsa Loquitur.* It is Latin for, "The thing speaks for itself." Let the "hate" speak for itself instead of trying to silence it. There is one glaring problem with letting the hate speak for itself. What is considered "hate speech" is more often than not, open to interpretation by every individual. The very nature of a debate is a challenge between different viewpoints, which either side can call 'offensive.' Who is to decide who doesn't get to be offended?

Yet many Democrats do not look at it this way, as many assume that they know what's best. Their reasoning for trying to silence opposing viewpoints appears to come from at least one of two premises. The first is that the American public is too stupid to properly recognize certain speech or expressions for themselves. Therefore, there is no need to give more than one viewpoint.

The other possibility is that the speech or expressions they oppose, expose the fact that their argument has no logical standing and cannot be debated. It could also expose deceit, hypocrisy, or anything that may make them look even worse and thus must be silenced to keep up the narrative, under the guise of standing against 'hate speech.' It is nothing new to the left. Many of them tried to get Rush Limbaugh off the air for decades without success. He successfully thwarted those efforts until the day he died.

Despite being told as children, "Sticks and stones may break my bones, but words will never hurt me," words are an effective way to bully people into submission if challenged, as well as to condition them to a certain degree. One of the most effective

The Freedom Scale

ways to bully someone into submission is with labels. Such labels include, but are far from limited to, *racist*, *sexist*, and *homophobe*.

- Did you disapprove or were you critical of any Obama policy? Yes? *Racist*.
- Are you a biological male who disagrees with abortion being legal? Yes? *Sexist*.
- Are you against gay marriage? Yes? *Homophobe*.

Both sides have been guilty of such name calling, but there is something important to consider. One side will encourage further discussion and elaborate their reasoning to create a dialogue unless they back down. The other side looks to shut down the dialogue with labels, as they may assume they already know the 'dissenters' arguments and reasoning. In their mind, it is because *the dissenters* truly are the racists, sexists, and homophobes. This becomes their justification for dismissing and trying to silence those people in a variety of ways.

Whenever I see someone try to suppress an individual's viewpoint for any reason without an honest discussion, I am wary. My grandfather and I used to have weekly political discussions, and he never let me dodge questions. Nor did he allow me to use labels without providing details. He made me defend my positions from a logical standpoint without fear. He said open dialogue was the best solution to any problem, as it helps ensure every angle has been explored.

That was fine with me. I am the type of person who wants to hear everything relevant that each side has to say completely unfiltered. I learned over the years, that people who refuse such dialogue, leave themselves to blindly accept what those with power tell them what is true, as has been the case throughout history. History has shown the people in power usually have a personal agenda and rarely is it foremost in the peoples' best interest. This is why those who don't know history are doomed to repeat it.

Media Bias

Certain forms of censorship have been accepted in society for years. Graphic violence, sex, nudity and profanity were considered taboo on most print and on television and radio programming in the 80s and 90s, and to an extent are still banned on many platforms today. Movie ratings have been in effect for several decades ranging from G to XXX, where people can choose what they want with warnings for various ages. This was done to maintain a level of civility and to protect children from being exposed to certain elements until the parents felt it was appropriate. While such a rating system censored graphic violence, sex acts, vulgar language and the like, ideas and viewpoints, not as much. That started to change more and more over the past few decades. Bias in the mainstream media was noticeable here and there for many years, but for the most part, partisanship was kept under the radar as much as possible despite warnings from Conservative talking heads. Much of that effort to try to maintain the appearance of being non-biased, was lost during Obama's presidency and especially Trump's presidency.

The Freedom Scale

> *"The media's the most powerful entity on Earth. They have the power to make the innocent guilty and to make the guilty innocent, and that's power. Because they control the minds of the masses."*
> *– Malcom X*

In much of mainstream media and entertainment, the more partisan they got over the years—and one specific party—the more they discredited themselves. It is why Fox news was so popular for a while. Many Fox News detractors pointed to certain news commentators, such as Sean Hannity as arguing Fox was biased towards the other side, but news commentators are different than reporters. They are not supposed to be neutral, but to offer their viewpoint. Other 'journalists' on other networks, show as much bias while claiming to be impartial anchors. Mr. Hannity has never made such a claim. He wears his affiliation and beliefs on his sleeve for everyone to see, while other self-proclaimed impartial 'journalists,' actively steer the narrative in their desired direction. This is done primarily through two courses of action.

1. *By deliberately misquoting someone—taking situations and words out of context.*
2. *By giving more attention to stories that fit the narrative and downplaying, censoring, belittling or ignoring the stories or viewpoints that don't fit the desired narrative.*

This is why we need the media and the judicial system to be fair and impartial—without bias or prejudice. Play it straight

15. Speech and Expression

for everyone, and let the chips fall where they may. Good news reporting should be like good teachers. If you don't know their personal politics, they are doing their jobs properly.

NBC Nightly news anchor Lester Holt did his best to justify the mainstream media's bias to a virtual audience in March of 2021, saying "I think it has become clearer that fairness is overrated." He went on to clarify saying "The idea that we should always give two sides equal weight and merit does not reflect the world we find ourselves in. That the sun sets in the west is a fact. Any contrary view does not deserve our time or attention."

Mr. Holt neglected to make the distinction between apples and oranges here. The science of the sun setting is old news proven beyond a reasonable doubt. That science was put to bed many years ago. Different viewpoints and the facts on modern political issues is something else entirely. Yet he finished by essentially saying it is fine to ignore reporting one side, because he and his team have already determined what is important for us to know from both sides.

These are current political issues and events with new facts coming out every day on these issues as they develop, and yet this is Mr. Holt's argument? Why should we trust what they say is not misinformation? Their good word? Do they think we believe the media heads never have their own agenda or biases? While the media may think that, I and most people are not that gullible. That is one of many reasons so few people trust the media today.

The primary reason is they have been caught too many times trying to control the political narrative. Remember when multiple news outlets tried to twist President Trump's words, saying he called "neo-Nazis and Klansmen fine people" to push a narrative. Look up the unedited videos and transcripts if you haven't already seen them. You will clearly see an anti-Trump narrative being pushed and just how dishonest the outlets were that ran with that narrative.

Mr. Holt forgot one of the most important aspects of good journalism. Reporting both sides as news equally and in the proper context is the only way to conclusively get all the facts. It also clearly distinguishes between news and propaganda. Ignoring one side by not reporting it, or twisting the facts, is a modern way of silencing dissent for the desired narrative. In such cases, truth is always a potential casualty. I doubt that is how many media outlets see it. They don't see it as denying anyone's free speech or misrepresenting facts; it is them denying certain speech on a platform that they control, so people will believe what these reporters and their bosses want them to. I would image in at least some of their minds, they believe that most of what they are saying is the truth, so it is OK. No need to muddy the waters with what they decide is misinformation. Let other side present it if they are so inclined.

If Hannity and numerous other conservative commentators spread nothing more than "misinformation," why have they not been sued into the poorhouse for defamation of character by the left? It is because drawing conclusions from opinions based on facts is one thing. Making claims on statements that cannot be supported is something else. This means any lawsuit for defamation of character would draw unwanted attention, and the facts of each side would have to be heard in court. Better to carefully pick

15. Speech and Expression

your battles, rather than draw attention to where it is unwanted.

In some cases, we have seen threats of a huge lawsuit. Sometimes it is legitimate, and other times it is a stunt to keep things tied up for years, hoping for a judge biased in your favor. Even if it is a stunt, in the short term, it sends a message scaring those who refuse to be quiet.

However, framing of one's words is equally important to avoid such lawsuits. Even that is no guarantee, as a partisan judge can choose to allow lawsuits. There is no way the average blue-collar worker has the resources to fight back legally, because more often than not, they won't be as outspoken.

For a while Fox News called out everyone and was labeled biased in favor of Republicans by other news networks, politicians, and individuals that have shown a Democrat bias. Fox didn't spare one side because they favored their politics. Some of their commentators did, but the reporters were mostly impartial—with some exceptions—when it came to reporting the news. Sadly, at least in my view, Fox gave up a fair amount of credibility in November 2020, with how they approached the election and what followed after that, refusing to stray from the established narratives of the 2020 presidential election, January 6th and COVID-19.

In most cases, Fox News followed the lead of other mainstream media news outlets in developing the desired narratives. They labeled claims of voter fraud in the 2020 presidential election as unfounded and baseless without appearing to look deeper at the claims. There were some outspoken commentators which landed a huge lawsuit with Dominion and a large settlement.

It was not proven there wasn't election interference, but because of careless wording, the result was large cash settlement.

January 6th protestors in the capital were largely labeled as insurrectionists, despite a large amount of evidence to the contrary. People skeptical on the manmade climate change narrative, are labeled climate deniers, and medical professionals who argued against the established narrative established by Dr. Fauci, the Center for Disease Control (CDC) and others towing the line on COVID-19 were dismissed as quacks. Why?

Controlling what people think on certain issues has become the focus of many media outlets, rather than putting out the entire unvarnished truth without labels and letting people make up their own minds. While they have presented their conclusion based on facts (with or without spin) they move to the category of being commentators like Hannity and Tucker instead of being news reporters. As I alluded to earlier, actual news reporting presents all the relevant facts without bias and lets the audience decide for themselves.

It all comes back to the desired narrative. As I stated, not all people will come to the media's desired conclusion, and their job is to get as many people to believe that conclusion as possible. Get the people believing what you want them to believe, and you no longer have to worry about their free speech.

There is a saying in research I heard on the radio one day in discussing COVID-19. I haven't been able to find the original quote, and I am sure there are variations. Nevertheless, it hits home. The saying is *"You won't find what you're not looking for, and you don't go looking for things you don't want to find."* This

15. Speech and Expression

best explains how to protect the established narratives. While such actions (or inactions) are utilized throughout a wide range of political beliefs, it is especially noticeable in the topics mentioned in this book.

While what *is not* reported is as important as what *is* reported and *how* it is reported, the media outlets are privately owned. It is their right to broadcast or print what they see as news, being as biased as they want, turning words into one-sided propaganda. In turn, we are free to voice our dissatisfaction and not watch or read them if they do not meet acceptable standards of journalism.

Something else can be done about media bias without violating the freedom scale, though. Allow news agencies to be open to lawsuits from the public for misleading, misquoting, taking statements out of context, or doing anything else that twists the truth to a desired narrative to benefit a specific political party, candidate or agenda when there is no defamation. Lower the bar and make lawsuits easier.

The exception will be news commentators like Sean Hannity. Reporters claim to be neutral instead of commentators, but instead clearly have a specific political axe to grind for Republicans, Democrats or another political ideology. Let that be stated outright by those news outlets. Let it also be a requirement for exemptions from those lawsuits. Would the media be so brazen in pushing a political narrative under those rules if they have to wear their bias on their sleeves as commentators?

It would also probably be best if all special incentives and benefits from the government, such as tax breaks, were eliminated for every form of media, regardless of how essential some may deem them to be. Let them survive on their ratings alone and see how long they last.

Entertainment Bias

"The perfect dictatorship would have the appearance of a democracy, but would basically be a prison without walls in which the prisoners would never dream of escaping. It would essentially be a system of slavery, where through consumption and entertainment, the slaves would love their servitude."
– Aldous Huxley

Politicians learned long ago that with the population distracted, they can more easily incorporate measures the population would normally be outraged over. This is accomplished through entertainment as that is our escape from reality, whether it be books, sports, television, whatever. This was done with the gladiator games in the Coliseum in ancient Rome, and was highlighted in George Orwell's book, *Animal Farm*, when television was discovered and used by the pigs as a distraction for the other animals. Unlike those examples, though, the distraction works best when political messaging is fed directly through entertainment.

Political bias in entertainment, is undeniable, but it has caused much backlash in some areas as many are seeing it as indoctrination because the messaging has become less subtle over the years. Quality stories are sacrificed for the sake of checking boxes for political points. Sadly, much of Hollywood, where most Americans have gotten their entertainment for many decades, is

15. Speech and Expression

all too happy to comply with pushing a less subtle political aspect.

The floodgates broke after Donald Trump was elected in 2016. I guess Hollywood felt they had to push it further to ensure people would think and vote the way they wanted them to. With Trump getting elected, the American public apparently didn't get the memo.

Media went from leaning toward one political ideology in their storytelling to shoving that ideology down our throats outright with their 'woke and inclusive' leftwing way of seeing things and right-wing talent being blacklisted. They didn't even try to hide it. When people got upset at the quality of the programming, they were insulted and called 'toxic' fans among other things. Alex Kurtzman with *Star Trek*, Kathleen Kennedy with *Star Wars* (actually all of Disney to be honest) and a number of others were in on this. You can easily find their comments online, but the message was clear. *Accept our way of thinking as the norm, never electing someone like Trump again, or we will see to it that you and others like you are considered social outcasts at the very least. We are tired of playing nice.*

They forgot the first rule of entertainment, and that is to entertain the people regardless of who they are and what they believe. Overall, people regardless of their beliefs, want to be entertained and not preached to. Movies, TV, and sports are supposed to be an escape from all of that. Most programming and movies were just that—a perfect escape before Hollywood decided we needed a more direct wakeup call. Entertainment can be a perfect escape again—the norm instead of the rare examples here and there.

So, are you saying entertainment groups should be forced

The Freedom Scale

to create entertainment in a non-biased manner and hire actors and actresses with different viewpoints? As nice as that would be to some degree, the answer is *no*. Like mainstream media outlets, Hollywood entertainment groups are privately owned. It is their right to broadcast what content they choose regardless of what fans want, and to be just as biased as they want in doing so. Again, as with media outlets, we are free to voice our dissatisfaction and not buy what they are selling if they do not meet our entertainment standards. Like the media, let them survive on their ratings alone, and see how long they last.

As far as movies go, original movies, made from streaming services, will be only so successful, as movie theaters are where the big money is made. Take for example the most successful movie in years that doesn't follow the woke agenda. It premiered in 2022 after most COVID restrictions were lifted. I am of course talking about *Top Gun: Maverick* and it has become one of the highest grossing films of all time. No political posturing or agenda to push, no political boxes to check off. Just a fun movie with a respectable script, serving as an enjoyable escape from our daily life.

The wakeup call has already started in a number of streaming services, now splitting their original programming between the shows more interested in checking political boxes and pushing political messaging, and those focusing on good entertainment. Look at the fans' reviews as opposed to the critics. Entertaining streaming series like *Yellowstone, Cobra Kai,* or *Reacher,* have no problem getting renewed. People understand entertainment critics want to be "in," especially now, and they will brownnose certain projects that are less than stellar to avoid being excluded. This is the reason for such a sharp divide between what fans say, and what critics say on some projects.

Many in Hollywood (and for now correctly) figure insulting certain fans who dislike their direction with certain programming by calling them "the toxic fandom" may get initial interest, especially with spinoffs or reboots. They may get the free publicity that comes with it, but despite that fact, my guess is that it will ultimately fail for one simple reason. I don't think it will keep the interest of enough fans, and that will work against long-term profits, as the movie or TV series franchises become spoiled for many longtime fans. I can't see there being sufficient interest in watching the new programming added to the established, loved franchises, or even breaking box office sales, despite their efforts to push it. Maybe Hollywood thinks they will convert enough people to their way of thinking and will thus create a new normal that people will accept. Good luck with that.

Online Journalism and Entertainment

The age of online journalism and entertainment was the biggest breakthrough in media since the early days of Rush Limbaugh with a microphone on the radio. With the progression of the internet, anyone could more easily create new entertainment, or investigate things for themselves, or even become an online celebrity reporting on events. It would certainly be easier to find the facts online than go to the library and look through old newspaper reels to research for verification. That was until the "Thought Police" as they came to be known, started cracking down on online social networking sights. It was slowly spread, with double standards here and there on the main social networking sites, like Facebook and Twitter until the beginning of 2021 when censorship reared its ugly head. The free flow of information and free speech was attacked in a bold way we have never before witnessed in my lifetime.

The most notable aspect started with questioning the 2020 election results by the Trump campaign. There was much speculation on the validity of the results, especially by Donald Trump himself. Looking at all the facts, the speculation was valid and warranted further investigation, at the very least. Well, this is where the social networking sights began with heavy censorship, in the manner of a police officers at a crime scene saying to the crowd, "Move along. Nothing to see here."

When the results were finally tallied after a pause in counting the votes by multiple swing states in the middle of the night, it was reported that Joe Biden overcame Trump's lead, and won. Looking at numerous factors, the Trump campaign set out to challenge the results with claims of election fraud and irregularities. Almost immediately most mainstream media outlets started calling all of it baseless accusations and false claims without reporting the details of what was said nor covering the hearings the Trump legal team had with state legislators. Many online networking sights soon followed suit.

Nearly every pro-Trump political post or any post questioning the results of a Joe Biden win in the election soon afterwards on Facebook, was either flagged by an "independent" fact-checker or had election update tags added at the end, saying things such as, "Joe Biden is the projected winner." or "voter fraud, which is historically rare, has not affected any outcome in this election." Such tags were common while the election challenges were going on, as though they didn't want the narrative of a Joe Biden victory to get interrupted or questioned, and wanted to help ensure its users saw it the same way and did not question further.

Let's discuss the "independent" fact-checkers a little more and share an experience from something I posted on Facebook. I had reposted a video from Media Research Center TV in my Facebook page. The "independent" Facebook fact-checkers had flagged the video as partly false shortly afterwards, with a gray line across the post labeling it as partially false information and a labeled link stating, "Biden did not suddenly go up to 138K votes in Michigan with no change to Trump." The link backs it up, showing how this was the result of an input error that was in fact corroborated.

So, what's the problem? The problem is that the MRCTV video had already addressed and acknowledged as true that specific fact check in the video. A number of other voting issues were the focus of the video and were not addressed in their fact-check. So, what was the partially false information? These fact-checkers either made a mistake, (a mistake repeated on a number of other posts); were negligent in their fact-checking, or deliberately trying to mislead the Facebook user, by pointing to one fact mentioned and addressed in the video already, hoping viewers wouldn't bother clicking on it and learning what else was said. Maybe the latter didn't work and people still clicked on it.

Maybe this is why the video was taken down. Although to be fair, I can't say for certain whether MRCTV or Facebook took it down.

The fact-checkers—when you look more closely—are not impartial. At least this appears to be the case for the group called Lead Stories, which at the time I write this, performs 76 percent of fact-checks on Facebook. Their fact-checks are done by at least eight former CNN staffers. CNN from their broadcasting, shows their line of thinking is very much in line with Democrats and hostile to conservatives, especially under Donald Trump's leadership. Between January 1, 2020 and March 9, 2020, more than 4.5 times more stories were focused on Republican-leaning social media users and news outlets as opposed to Democrat leaning by the fact-checkers. Is this because there were not enough Democrat-leaning stories in comparison that warranted fact-checking, or did they simply choose not to fact-check certain stories based on political ideology?

Look at the attempt by numerous fact-checkers on Facebook to explain away one of Joe Biden's statements in campaigning for President, which turned into a popular meme. In the meme, it has Biden saying "I don't work for you." This was in reference to a heated argument between Biden and a Detroit auto worker over gun rights, in which Biden eventually says, "I'm not working for you." or more details of that statement after the auto worker made the statement that he does. The arguments presented by three fact-checkers for Facebook, argue it is half true or missing context, trying to bring the gun argument into it to lessen the damage by Biden's statement. This gives the appearance of deflection as the real focus should be on the context of Biden

15. Speech and Expression

saying, "I'm not working for you". They can only speculate on the context of what Biden's response meant when he said, "I'm not working for you". Was it meant as an individual or as a taxpayer? Surprisingly, none of them address that.

The most telling thing about the bias of some of these fact-checkers, came in the latter half of 2021, when John Stossel sued Facebook for defamation, when 3rd party fact-checkers labeled his public posts as misinformation. On page 2 of Facebook's court filing, Facebook admits that fact-check labels are just "protected opinion." If the fact-checks are just "protected opinion," why label it fact-check instead of opinion-check? Because actual facts are hard to argue with, and Facebook appears to want people to believe their fact-checkers deal with concrete facts instead of opinions. The fact that Facebook was in a position to lose money because of their "fact-checkers" is apparently the only reason they labeled what was written as "protected opinion." It isn't like they broadcast that admission loudly or highlight them in their fact-check tags.

Beyond "fact-checkers," we saw the shutting down of platforms for the dissenters to speak out all together. On Wednesday, December the 9, 2020 after the electors were certified in each state, YouTube announced it would remove any new videos that either alleged widespread voter fraud or errors that changed the outcome of the 2020 presidential elections. As part of the official statement, they said *"Yesterday was the safe harbor deadline for the U.S. Presidential election and enough states have certified their election results to determine a President-elect. Given that we will start removing any piece of content uploaded today (or* any time after) that misleads people by alleging that widespread voter fraud or errors changed the outcome of the 2020 U.S. Presidential election, in line with our approach towards historical U.S. Presidential elections."

Here is the official link:

https://blog.youtube/news-and-events/supporting-the-2020-us-election/

A few issues here. First: Did YouTube go this direction with Hillary Clinton supporters posting videos, echoing her claims that the Presidential election in 2016 was stolen from her? What about after the Russia collusion debacle that was supposed to prove Trump conspired with Russia to steal the U.S. Presidential election—completely debunked? In both cases, the answer is *no*, so the reasoning they gave of 'keeping in line' with their approach towards historical U.S. Presidential elections sounds like a bunch of B.S, with Safe Harbor day (the deadline for states to certify the result of the presidential election) just being an excuse.

The second issue is the use of the term "misleads" when referring to voter fraud or errors. I ask: "Misleads according to whom?" YouTube executives? Politicians? People with something to lose if caught having committed fraud? While some allegations have been explained, a large number were not conclusively proven or even addressed. They were simply ignored. How can anyone honestly say any accusation is misleading or false if it has not been thoroughly investigated and proven beyond a reasonable doubt otherwise?

It must also be noted that on December 9, 2020, when You-

15. Speech and Expression

Tube set this policy in place, legal challenges were still proceeding from Mr. Trump through the court system. When considering the fact that two sets of electors were sent from multiple states to Washington D.C. because of questions regarding the validity of the vote, it looks more and more like the concerns brought up by Trump and his supporters were silenced because the election was not conclusively decided.

The next big issue in what can be considered censorship came from online companies on January 6, 2021, when President Trump's Twitter account was temporarily suspended under the claim that his tweets incited violence among supporters at the Capitol building. Two days later Twitter decided to permanently suspend his Twitter account, claiming it was due to the risk of further incitement of violence. This was a policy enforced by Twitter. So, what did President Trump tweet that allegedly incited this violence? Twitter used these last two tweets as their reasoning:

> "The 75,000,000 great American Patriots who voted for me, AMERICA FIRST, and MAKE AMERICA GREAT AGAIN, will have a GIANT VOICE long into the future. They will not be disrespected or treated unfairly in any way, shape or form."

> "To all of those who have asked, I will not be going to the inauguration on January 20th."

What was so wrong with either of these statements? The first points out that despite Biden being announced the winner, Trump received more votes than any incumbent President,

The Freedom Scale

which is around 10,000,000 more than he received in 2016. Highlighting the number of people who voted for him is a polite way of saying there are too many Trump supporters for politicians to ignore and do as they see fit. That is the giant voice being referenced. To ignore that giant voice meant a serious risk to their political future at the ballot box depending on the state or district they represent.

The second statement directly and simply answered a big question on the mind of many at the time. It is Trump's belief the 2020 Presidential election was stolen from him, and thus he had no intention of attending Biden's inauguration. No clear call to violence in either case, but the decision-makers at Twitter saw things differently. In their justification, Twitter stated the following on their blog titled 'Permanent Suspension of @realDonaldTrmp' citing the violence at the Capital as the main consideration in their decision:

"...these two tweets must be read in the context of broader events in the country and the ways in which the President's statements can be mobilized by different audiences, including to incite violence, as well as in the context of the platform of behavior from this account in recent weeks. After assessing the language in these Tweets against our Glorification of Violence policy, we have determined that these Tweets are in violation of the Glorification of Violence Policy and the user @realDonaldTrump should be immediately permanently suspended from the service."

Look closely at the words in bold print. "...must be read in

15. Speech and Expression

the context of", and "...the ways in which the President's statements can be mobilized by different audiences." In other words, you must look at it the way they chose to see it and how they see messages. Even with no direct call or implied call for violence, their decision is based on how what he said *might* be interpreted by some. Sounds like following their rules under their guidelines, they could justify censoring anyone using their platform if they don't like what is said. But let us look closer at their assessment to ensure I am being fair.

In the details of their assessment, Twitter does not provide examples that show he incited the violence but does refer to a few other tweets. The justification of their assessment under their Glorification of Violence policy focused primarily on Trump's last two tweets. The factors they listed are as follows:

> *"President Trump's statement that he will not be attending the inauguration is being received by a number of his supporters as further confirmation that the election was not legitimate, and is seen as him disavowing his previous claim via two Tweets, by his Deputy Chief of Staff Dan Scavino, that there would be an "orderly transition" on January 20th."*

Is seen as by whom? Trump supporters or Twitter decision-makers? Why is it seen this way? Because he and many of his supporters do not see the election as legitimate? So what? How is that him disavowing his previous claim of an orderly transition or promoting violence, especially when it is not required for an outgoing President to be present at the inauguration of a new

President?

> "The second Tweet may also serve as encouragement to those considering violent acts that the inauguration would be a "safe" target, as he will not be attending."

So again, it *may* serve as encouragement. Not it *definitely* will. It *may*. Then again it may just as easily not serve as encouragement. But the Twitter decision-makers chose in part as their reason for restricting free speech that it *might* encourage violent acts. So, can any number of things. It all depends on how you look at it.

> "The use of the words "American Patriots" to describe some of his supporters is also being interpreted as support for those committing violent acts at the U.S. Capital."

The Twitter decision-makers need to go back and reread that tweet. "American Patriots" was not used to describe some of his supporters, but all of his supporters who voted for him. Said it clear as day. But being interpreted by whom is the real question. The Twitter decision-makers? Looks like they decided to make an assumption rather than seek clarification. Is that something they do for Democrat politicians, or do they just not bother and assume differently?

> "The mention of his supporters having a "GIANT VOICE long into the future" and that "They will not be disrespected or treated in any way, shape or form!!!" is being interpreted as further indication that President Trump does not plan to facilitate an "orderly transition" and instead

15. Speech and Expression

that he plans to continue to support, empower, and shield those who believe he won the election."

Those same key words are presented and interpreted and repeated without clarification by Twitter regarding who is doing the interpreting. Whatever happened to taking something at face value? It is also possible to plan to continue an orderly transition while supporting and empowering those who believe he won the election. Every day numerous outlets encourage people to make their voices heard. How is this different? Because of how the Twitter decision-makers *chose* to interpret it?

I must admit I don't fully understand the *shield* comment of the statement as once again, it is not clarified. Shield them from the fact Biden will be sworn in as President? I think that was already a given for most that Biden would be sworn in. Shield the rioters at the Capital from prosecution? I doubt it.

"Plans for future protests have already begun proliferating on and off-Twitter, including a proposed secondary attack on the U.S. Capital and state capital buildings on January 17, 2021." The assumption there would be future protests was already a given. Whether there would be violence is another matter. A proposed, secondary attack of the U.S. Capital and state capital buildings? Again, I ask according to whom? The FBI? The Justice Department? Or are rumors swirling around the water cooler among the Twitter decision-makers? They don't clarify. Nor did they clarify whether or not the sources were vetted or the political leanings of those making the claims of a secondary attack.

I will address the need for such reasoning shortly.

There is Twitter's reasoning in their own words. When you look at it, their reasoning was based on nothing more than how they chose to interpret how Trump's tweets would be received by his supporters, rather than any direct statement or strong suggestion in tweets to commit violent acts at the Capital.

Twitter CEO, Jack Dorsey came out and defended the decision, saying that while it set a dangerous precedent, he believes banning President Trump was the right decision because they were forced to focus on public safety. Is that what it takes to justify banning free speech with no clear-cut incitement of violence? Just say you felt it promoted violence? What speech is safe under those guidelines except the speech they like?

Here is the link to read the Twitter decision for yourself: *https://blog.x.com/en_us/topics/company/2020/suspension*

Numerous popular media platforms soon followed suit and banished Trump from their respective platforms including, but not limited to Facebook, YouTube, Shopify, and LinkedIn. Facebook also took down and banned the #WalkAway Campaign, shortly before Donald Trump's Twitter ban. Walk Away is a movement started by former Democrat supporter, Brandon Straka who shared his testimonial about walking away from the Democrat party and encourages other Democrats to do the same and share their story of why. This is what his Facebook page was created for, and according to Straka the only thing it was used for. The page at the time it was taken down had around 500,000 followers.

15. Speech and Expression

It wasn't just Straka and the Walk Away campaign page that was removed, but every volunteer and paid employee associated with them. From what I can find at this moment, Facebook has not made an official statement as to why. All we have is screenshots from Straka, with Facebook stating they had violated their terms of use. Facebook also decided to crack down and punish users referring to the term "stop the steal" for those believing the 2020 presidential election was rigged.

That in itself shows the discontent the above companies have for free speech. Conservatives were constantly told if you don't like what is being said, go work on your own platform. Yet when they did go to a platform that doesn't discriminate based on political beliefs, there appeared to be a coordinated effort to shut them down. There are other small free speech platforms that have not gone along with platform censorship, such as GAB.com. My guess is they haven't become big enough to be considered a threat.

Ok so it appears censorship seems to be politically motivated and an attack on free speech, but nothing can be done without infringing on these private companies' right to free speech, right? Wrong. There is a law regarding social networking sites called Section 230 in Title 47 of the United States Code.

To my understanding, it gives them legal immunity from being sued because of content posted by its users. In essence think of it along the lines of the phone company. The phone company cannot be held liable for anything illegal planned by a phone conversation. They simply provide a platform from which to speak. Now there are some differences. For example, social media is still required to police their platforms for certain material that may be posted, such as child pornography.

Google was sued in 2017—after 2015 ISIS terrorist attack in Paris that killed 130 people—by the family of Nohemi Gonzalez, who was an American student killed in the attack. YouTube, which is owned by Google, was used by these terrorists to:

- actively recruit terrorists
- plan attacks
- incite followers to carry out violent acts
- give instructions for terror attacks

Google conceded to all of these facts, but successfully argued it cannot be held liable under Section 230, as it was just a platform, not the "publisher." Google did not create any of the videos, or endorse them. Their service was just used as a platform like millions of other people.

However, everything regarding the results of the 2020 election, officially turned many platforms from a place for people to freely communicate their beliefs to an area where the platform feels the need to force their two cents on everyone else as a "publisher." Imagine having a phone conversation, and an operator suddenly jumps on the line, injects his or the company's stance, and then possibly warns you to stop your current conversation, or they will disconnect you. You would be pretty annoyed at that happening and rightfully so. That is the equivalent of what is going on with popular social media sights now as many have decided to stop being the neutral platform.

15. Speech and Expression

So why did so many big-name online tech companies almost immediately jump on the bandwagon with the police officer—move along, nothing to see here attitude—when they had immunity from the consequences of what people express using their platform? Are all of them such big believers in the integrity of the electoral process? Did they not want to risk Joe Biden losing, and thus feel a need to dissuade people from looking at the claims of fraud? Do they hate Donald Trump that much? Is there a quid pro quo, any bribery or extortion from Democrats to get social media to act in this manner? It is hard to say what the reasoning is. Only certain politicians and certain people at the top of these companies know for sure. However, with the billions lost by so many social media sights for taking such action without reversing course or even rethinking their position, it sounds like rather plausible reasoning to think there was indeed government influence affecting such decisions. Oh wait, the Twitter files released by Elon Musk after he purchased Twitter point to exactly that.

What is the solution in regard to Section 230? Should it be repealed? No. I think the best course would be for the big tech companies to keep their mouths shut regarding their beliefs, and media should return to being a non-bias platform, instead of injecting their beliefs on every post they feel needs it to help ensure their users will think like they do.

Let them be subject to the lawsuits they are protected from when they feel they must force their opinion and make mistakes such as using fact checks that are not fully vetted and can be refuted. If it is an opinion that they don't like being stated on their platform, let them create a profile(s) and comment on posts under the same rules as everyone else to avoid losing the protection under Section 230. Let them make their argument that way, the same as everyone else and allow people the choice in following that profile, rather than using special abilities to determine what they do and do not want not open to the public.

Yes, these Big Tech platforms such as YouTube and Facebook are private platforms, and they are free to deplatform whomever they want, in a free society. The platform is after all *their* property. I never said otherwise, as some are probably already arguing. I said let them lose the special protections they have under Section 230 if this is how they want to play. Let them be held personally responsible for such actions, in the same way people who riot should be held accountable for their actions. It would have made a world of difference in how they handled what was allowed to be said with the China virus. Let them either play the role of a bias censor on their platform and lose the protection under Section 230, or stay completely neutral when it comes to political expression and stay safe from those lawsuits under Section 230. When you think about the current politically charged atmosphere in this country, people will sue for any reason. That is all the more reason for them to play it safe.

The New Free Speech in DC

Donald Trump has been lambasted by the media and a wide range of elected officials from the time he came down the escalator in 2015. However, by the end of his first term, the Washington establishment in both parties seems to have set a new

15. Speech and Expression

precedent regarding free speech among their own.

I already pointed out the flaws in the argument Twitter used to ban Donald Trump from their platform, and how numerous other Big Tech companies soon followed suit, under the same faulty reasoning.

The United States House of Representatives had other plans after the alleged riot at the Capital Building on January 6, 2021. They still held Trump accountable, but expanded to include his speech in front of the White House that day, as a reason to impeach him a second time, saying he tried to incite an insurrection with his words. The House of Representatives impeached him a week later. We have to ask some simple questions? What exactly did he say to incite insurrection? What were the exact words he used to try to convince his supporters to overthrow the government of the United States, or to break into the Capital Building and cause a riot? Surely there must be a smoking gun proving his words incited violence. Actually, there isn't. If there were, we would have heard that sound bite repeated on news and social media so often that we would have it memorized. Yet all we heard was the narrative repeated over and over again saying Trump is responsible for the violence and an attempt at insurrection occurred because of him. Whether you like Trump or not, there was no smoking gun or any evidence coming close to proving it. There was only the reasoning that certain people chose to believe.

Like with Twitter, the "evidence" is *their interpretation* of what Trump meant. It is what they want to believe. They chose to believe it so strongly that they felt the need to rush things and vote on his impeachment before the facts were even investigated or gathered and with only days left in his presidency, and a very limited time for debate. Many outlets also neglected to mention or they casually dismissed one specific thing Trump said in his speech in front of the White House on January 6, 2020 at around the 18 minutes and 16 seconds into his speech.

> **"I know that everyone here will soon be marching over to the Capital building to peacefully and patriotically make your voices heard."**
> **– Donald Trump**

If anything, this alone destroys their claims of inciting insurrection. But like I said, there are those who will believe what they want to believe. They will insist that what was said is code or a dog whistle to mean something else. However, they will ignore worse actions and words from their political allies or their supporters, even going so far as making excuses for them when the opposing side calls them out. Vice President Kamala Harris is the prime example.

In June of 2020 then VP candidate Harris, said the following in an interview on, *The Late Show* with Stephen Colbert in regard to the protests of surrounding the death of George Floyd.

"And everyone beware because they're not gonna stop, they're not gonna stop before election day in November, and they're not gonna stop after election day. Everyone should take note of that on both levels. They're not gonna let up, *and they should not,* and we should not."

Rioting and looting was not specifically addressed in this in-

15. Speech and Expression

terview, and Harris has indeed condemned the riots and says she supports peaceful protesting both before and after this interview. However, if you are going to condemn and impeach Trump for the actions of a handful of his political supporters, and what his opponents feel he meant when he didn't differentiate between his protestors in his final tweets, shouldn't Mrs. Harris, be just as strongly condemned and even impeached for not doing the same, when she said they should not let up, which could easily be seen as encouragement for all those protests, peaceful or otherwise? It follows the same guidelines.

There are numerous examples of politicians like Mrs. Harris not being held to the same standards; her controversial comments at best in some cases can be seen as openly encouraging violent behavior. Such an example can be found with comments by United States Senator Maxine Waters, who at a rally of her supporters in Los Angeles in the summer of 2018, said the following:

> "If you see anybody from that Cabinet (Trump's) in a restaurant, in a department store, at a gasoline station, you get out and you create a crowd and you push back on them, and you tell them they're not welcome anymore, anywhere."

This sounds like a call strongly hinting at political violence against political opponents. At the very least, it is more provoking than what Trump said.

There are more comments made during the rioting, looting, and arson that occurred during the BLM protests in 2020.

"Show me where it says that protests are supposed to be polite and peaceful." - Chris Cuomo, New York City Mayor

"I just don't know why there aren't uprisings all over the country. Maybe there will be." - Nancy Pelosi, Speaker of the House for the United States House of Representatives.

We have been over what President Trump said and tweeted. Can anyone say these other comments are not worse, if you are looking to incite insurrection or encourage violence? Even if you think any of those comments are taken out of context at all, their words are still pretty damning. There were no serious calls to have them removed from office for these comments that I can remember.

This is not looking to downplay or shift focus from the Trump supporters that breached the Capital. Far from it. Everyone who breached the Capital needs to be held accountable without excuse. Keep something in mind though. Years later we don't know all of the identities, backgrounds, or political leanings of all the protestors who breached the Capital on January 6. Were they Trump supporters, people opposed to Trump, or even opponents' subordinates to make Trump's supporters look bad? After all the FBI refused to acknowledge if they had agents as part of the protest, how many, and their exact role. I am inclined to believe it was a mixture of all three groups. One group is as capable as another, and there are always people who will convince themselves that the ends will justify the means. In fact, BLM activist, John Earl Sullivan, was arrested for entering the Capital building on January 6, 2020, on numerous charges. A video he made of the event shows him actively encouraging those around him

15. Speech and Expression

to continue to push forward. Yet interestingly enough, he was released shortly after being arrested, while others were still being held years later without bail for nonviolent actions in the Capital on January 6.

The calls for removing politicians haven't stopped with Trump. There were also calls for actions to be taken to remove 147 elected Republican officials, especially Senators Josh Hawley and Ted Cruz, simply for voting to *not certify* the presidential election results right away. Many media outlets have called it a vote to overturn the election results, and to justify the riot at the Capital building. Their reasoning for calling to remove them comes from Section 3 of the Fourteenth Amendment to the United States Constitution, which states:

> "No person shall be a Senator or Representative in Congress, or elector of President and Vice President, or hold any office, civil or military, under the United States, or under any State, who, have previously taken an oath, as a member of Congress, or as an officer of the United States, or as a member of any State legislature, or as an executive or judicial officer of any States, shall have engaged in insurrection or rebellion against the same, or given aid or comfort to the enemies thereof. But Congress, may by a vote of two thirds of each house remove such disability."

Sounds serious, but did they really violate this section of the Constitution, which would warrant their dismissal? Earlier Cruz and other Senators had called for Congress to "immediately appoint an Electoral Commission, with full investigatory and fact-finding authority, to conduct an emergency ten-day audit of the

The Freedom Scale

election returns in the disputed states. Once it was completed, individual states would evaluate the Commission's findings and could convene a special legislative session to certify a change in their vote *if needed.*"

This group cited the Presidential election in 1876 between Rutherford B. Hayes and Samuel J. Tildmen, in which there was widespread allegations of voter fraud. In Florida, Louisiana and South Carolina, two sets of electors were sent, one for each candidate at that time, just as two sets of electors were sent from seven states for the 2020 election, so the Congress in 1876, in a bipartisan manner (as the house was controlled by one party at that time and the Senate controlled by the other), agreed to a bipartisan electoral commission that would investigate any electoral disputes. The resolution in that case was resolved along party lines, but they decided to work together to end concerns of voting fraud.

Now go back and look at what the Senators who supported it, said about forming an Electoral Commission for the 2020 presidential election. The Commission investigates and sends its findings to the states in question, and then the states could (not must) convene a special legislative session to change their vote if needed. Doesn't sound like a call for insurrection to me. It sounds like these Senators were saying to have all of these allegations of voter fraud thoroughly investigated; to have the states decide based on that evidence and let the chips fall where they may, whether it be for Biden or Trump. Where do they say overturn the election? They didn't say that. The media and Democrats said it.

If anything, the call to use the Fourteenth Amendment sounds like a call to muffle free speech through extortion to any elected

15. Speech and Expression

official that challenged the desired narrative. Biden won. Don't make waves and accept it or measures will be taken to ensure you will regret it. Maybe that is part of the reason a number of Republican politicians jumped on board against Trump with the January 6th committee. It was a way they could show their loyalty to the establishment and maybe secure a promise from the establishment they will be left alone for doing so, and possibly more.

Free Political Speech Amongst the People

The attacks continued on Trump supporters after January 6 as well. Protests had gotten out of hand for a long time in this country, many of them in recent years. However, none of them were labeled insurrectionists, until January 6. It has even been suggested supporting Trump is cult-like behavior, and that Trump supporters need to be deprogrammed. Did we hear the mainstream media provide such an analysis during BLM and antifa riots or any other left-wing protest that has gotten out of hand? I haven't. Could this be a double standard based on political beliefs, as opposed to actions? Either way, it is a call to silence free speech.

In regard to the protestors being insurrectionists, there are several reasons to question that claim and even the very creation of the January 6 Committee, but I will keep it to the five most important reasons to be skeptical.

1. *Most Trump supporters are staunch Second Amendment activists. If insurrection was the objective, I find it doubtful they all would have left*

their guns at home or that there would have been such little bloodshed.

2. Why did it take years, and a Republican Speaker of the House to get complete audio and video surveillance tapes inside and outside of the Capital Building showing all of the protestors from January 6? Why was it not released immediately to prove an attempted insurrection by the J6 Committee? We now know what that footage shows, but the media pretends that the most damaging footage was never released.

3. Why was Ray Epps not of interest to the January 6 Committee or even jailed awaiting trial, with video evidence of him insisting on storming the Capital Building on more than one occasion? With the belief of an attempted insurrection, he seems to be someone who would be of particular interest. The only reason I can think of to ignore him is if he was a plant with the intention of having protestors enter the Capital Building, so the event could be called an insurrection.

4. If the goal was to get at the truth, why were only people hostile to Donald Trump on the J6 Committee? Why not have differing viewpoints? Was the goal to control the narrative or get to the truth? Would the evidence against Trump supporters not hold up under scrutiny with a bipartisan committee?

5. Why of all the people arrested for January 6, has not a single one of them been charged with attempted insurrection? The best guess would be political theater

15. Speech and Expression

> *to keep those opposed to Trump motivated to vote. After all, if it were a definite attempt at insurrection, it should be easy to prove for at least a few people.*

To any rational person, these things are reasonable considerations. However, according to others, like former Facebook chief security officer, Alex Stamos in an interview with CNN, the answer to dealing with Trump supporters is something we have already seen and discussed with various social media sites, and that is to shut down the opposing viewpoint at least to a degree. He claimed they had to turn down those influencers' ability to reach huge audiences. In other words, shut down or limit the platforms these people can speak on and get their information from so they cannot influence or be influenced anymore. Problem solved. After all you can't be trusted to choose for yourself and make up your own mind. You may not make the right decision in the mind of Mr. Stamos and other like-minded individuals. This gets the people another step closer to the approved groupthink that doesn't ask unwanted questions.

Never mind looking at opposing arguments and dissecting them one at a time to prove beyond a shadow of a doubt that they are false. Forget about being just as critical of President Joe Biden as President Donald Trump. Don't even think about at least listening to and directly addressing the concerns of Trump supporters. There is no reason to even acknowledge the concern of insurrectionists. This is the answer for power hungry political elites who control the narrative by authoritarian means, not the way of freedom.

Remember how I mentioned many of the so-called insurrectionists were held for years on end without bail, pending trial? This can be confirmed as true from the court records and prison records. There were also reports of poor treatment in jails such as being housed in solitary confinement the whole time or given limited access to legal representation. Whether that is true or not we can't know for certain without seeing for ourselves.

In any case it sends a clear and intimidating message. Shut up and fall in line, or suffer the consequences.

Adolf Hitler had similar thoughts on the need to suppress differing viewpoints, though his methods for doing so often ended in people dying if they were not put in prison. That way there was no open and peaceful disagreement or discussion with those openly opposed to him. The opposition was either silenced or eliminated. In Nazi Germany such practice was known as *gleichschaltung*. It is defined in Merriam Webster online dictionary as:

> *the act, process, or policy of achieving rigid and total coordination and uniformity (as in politics, culture, communication) by forcibly repressing or eliminating independence and freedom of thought, action or expression: forced reduction to a common level: forced standardization or assimilation.*

"If freedom of speech is taken away, then dumb and silent we may be led, like lambs to the slaughter."
– George Washington

Lies and false information wherever they come from are not crushed by shutting down what some people see as lies and false information. They are crushed by shining the light of truth

15. Speech and Expression

on them, presenting all the facts, and not just the facts that are beneficial to a specific argument. They are crushed by the important questions being asked and answered. They are crushed by making a better argument than the other guy. Only those with an agenda or something to hide look to actively suppress or control what is said to achieve their desired result.

Control of what is said and thought, as well as information available is essential to taking away freedom of expression. Following that path helps ensure people will blindly follow without question. Despite what many will have you believe; no side is always right or wrong. It is why we must ask the questions many people have not asked or even thought to ask. More importantly, asking such questions and challenging the narrative, is necessary for those who value freedom, even if you agree with the narrative being touted. It is especially essential to do this when you agree with the narrative, because sooner or later, you will likely be on the other side of the fence. Where does that leave everyone though if free speech is already silenced?

16. Elections: Controlling the Choice

"Those who vote decide nothing. Those who count the vote decide everything."
– Joseph Stalin

The 2020 presidential election was by far the most memorable in my lifetime to date. It was an election rife with various accusations of voter fraud. Since COVID-19 was such a big issue during the election, and the first time any type of mail in ballots were used on a massive scale, it was practically a given assumption that such accusations would arise, hence the need for even more scrutiny than usual.

Before we get into the 2020 presidential voter fraud allegations, I want to throw something out there. What I have to say will piss off a whole lot of conservatives, but I don't care. Trump was wrong in saying the election was rigged. With that said, I believe his conclusion was correct; he followed it up in the wrong manner. Believing the election was rigged and saying it out loud as fact without presenting concrete proof to the public are two different things. By following the latter, Trump allowed the narrative to be redirected putting him on the defensive to try and prove everything.

What Trump should have done was point out all of the possible ways the vote could have been rigged, and make the argument that the government didn't conclusively prove that Joe Biden won, putting the election process on the defensive instead. It could have saved the hassle, especially when people were later questioned by the government if they now believed Joe Biden was legitimately elected.

Coulda, woulda, shoulda. No sense crying over spilled milk at this point no matter what you believe. This isn't to argue about who really won. It is to look at freedom and elections and how that freedom can be compromised if the elections are questionable. We'll start by looking at various laws used and arguments against alleged voter suppression, to see if they conflict with what is needed for a free and fair election, and how, if possible, it can be used to skew the outcome.

Voter Suppression

Voter suppression is a tactic that has been used the world over in an effort to determine the outcome of various elections. It is, as the name suggests suppressing the vote of certain people who don't support certain politicians or ideologies. The goal is to ensure more votes are preserved or gained for one side and more votes are lost or not placed for the other side. In some authoritarian countries, people face punishment for voting a certain way making intimidation the means for suppressing a free election. That is just one tactic among a wide variety of methods that can be used to ensure the desired result. How else do you think ruthless and oppressive dictators or other authoritarian governments stay in power if they even bother to hold elections? Do you think the people of those countries willfully keep electing those leaders be-

The Freedom Scale

cause they believe they are doing a great job? Stew on those questions in the back of your mind as you finish reading this chapter.

To keep it simple though, we will focus on accusations of voter suppression in the United States. The most famous voter suppression came from Jim Crow voting laws in the south to prevent blacks from voting despite the newly amended Constitution. Examples include but are not limited to:

- Threats and the use of violence against blacks, especially from the Ku Klux Klan.
- Literacy tests primarily determined whether or not someone could vote. Many whites had a way around this literacy test with a grandfather clause which stated a person could vote if their father or grandfather voted prior to 1867, which was before the Civil War ended.
- Blacks were purged from the voter rolls, so they could not vote. The excuse could easily be, well it may well be a mistake, but there is nothing we can do about it now, so you will have to wait till the next election.

These were some of the most egregious and undeniable examples of voter suppression in this country and have long since been removed from state laws. It targeted a specific group of people to help ensure a specific party didn't lose power. What about modern-day voter suppression? What are the examples, and do they infringe on individuals voting, or are they voting laws that some people simply don't like? Let's look at some of the biggest claims of voter suppression that Democrats say Republicans are guilty of.

16. Elections

The claim of preventing felons from voting is said to be a form of unjust voter suppression. Is it really though? If a person commits a crime and becomes a convicted felon, they have knowingly and willfully committed an act that they knew would strip them of their right to vote, and their Second Amendment rights. Nobody forced them to commit a crime.

This argument is often approached from a racial standpoint, rather than an individual standpoint. Since more blacks are convicted of felonies per capita and thus lose their voting rights, it is addressed as voter suppression of the black community. There is no legal distinction in any of the laws saying only black felons lose their voting rights. Every convicted felon regardless of race who has lost their voting rights made an individual choice, and the actions of those choices have consequences. Convicted felons released from prison, are more likely to be seeking a government handout because of the difficulty in getting meaningful employment that comes with their criminal record.

Making it difficult for people to vote is also a big claim of voter suppression. State legislators under the U.S. Constitution have the power to determine the number of polling stations and the times during which the polling stations are opened. That ability is directly granted to them in the U.S. Constitution. The argument narrows down to early voting, and once again the argument goes to race among other things. The claim is that early voting allows poor people, or those working long or inflexible hours to vote before going to work and by not going along with some early voting measures disenfranchises them. This process disproportionately affects the black community according to their claims.

Let me put myself in the shoes of these people that are claimed to be disenfranchised. At the time I write this I live 45 minutes from my work. If I were to work a 12 hour shift that day, I would not have time to get to the polls before they close. Here we circle back to personal responsibility. If the rules for voting don't coincide with my work schedule, I adjust my work schedule in advance, if I want to ensure I vote that day. I could also try to work extra time or work other day(s) to get election day off, or I could schedule a vacation day on election day. If worse comes to worse, I call in sick. If I want to vote, I am responsible for adjusting my schedule to arrive at the polling place during the scheduled hours. It all depends on whether voting is that important to me. Everyone knows when election day is, so it is a matter of requesting that specific day off or requesting specific hours off. As the majority of the country chooses not to vote, that should not be too difficult for most people.

Next, we get to the purging of the voting register. There are complaints such as in Ohio of a law being passed removing voters from the registers if they have not voted in 2 years and did not return a voter card mailed to the registered address. The argument for such laws is to reduce voter fraud. Makes sense. Sometimes when people die, their name doesn't get purged from the voting registers for years. Regularly purging names of deceased individuals makes it less likely that a fraudulent vote will be cast in their name. It also requires personal responsibility of every individual to ensure if they want to vote that they are not purged ahead of time. We live in the digital age where practically everyone has online access. It is easy for most everyone

16. Elections

to go online and check the status of their voter registration. You can also call and verify you are not scheduled to be taken off the roles. I personally did this to ensure that when election day came, I could vote without worry. It wasn't that hard.

Gerrymandering is another complaint about voter suppression. It involves creating voting district maps that look very disorganized—often linked by splinters of land connecting two or more larger parts to maximize votes of a particular party. This appears to be a legitimate concern. Pack enough people supporting the opposing party into a district to make the vote close, but not close enough so that there is a remote chance their party will lose. In areas you can't win, someone packs as many opposition voters into that district as possible. These decisions are normally determined by the state legislatures.

However, populations are constantly changing across the United States. People are dying and being born every day. Citizens and new immigrants alike are constantly changing the demographics all over the country by moving or coming into the country and becoming citizens creating the need to redraw the districts from time to time. The main political parties utilize gerrymandering whenever they get the chance, so what is the main complaint? One main political party uses it more than the other? Gerrymandering will happen on both sides depending which party has more power in the states and local governments. To complain only when the other side does it is outright hypocritical.

What is the solution to gerrymandering? Make a better argument than the other guy. In the 2020 presidential election for example, Donald Trump won over numerous counties in Texas that historically would have gone for Joe Biden or anyone from Biden's party running for president.

We now get to the most interesting argument in the claims of voter suppression, which is requiring a photo I.D. to vote and in many cases a government issued photo I.D. such as a driver's license or passport. It is said this requirement, disproportionately affects elderly, poor, and black voters' ability to vote because they are less likely to have a government issued ID. The elderly? If they are of sound mind, they can go to the DMV and get a standard photo identification card. They may need a ride, but people arguing against photo ID requirements, would surely give these folks a ride! Right? At least the ones likely to support their candidate. You know to make sure they are not disenfranchised. The poor? They cannot afford an ID at the DMV, and thus they are disenfranchised from voting. There are several arguments to be made here. Let us start with the most basic question. What poor person doesn't have a photo ID (besides a homeless person)? You need a photo ID for practically everything. You need one to board a plane, to buy a gun, to rent an apartment, to apply for most jobs and numerous other things. It is practically impossible to advance anywhere in life without one, so it seems like having one would be a high priority in life. This brings up another concern. Photo IDs may be too expensive for the poor. It wasn't too expensive for them to buy God knows how many masks for COVID-19, and the cost of those can easily exceed that of a photo ID many times over. Yet we saw no outcry in response to mask mandates anywhere for the poor. Maybe give up a luxury once every four years to obtain one, so you can vote and start to advance beyond being poor?

We also cannot seem to escape the racial cry of voter suppression. Are blacks less capable of obtaining a photo ID than other races? Are they turned away at the DMV nowadays or prevented from being registered to vote? The answer to all of these situations is an emphatic *no*. Once again it comes down to individual choice. What are your priorities? Making sure your vote is counted or doing what you want?

From these arguments, I see nothing targeting any specific group of people. All of these laws and requirements that are claimed to be voter suppression apply to everyone, not just one group. It comes back to personal responsibility.

The Indicators of Presidential Elections

Before diving into accusations of voter fraud in 2020, we must ask if there was sufficient reason after the votes were counted to think something might have been off with this election. Something that warrants further scrutiny. There is a pattern of indicators that are normally constant and consistent on determining who wins a U.S. presidential election. That applecart was completely turned on its head in the 2020 presidential election. At the very least, it should have warranted a deeper look before claiming a victor.

Reasonable doubts existed for the 2020 presidential election since November 4, 2020, except for those who merely accepted what they chose to believe without question. Deep down, I doubt most of Biden's supporters believe that he really won the presidency, but they didn't want to rock the boat so to speak, and possibly feared learning that Biden lost. It would make sense they would turn a blind eye to anything that didn't fit the desired narrative. So, what made that presidential election different from others?

In all honesty, heading into the 2020 elections, it looked to me like Democrats were intentionally trying to lose not only the presidential election, but a number of other elections on the state level as well. They had the strictest lockdowns from COVID-19 from the mayors and governors that ran those cities and states where countless businesses went under as the result of being forced to close for so long. Cities run by left-wing mayors experienced widespread riots, arson, and looting because of outrage over past alleged racist actions by police. Many of those mayors did nothing to crack down on the actions of the rioters. Instead, these mayors and governors—in some instances—slandered the police and brown-nosed all protestors, not even calling them out, because they represented groups that normally align and vote in lockstep with the Democrat Party.

On top of that, Joe Biden, who was their candidate running for President, often didn't appear able to talk coherently. This happened and continues to happen so often that it was speculated he may have early onset Alzheimer's or dementia. He barely drew any attendance at his drive-in rallies, while Trump still drew in overwhelmingly large crowds in the tens of thousands (at minimum) on short notice and campaigned tirelessly.

The person Biden picked for his running mate was so un-

16. Elections

popular, she was the first to drop out of the Democrat primaries. Trump ignored warnings from the media that Biden was far ahead all over the country according to the polls. It was even suggested by those opposed to Trump to not worry if it looks like he is initially winning over Biden, because it was likely to turn around after all the mail-in votes were counted. Low and behold that is exactly what started happening in the early morning hours of November 4.

Looking at the data from past elections, the results didn't make sense. There are specific indicators that predict how an election will go. What were the indicators in Trump's favor?

- Trump garnered more than 10 million more votes than he did when he won in 2016. No incumbent president in nearly 150 years has gained votes in reelection and lost, let alone so many votes.
- Trump won 18 of the 19 main bellwether counties by an average of over 16 points, while losing the 19th county, (Clallam County in Washington by 3 points). These counties have had a near perfect record for the past 40 years in determining who would win the presidency. Whoever won these counties was practically assured of winning the presidency.
- Trump received 94 percent of the primary vote for the 2020 election, which is the fourth highest in U.S. history. No incumbent president had ever lost reelection with less than 75 percent of the total primary vote.
- Trump gained more votes from all minorities and other

217

demographics than his Republican predecessors in the 2020 elections. The only demographic he lost in was white people.
- Trump gained a higher percentage of votes or stayed at the same percentage in every major metropolitan area, except four where Biden super performed outdoing both Barrack Obama and Hillary Clinton. Those four cities were Milwaukie, Detroit, Philadelphia, and Atlanta. All were in states where we saw a large number of voting irregularities. Coincidence?
- Trump lost despite a significant number of seats in the House of Representatives being picked up by his party. This is practically unheard of.

There is a first time for most everything. Is it possible that Biden won despite all of these anomalies? Of course, it is. However, being the first time that mail in voting and especially drop boxes were used on such a massive scale, a large-scale analysis and detailed audit of the vote should have been warranted no matter who won. The analysis would have looked for flaws in the system where states may have been lax in their voting laws or evaluation of the mail-in votes. This analysis would have shown where processes needed to be shored up. This analysis was needed *before* votes were counted. Yet, practically nobody but Trump and his supporters called for a closer look at the election results. Most people in the media and on the left, wanted the results of Biden winning accepted without any further scrutiny. Again, being the first time, this was done on such a massive scale, how do we know for sure this was a free and fair election without examining the results and thoroughly investigating the thousands of sworn affidavits of voting irregularities?

It was more than just not wanting to look though. There was near universal, steadfast, opposition for detailed recounts and audits of the 2020 election from Democrats, and even some Republicans. The more (though not fully) detailed Arizona audit of Maricopa County was opposed vehemently by Democrats and the Biden Administration, instead of trying to put the doubts of all the American people to rest. Several dozen lawyers were brought in to fight that audit. The main question is why the opposition?

"Never interrupt your enemy when he is making a mistake."
– Napolean Bonaparte

If it is so certain that Biden won the presidential election, why not agree to the recount and to a fully detailed, forensic audit in fair and transparent manner—that both sides can agree to—in order to prove beyond a shadow of a doubt that Biden won? Doing so would not only have silenced Trump's base and severely demoralized them, but it would also have been an olive branch from Biden showing they were reasonable about addressing political opponents' concerns. After all Biden claimed he was going to be the *uniter*. Yet every elected Democrat I saw addressing the issue, refused to give even a centimeter. Why? Simple logic shows us, they had much to gain and little to lose with the recounts and audits. That is however, only if Biden legitimately won. If Biden actually lost, the Democrats had a lot to lose. In addition to the most logical conclusion that the vast majority of Democrats held the belief that Biden didn't really win, there is also the disturbing possibility that there are elected Democrats and other Trump opponents who had a hand in rigging the Presidential election for their candidate and don't want to be found out as well as have Biden removed.

Also consider the fact we saw many of our elected and government officials playing quite fast and loose with election laws in 2020, both before and after the election. Was such behavior another way the 2020 presidential election could have been manipulated to achieve a specific outcome? Time to take a closer look.

3 Strikes in the 2020 Election

"Elections belong to the people. It's their decision. If they decide to turn their back on the fire and burn their behinds, then they will just have to sit on their blisters."
– Abraham Lincoln

What should be the consequence of anyone not following state election laws? Quite honestly that is something that should be determined by their position, the role they played, and the degree to which their actions could have affected the election. Regardless of these factors, at the very least, the ballots in question as the result of the broken election law should not be counted, as they are by definition illegal ballots being in violation of the law. Who would be the expert to decide if ballots are in question or election laws were broken? It would have to be the courts, who

16. Elections

in some cases can be as corrupt as some politicians. Specifying ballots to be disqualified will have to reside in the government proving beyond a reasonable doubt, no fraud could have occurred. I'll explain the details soon enough.

In 2019, in Pennsylvania, the state legislature passed Act 77. This was a measure to allow mail in voting in response to COVID-19. It set out specific guidelines that must be followed in regard to mail in voting. It specifically states that:

"No absentee ballot under this subsection shall be counted which is received in the office of the county board of elections later than eight o'clock P.M. on the day of the primary or election."

Act 77 goes on to state that many sections of this act are non-severable. It also clearly states that:

"If any provision of this act or its application to any person or circumstance is held invalid, the remaining provisions or applications of this act are void."

In a nutshell it says, 'break the rules we lined up here for mail in voting, and all of the mail in ballots we are allowing under this law become invalidated.' As it turns out, *'held invalid'* apparently meant by the courts instead of the legislature, as Pennsylvania had a challenge to this specifically in Act 77 in 2022 in the court case McLinko v. Degraffenreid, in which the Pennsylvania State Supreme Court ruled against Republicans trying to enact this provision. In all honesty the Pennsylvania Supreme Court should have been forced to recues themselves because of the 2020 election. Let me elaborate.

Shortly before the 2020 election, the Pennsylvania Supreme Court decided by a vote of 4 to 3 (with a majority representing Democrats), to change the rules of Act 77 on its own declaring that Pennsylvania residents had an extra 3 days for their ballot to be received and counted so long as they were postmarked by November 3, rather than rule Act 77 unconstitutional, and send it back to the Pennsylvania legislature to be rewritten. As a result, on October 28, 2020, Pennsylvania Republican representatives challenged this ruling by the Pennsylvania Supreme Court by filing a Writ of Certiorari, which is a petition for a higher court to review the decision of a lower court. It was reported by much of the mainstream media to have been rejected by the United States Supreme Court. That was not the case, however. The U.S. Supreme Court only refused the request to have the review expedited, not the review itself. The law was sent back to the Pennsylvania Supreme Court for further review.

Two arguments have been made regarding Act 77 for the 2020 election. The first is that in changing the deadline for mail in ballots, the Pennsylvania Supreme Court ruled blatantly and unconstitutionally overstepping their authority, and also violating Act 77 making all the mail in ballots void. The second argument was that Act 77 violated the Pennsylvania State Constitution and was thus an invalid law to begin with.

The Pennsylvania Supreme Court did indeed knowingly and willfully violate the United States Constitution in extending the mail in ballot deadline 3 days. Article I, section 4, clause 1 of the United States Constitution specifically states:

16. Elections

"The Times, Places and Manners of holding Elections for Senators and Representatives, shall be prescribed in each State by the Legislature thereof; but the Congress may at any time by Law make or alter such Regulations except as to the Places of chusing Senators."

This means that as far as State elected officials go, only the State Legislatures may choose how to alter election laws. The state courts do not have that right being part of the judiciary, and neither do the governors of those states, being part of the State Executive Branch.

What about Act 77 violating the Pennsylvania State Constitution? Does it actually do that? No it does not. The exact words of Article VII, Section 14 of the Pennsylvania State Constitution which addresses absentee voting, states that the Legislature **shall**, by general law provide a manner for certain people with certain circumstances to vote absentee in an election. I have found nothing prohibiting or restricting them from extending any absentee ballots to state residents as they see fit. Only that they must do it for certain people with certain circumstance. Going back to the U.S. Constitution, it looks like that is their right.

Looking at everything, it shows that the Pennsylvania Supreme Court not only violated the U.S. Constitution extending the deadline for ballots by three days, but they also violated Act 77 in the process, making all mail-in ballots illegitimate. This could have been avoided had they simply ruled Act 77 unconstitutional, but they didn't, meaning it was still law. Considering Biden voters, voted much more heavily by mail when compared to Trump voters, and that Biden took Pennsylvania only by 81,660 votes, Trump would have easily won Pennsylvania, if Act 77 had simply been enforced as written.

The U.S. Supreme Court did order the segregation of the ballots that came in after 8 pm on November 3, and Biden still won, so what does it matter? First there is no way to prove how many, if any ballots slipped through for whatever reason after 8 pm on November 3, before that order came through and was enforced. Some ballots had no postmark. Who is to say for sure they arrived before the deadline? Ballots were separated from their envelopes with no way to tell what ballots went with what envelopes afterwards, so it is anyone's guess the number of legitimate votes received by each candidate.

A full forensic audit was denied when it may have ascertained with more certainty if any mail-in votes violated Act 77. Such action was repeatedly denied by Governor Wolf, who ultimately said he would not stand for this. Such is not his call, as that power resides with the Pennsylvania State Legislature.

While it cannot be proven if any of those votes were counted, it doesn't matter. Legally Act 77 still should have been invalidated by the Pennsylvania Supreme Court's three-day extension to count mail-in ballots at the time the election took place. Harmful, vagrant violation of election laws were carried out by those who had power, but did not have the authority. None of them suffered the consequences for their actions. It must be taken into consideration, if such actions are allowed to stand, what other election laws can be ignored or violated on a whim by those without the authority? What is the purpose

16. Elections

of election laws in that case? With the number of mail-in votes cast, Trump would have won if those votes had been thrown out and Act 77 had been enforced and invalidated. Strike 1.

Before continuing, there are probably those already screaming that I am arguing that we must rob people of their vote so Trump would win. My argument is to simply follow the law in an unbiased manner. Any violation of the law must have consequences. In the case of Act 77, those consequences were specified very clearly.

Wisconsin has in place some of the strictest laws for absentee voting, but they still had problems in that regard. Under Wisconsin state statute 6.87 (4) (b) 1, the rules are spelled out very clearly. It provides that the absentee ballot envelope into which the absentee ballot is specifically placed must be "mailed by the elector or delivered in person to the municipal clerk issuing the ballot or ballots." This would in essence make drop boxes illegal in Wisconsin without legislation passed by the Wisconsin State legislature allowing an exception. So why were drop boxes utilized in the 2020 election? The Wisconsin Election Commission (WEC) sent guidelines or instructions to various election officials throughout the state in both March and August of 2020, which gave officials the authority to use drop boxes very liberally, or so they thought. The Wisconsin State Legislature was supposedly sent the request for approval authorizing drop boxes, but they never officially gave approval. The WEC jumped the shark big time.

So official permission through proper legislation was given eventually by the legislature after the fact, right? Not exactly.

In early 2022, Waukesha County Circuit Court Judge, Michael Bohren presided over a case involving drop boxes in the state and ruled them unlawful in Wisconsin. How could he do that if state legislation officially exempted drop boxes? If he was just playing politics, his ruling would have been overturned almost immediately on appeal, citing the proper statutes. It wasn't.

It doesn't end there though as even more laws were not followed in Wisconsin. While everyone is sent an application for a mail-in ballot, 170,140 of these ballots were allegedly cast without the application having been received by the state of Wisconsin. Requesting absentee ballots creates a paper trail; yet apparently the state of Wisconsin could not provide the signed requests for absentee ballots for more than 8x the margin of victory for Biden, which was 20,682 votes, most of which were in districts that are Democrat strongholds. Where is the proof that the state received the applications from the individuals? There should be a request on file for everyone else that requested an absentee ballot. Are we supposed to believe all of these 170,000+ requests were accidentally lost and should be counted without a second thought on blind faith? How do we know for certain this was not an attempt at fraud? Just as important, how do we track the person(s) responsible for the missing applications or know conclusively where these ballots went without applications, and what is the punishment for these officials? After all any number of those ballots without a request to back it up could have easily been a fraudulent vote. There is no way to prove one way or the other, which is why ballots without this request on file should never have been counted. The Wisconsin Supreme Court did address this issue which will be discussed shortly.

As there is no way to determine who these 170,140 ballots were cast for, being mixed in with all of the other ballots, any candidate on those ballots could not claim victory if their margin of victory was not greater than this number, not just the presidential candidate. Best option is to either have a brand-new election for everyone in the state or throw out all the contaminated ballots and go with the results of the uncontaminated ballots. When government doesn't do its job, there must be consequences on the officials responsible (preferably criminal) that assure the public it won't happen again.

Implementing such measures of keeping track of the applications are not difficult in this day and age. Each returned application could be scanned and sorted by date, verified by the government official who did it, by a means that personally identifies them. These scanned applications can be stored on the computers, flash drives, the cloud, as well as the hard copies locked up in a secure location, sorted in much the same manner. Redundancies on top of redundancies. There is no excuse for what happened in Wisconsin. Strike 2.

The final state is Arizona. The largest category of ineligible ballots in Arizona comes from ballots cast after Arizona's registration deadline to the tune of 150,000. In a display of what appears to be judicial activism, the courts agreed to extend the registration deadline from October 5 to October 23, 2020. Why do I call it judicial activism? Go back again to the U.S. Constitution, art 1, sec 4:

The Freedom Scale

> "The Times, Places and Manners of holding Elections for Senators and Representatives, shall be prescribed in each State by the Legislature thereof; but the Congress may at any time by Law make or alter such Regulations except as to the Places of chusing Senators."

The power in deciding rules for state elections resides in the state legislatures, not the courts, and not the governor's office. If an extension was needed, on the state level, it was solely within the power of the legislature to remedy the situation and their sole responsibility to officially authorize it as they were the only officials in the state authorized to do so. The judiciary had no authority to act in that manner, and thus those 150,000 ballots were counted as legitimate votes. If people were so concerned about being registered to vote, it was their responsibility to register in a timely manner before the deadline established by the state legislature. Strike 3. Biden should have been out.

Looking at these his presidency should never have happened. Without the needed majority of electoral votes, the Fourteenth Amendment of the Constitution would have been invoked, where the fifty individual state legislatures each cast one vote to choose the president. In this case Trump wins as the majority of state legislatures are governed by Republicans both before and after the 2020 election cycle and must vote in line with their party. Thus, it is reasonable to conclude looking at this analysis, that the 2020 presidential election was stolen from Donald J. Trump.

It is just technicalities you say, but in essence it is denying the lawful choice of the people. There is a line between technicalities and following the law, and that line was clear as day. It must be about following election laws as written that apply equally to everyone, no matter who wins as a result. If you don't like the law, push to get it changed. We cannot have elections, where we get to pick what election laws we follow and what ones we don't. The system would fall completely into chaos. This is why there must be severe consequences for government officials that drop the ball.

Voter Fraud in 2020?

"...and it is only prudent of us to question your motives. After all aren't there times when you feel it's in your best interest to deceive us? ...Tell me advocate... isn't it possible?"
– Benjamin Sisko, Star Trek: Deep Space Nine

Despite many Democrats and the mainstream media claiming voter fraud is rare, and that the 2020 election was the most secure in American history, it doesn't answer the question: How possible was it to commit voter fraud in the 2020 election. You can't simply say it was secure with little to no fraud when many opportunities were left open for fraud to occur. This brings us to one of the best examples of potential ballot fraud that was brought up in May of 2022 by an organization called True the Vote.

According to True the Vote, in investigating the use of drop boxes, thousands of ballot mules made numerous trips to the drop boxes in the key battleground states, with 40 percent in Atlanta being between midnight and 5 am. Their evidence comes from utilizing whistleblowers', publicly available cell phone geo tracking data, and security videos from local businesses. This ping data from the geo tracking was used to track the movement of the whistleblower-mules' to see who was repeatedly at the drop boxes, and the security video showing the drop boxes were used to verify these people were indeed dropping off multiple ballots in the drop boxes and taking cell phone pictures of the event, supposedly to get paid by the NGOs (non-governmental organizations.)

The TTV criteria was specific to raise a red flag. All activity fit into a specific grid where the drop boxes were within a specific timeframe October 1–November 3, and even later in Atlanta because of the Senate runoff election. Someone was identified as a mule by the geo tracking if they went to at least ten different drop boxes and five different NGOs within that timeframe. This wouldn't be useful in catching all ballot mules—just the worst offenders. There were also locations where video evidence was not produced. In some places because the ball was dropped, and they have no surveillance, and some like Philadelphia where government officials refused to share the video surveillance to those requesting it.

All of this and much more was highlighted in the political documentary by Dinesh D'Souza, *2000 Mules*. A few articles such as *Fact Focus: Gaping holes in the claim of 2K ballot 'mules'* by Ali Swensen of the Associated Press, have responded to this documentary with many of them primarily saying there is no definitive proof.

Here is what I observed in the articles I read. I didn't see them asking the necessary questions to see if it might be true, but instead playing the word game to misdirect and make vague claims

16. Elections

saying it was wrong for a variety of reasons. The most common argument is that geo tracking isn't that accurate, and according to Ms. Swensen, experts say geo tracking can only reliably track a smart phone to within a few meters. Even in the case of a few meters, it would still show the roads these people took constantly on several different days, passing several different drop boxes on a daily basis. All still just coincidence? Regardless not everyone is as easily convinced as Ms. Swensen's experts.

TTV's cyber expert, Greg Phillips, makes a different claim and is quoted as saying, "From these pings, it can be determined where you work, where you sleep, and even what floor you are on within inches." Chief Justice of the Supreme Court, John Roberts has cited the accuracy of geo tracking in deciding a case. Geo tracking has also been successfully used in the past for criminal cases, by the military, and is key in keeping track of felons walking around with ankle monitors. For Ms. Swenson's claim to carry real weight, we need to hear more than the vague claim that "experts say." What specifically did these experts say, and when did they say it? Give us the details.

The movie also points out interesting behavior patterns, such as the fact that around December 23, 2020, Arizona authorities announced fingerprints on absentee ballot envelopes helped uncover an illegal ballot harvesting scheme in that state. Coincidentally the day after this was brought to light, the video footage of ballots that were still being collected via drop box for the Georgia Senate runoff races, started showing people putting on blue medical gloves to deposit the ballots in the drop boxes and removing the gloves afterwards. It could be argued that fear of COVID-19 is the reason, but that doesn't explain why we didn't see this behavior earlier.

The hard questions have to be asked in regard to *2000 Mules* as well, instead of relying on the movie's skeptics. My main question is: Why did we not see any of these ballot mules more than once in any of the videos that were shown? The movie admits there were problems acquiring many surveillance videos, and some states had no footage or refused to share, but still make the claim that over four million minutes of footage was collected. Yet none of that footage conclusively showed at least one person at two drop boxes at specific times depositing ballots to round out the argument? Seems like it was too obvious to be missed, so why didn't we see it?

I found the answer in an interview with Mr. D'Souza on the YouTube channel, "Vince & Jason Save The Nation." D'Souza admits there is no video footage showing this in the four million minutes of video they have nationwide, and he blames the states for being notoriously delinquent in installing the video, despite election rules requiring it. That raises even more questions.

- How many drop boxes were in each state?
- How many drop boxes were in each geo spacial grid, and how many grids were there?
- What percentage of each state's drop boxes did they get surveillance video from?
- Was video quality too poor in some areas to make a definitive determination?
- How many cameras were on each surveilled drop box?

- Are certain days and times missing from the video surveillance on drop boxes where video footage was acquired?
- Did TTV attempt to match the clothing for these mules who were going to different drop boxes on the same day?

The answers to these questions are crucial. Part of the criteria for being identified as a mule by TTV is visiting over ten different drop boxes. If each geospatial grid has twenty drop boxes and only one is being videoed, it would make sense. If only half had cameras monitoring drop boxes, odds are a few people would show up more than once unless the mules were instructed to go to specific drop boxes, and maybe at specific times and/ or days when the cameras were not on.

The other problem is a concrete money trail from the NGOs to the mules. If everyone were paid in cash, it would be nearly impossible without confessions, and only a few admitted to being paid. Using any kind of electronic payment instead would leave a paper trail that could be followed. Maybe that evidence exists and is being withheld from the public for the time being to allow law enforcement and state officials to investigate. Maybe it doesn't exist.

TTV has promised to release their data to the public in the near future for everyone to view. Whether it will be organized for people to see and easily critique and is something we can only hope TTV will follow through on so the questions above and others can be answered. Until that evidence is released to the public, we can only rely on their word that what they have presented and whatever else they have is accurate.

Sadly though, the first we hear about such a possibility of massive voter fraud is from a private organization, and not our elected officials. This very scenario should have been investigated by law enforcement on the local, state and federal levels the day after the election to rule out fraud. While a warrant is needed by law enforcement for the ping data, it is not needed to review the video surveillance, which could have given enough reasonable suspicion for an investigation. In all fairness, since TTV did not have evidence showing more than one person dropping off ballots, aside from the missing required video, establishing probable cause is iffy at best for obtaining the geo tracking data.

Despite the two shortcomings I mentioned from *2000 Mules*, it presents a compelling argument that the matter should be investigated further, and the undeniable flaws with the drop boxes must be addressed. A number of sheriffs of the counties in question have already opened investigations as a result. TTV is not shy about answering questions from the public, and they set up a chat on Mondays for that purpose. In my opinion this adds credibility as it shows a willingness to answer hard questions. One would think considering TTV's openness to discuss their findings, despite flaws in the film, a compelling argument was made, making it worthy of further media investigation. Yet the largest media corporations created a blackout where they refuse to allow it to even be mentioned by anyone on their network.

It is very odd for the most secure election in history, that these issues are so feared that the main networks won't even discuss it. Perhaps it is likely those who made those claims see that they would very easily be proven wrong. Perhaps there was fear of even more backlash for the midterm elections.

Ultimately the fault lies with the government for the issues with the drop boxes. No drop box should have been placed or used without multiple high-definition surveillance cameras present and working to monitor activities. No ballots should have been counted from drop boxes where that surveillance was not present. It is highly likely those who failed to make sure appropriate surveillance was in place for the drop boxes will ever face consequences. With nobody held accountable for the missing footage or for it not being set up in the first place, we can likely expect it to happen again.

Despite the media blackout, the news is out over the potential fraud with drop boxes. It is likely if they are used again, even more measures would be used to cover up potential voter fraud by mules. I mentioned that we saw how medical gloves appeared after the announcement in Arizona. Now these mules will probably leave their regular cell phones at home and use burner cell phones bought with cash to take the pictures which will allow them to get paid. That is what I would do if I were ballot trafficking to avoid getting caught breaking election laws. It makes getting caught practically impossible, unless new measures are created in using the drop boxes. There is also the possibility that ordinary people who want to ensure ballot integrity will take up measures of their own in response to *2000 Mules*, such as organizing groups of people to watch drop boxes and take photos or videos of supposed mules depositing stacks of ballots.

Voting Irregularities in the swing states

At this point we are not arguing whether Trump won or lost the presidential election of 2020. More than enough reasonable doubt has been raised in this chapter on just how free and fair the 2020 election was.

Moving forward, we will be looking at the allegations with the biggest examples of voting and ballot irregularities that alone could have swung the Presidential election in specific swing states including Pennsylvania, Arizona, and Wisconsin, (which we already touched on to a degree). Going over every irregularity in each of these states would take too much time. The questions most elected officials and media outlets apparently wouldn't ask and appear to not want answered, will be addressed. After all is said, we can determine for ourselves how possible and likely voter fraud could have occurred in the 2020 presidential election, and if these possibilities exist for future elections. For the sake of consistency, we will be using the "Navarro Report" when referencing the voting numbers and claims as some of the claims of questionable and possible fraudulent votes vary from different sources. Whether or not the claims are true is irrelevant at this point as well as arguing whether or not Trump really won. That will be something for you to decide after looking at everything if you so choose. The main question is do these opportunities for fraud exist and was it possible to swing the election using the methods in this report?

16. Elections

In going through many of the accusations of ballot irregularities and voter fraud in the 2020 presidential election, I and many others in asking questions and expressing our doubts were bombarded by "fact checkers." Sometimes they made legitimate points. Other times they appeared to be trying to spin the issues to fit their beliefs and the established narrative that this was a free, fair, and secure election. Neither the mainstream media nor any elected official came close to proving it was secure, leaving those claims easy to be seen as false, for anyone looking objectively at the facts. Possible explanations for irregularities don't those explanations are the reason. Just how much digging did any of them do into potential election fraud? How closely did any of them look? They rushed to claim accusations of voter fraud by Trump and his allies was unfounded, but they missed addressing the two big questions that should have been asked and answered before the accusations of voting irregularities and voter fraud were dismissed.

1. *How do you know for sure that no significant voter fraud occurred?*
2. *How possible was it that voter fraud occurred?*

You can't know the answer to the first question without answering the second.

Pennsylvania

One potential issue on the list for Pennsylvania that could have easily flipped the state, was the allegation that the number

237

of ballots exceeded the number of registered voters buy 202,377 ballots. This is a claim made by Pennsylvania State Representative Frank Ryan, making apparent reference to the Statewide Uniform Registry of Electors (SURE system). However, according to the communications director for the Pennsylvania Department of State, Wanda Murren, these claims rely on incomplete data. This incomplete data is because some large counties had not yet finished uploading data on the voting history of registered voters. This number has since been revised to a much smaller, though still significant number with the uploaded data complete.

Regardless of the number, there are still numerous questions that deserve an answer. Why was this information not first verified before certification of the vote? Why were these votes not set aside and then added to the total after the needed data was added? Seems like putting the cart before the horse. To ensure a free and fair election, wouldn't it be necessary to have all voter information present first before matching it up to the ballots? Otherwise, what is to stop election officials from creating votes as they need, and then going back through the registries in these counties and adding the names of registered voters as people who voted to cover their rear ends? Is there constant oversight from both sides in compiling and submitting the data until it is complete? How can we trust the results if it isn't? Why weren't these numbers compiled well in advance if nothing shady was going on? Do we simply rely on the good word of one party that everything is on the up and up?

One of the most significant issues brought forth with the votes in Pennsylvania, is that Republican-certified poll watchers were kept a significant distance away from observing the vote-counting process, so they could not supervise the count with a reasonable degree of certainty as to the accuracy of the count. Now it has been claimed, that both Republican and Democrat poll watchers were both kept at the same distance, so to say one party was given an undue advantage is indeed possible. As with other situations in the issue of voting, this begs a few questions as well. What is the party affiliation of those initially counting the ballots? Did the representatives of each party initially take turns counting the ballots? Were there representatives of the other major party counting ballots at the same time or directly afterwards without those ballots leaving their sight or is that the job of the certified poll watchers? Oh, that's right; we had COVID-19 social distancing measures in place. So, any sleight-of-hand was possible.

Peter Navarro, listed this possible sleight-of-hand as a reason to discount more than 680,000 votes in Pennsylvania in "The Navarro Report". The *Washington Examiner* pointed out that Navarro provided no proof that any of these votes were in fact fraudulent. Were all ballot boxes signed, sealed, and delivered under constant supervision by both sides? Did universal standards have to be met on each ballot before being counted? Assume for a moment there was none of that. Ballots that are not opened and verified with both sides present and able to equally supervise and scrutinize at this stage, leave the real possibility that fraud may have occurred. There is no way to conclusively prove fraud did not occur in many cases. Such flimsy evidence in a murder case would be thrown out because it no longer meets the standard of 'beyond a reasonable doubt.' After all, if only one side sees the ballots, how could the poll workers get caught if they decided to allow questionable ballots or ineligible ballots for their favored candidate, and/ or disqualify less questionable ballots for the candidate they oppose? What about slipping extra, illegal ballots in, with the other side none the wiser? Once mail-in ballots are separated from the security envelopes under these conditions, there is currently no way to separate them from legitimate ballots without additional security measures, especially if the security envelopes are destroyed as was rumored to be the case in Philadelphia. The appropriate action at that point was to void all ballots opened and counted without both sides present to observe. This as well could have easily erased Biden's win in Pennsylvania, and brings up an interesting statistic, which we have seen in many of the states in question and that is an unusually low absentee ballot rejection rate when compared to the 2016 election, despite a much larger percentage of mail-in ballots.

Comparing past elections, in 2016, the rejection rate of absentee ballots was around 0.95 percent for the entire state of Pennsylvania with 266,208 absentee ballots cast, and 2,534 rejected. For the 2020 election, the rejection rate was 0.03 percent with only 951 rejected. With millions more mail-in ballots in play, the number of rejected mail-in ballots, was more than 2.5 times less than 2016. According to Redstate.com, out of more than 1,300,000 mail-in votes of the six heaviest Biden counties, only 440 total were rejected. Two of those counties rejected zero ballots, as did the two counties with the lowest number of mail-in ballots. Are we expected to believe nothing shady was going on in counting the mail-in votes, without a thorough audit? The rejection percentage and number of rejected mail-in ballots is too low compared to previous elections. With so many questionable actions and inactions, it is increasingly probable that fraud likely occurred.

Georgia

The next state on the list is Georgia. Here again were multiple issues where—if the law had been properly followed—Trump would have picked up the necessary votes to win the state, especially considering that Biden took the state by only 11,779 votes.

The rejection rate of mail-in ballots was 6.5 percent in 2016, and dropped to 0.2 percent for 2020. Looking at such a statistic, it is no wonder the Trump legal team was fighting for a heavily detailed audit, rather than simple recounts because the rejection rate was more than 30 times lower in 2020, when compared to 2016. We must have answers to numerous questions here to alleviate concerns of potential voter fraud. Who were the people inspecting these ballots for errors? What party did each represent, and what specific ballots were assigned to each for inspection? Was the chain of custody kept intact the entire time?

Next up is the issue in Fulton County, Georgia where ballots were removed from under a draped table, and tabulated after poll watchers, observers, and the media were allegedly asked to leave in the middle of the night, supposedly due to a water leak. Those few who remained after everyone left were caught on surveillance video tabulating the ballots they pulled from under the draped table. The number of those ballots has been estimated to be in the tens of thousands, looking at the time the count started till the time it ended. Keep in mind a large surge in votes for Biden occurred during this timeframe in Georgia.

The chief investigator was Francis Watson from the Georgia Secretary of State's office. She filed a sworn statement in federal court saying the video does not show voter fraud. She claims from her investigation that people were left on their own, thinking they were done for the night, and that the ballots that were under the table were placed there at around 10 pm. while the media and everyone was still present. She also claims the ballots had been opened but not counted and were in sealed boxes. She acted as though this made it alright. Far from it. There was still no representative from the other party present. The mail-in ballots were already opened, compromising the integrity.

Here we have even more unanswered questions. Who were the handful of people who remained? With everyone else gone, how do we know for sure these were legitimate ballots? Were the checks and balances in place to ensure no one party was cheating since everyone had left? Why were the votes already open, but not already counted? Who verified the opening of these ballots? Who sealed the boxes containing these ballots, and is there documented evidence of who witnessed it and when? Were these ballots constantly supervised by both parties before arriving? Why were these ballots stored separately from the rest? If nobody told the workers to go home, and they thought it was done, why did no supervisor correct them as they walked out or

16. Elections

why wasn't a mass text sent to their cell phones?

In the Navy and Marine Corps, the fifth general order is "To quit my post only when properly relieved." Is a similar rule not in place for vote counting facilities in the interest of maintaining the integrity of the vote? Or is there one in place and there is merit to the story of people being sent home due to a water leak? Why did the counting continue after everyone had left? Why not close up shop to at least prevent the appearance of an election impropriety?

Digging deeper still, why was there not an immediate order for a full, detailed audit in this county by the Governor or Secretary of the State of Georgia after this was discovered? Why was a specific audit ordered for a different county? For Fulton County, the governor gave a strong suggestion but made no order. Did those two government officials know something we don't know? Did they simply want to 'stick it' to Trump? After all, they both fought hard even before the video surfaced against any kind of audit with the recount of the Georgia vote. The Trump team pushed for an audit from the beginning.

Regardless, knowing the county whose votes are most in question by a large portion of voters suggests this is the county to force a detailed audit and recount to help alleviate voter concerns of fraud. There is no reason to avoid or delay such action, unless of course you don't want to know what the results of that audit would say while it can potentially make a difference in the election, or you already know the results would be different and don't want them coming to light.

Well, the statewide Georgia recount didn't turn up any

anomalies, so why the need to continue with a deeper recount with a more detailed and signature audit? Think of a bank holding hundreds of thousands of dollars, but it is expected that some of the bills are counterfeit. To root out those, the answer is not to just recount the bills because you won't find the counterfeit bills that way. The best solution is to examine them all in painstaking detail to determine which bills, if any are counterfeit. Signatures that don't match or even come close must be tossed. In this case if the ballots had not been resealed in the envelope with the ballot verified by both parties, the number of ballots found fraudulent has to be subtracted from the victory margin because you would not be able to determine whom they voted for. If the total number of these votes end up surpassing the victory margin, the electoral votes for that state should be thrown out.

Numerous other allegations could have given Trump the victory in Georgia. They are listed below:

- 15,700 ballots from ghost voters. Ghost voters are those who requested and submitted ballots under the names of voters no longer residing at a particular address.
- 20,312 ballots cast by out-of-state voters.
- 40,279 ballots cast in the wrong county.
- 66,247 ballots cast by individuals under the legal voting age of 18.
- 136,155 voting machine irregularities.

"Wait a minute," you may say. Around sixty court cases were thrown out. They had been filed by the Trump team on instances such as this in Georgia and numerous other states. Doesn't that prove there was nothing to these claims? Actually, no it doesn't. To my understanding, the vast majority of judges in the states, did not hold evidentiary hearings before dismissing the cases. Without an evidentiary hearing, evidence cannot be presented. While it is easy to say, "I see no evidence of voter fraud", it is impossible to say fraud definitely wasn't present without an evidentiary hearing examining such claims.

Why would any judge not even look at evidence of such huge allegations? Aren't judges supposed to be impartial? The key words are *supposed to be*, but like other people, judges have personal beliefs, prejudices, preferences, and motives that may influence their decisions. Maybe they are hoping to be appointed to a higher court. Maybe they are scared of the possible ramifications of making a specific ruling that could hurt them, their families, or their careers.

The bottom line is Accusations alone wouldn't work. If the Trump legal team didn't have evidence to support their claims of the number of underage voters, or out of state voters, for example, why not allow evidentiary hearings in the court cases and then dismiss them if that was the appropriate action? The reason is you don't want to run the risk of the election outcome being changed. This argument will apply to the rest of the states where applicable.

Wisconsin

Wisconsin, which as I said earlier has in place some of the strictest laws for absentee voting, still showed problems with absentee voting. They have strict photo ID laws for voters and do not allow mail-in voting. The exception is for people listed as indefinitely confined. Indefinitely confined is usually reserved for people who cannot leave their home for a variety of reasons, such as a combination of old age and physical ailments. These people are exempt from showing a photo ID when voting and undergo a less rigorous ID check than other voters. This exemption was allegedly skirted illegally by a large number of Wisconsin voters residing primarily in counties that are Democrat strongholds. In March of 2020, county clerks Scott McDonnell and George Christiensen for Dane County and Milwaukee County respectively, issued guidance indicating that all voters should register themselves as "indefinitely confined" because of COVID-19.

Republicans filed a lawsuit in response petitioning for the Wisconsin Supreme Court to intervene, apparently recognizing it as a way to circumvent Wisconsin voter ID laws. In a unanimous decision, the Wisconsin Supreme Court confirmed the advice from these county clerks was incorrect and people are not indefinitely confined as a result of COVID-19. However, despite this ruling, the number of "indefinitely confined" voters went from around 70,000 in 2019 to around 200,000 in 2020. With the Wisconsin Supreme Court's ruling, the newly "indefinitely confined" voter claims should have been investigated further by the State for confirmation and voters given the opportunity to change their status of "indefinitely confined" as they may have filed that way based on the bad advice of these county clerks. Yet that approximate amount of 200,000 mail-in votes listed as "indefinitely confined" is what was counted. There have even

16. Elections

been claims of around 20,000 first time voters marking themselves as "indefinitely confined," meaning they never had to show ID in an election to prove who they were in violation of Wisconsin law and Wisconsin election commission guidelines. Did that many more people become legitimately "indefinitely confined" over the course of a year, or did they ignore the ruling of the Wisconsin Supreme Court? Was it a legitimate scare over COVID-19, or was it an attempt to scam the election process?

The most telling thing in looking at the Wisconsin vote was the fact that the Wisconsin Supreme Court gave the Trump legal team their full day in court, to include an evidentiary hearing. The Trump legal team sought to have more than 221,000 ballots disqualified in Dane and Milwaukie counties, which was approximately 11 times the victory margin by Biden.

The Trump legal team sought to disqualify votes in these counties through the following four areas:

- Absentee ballots cast early and in person, saying there wasn't a written request for the ballots. (This was addressed earlier in the chapter.)
- Absentee ballots cast from voters claiming their status as "indefinitely confined."
- Absentee ballots with missing information on ballot envelopes filled in by clerks.
- Absentee ballots collected at Madison parks by poll workers.

For clarification, the ballots cast at Madison Parks, were part of events known in Wisconsin as "Democracy in the Park." At these events, in direct violation of Wisconsin state law, ballots were cast, and witnesses were provided for granting absentee ballots. They acted in every way like legal polling places. However, it was claimed that many of the ballots received from these events were outside of the limited 14-day period that precedes an election; that is the period authorized by statute for absentee balloting and in-person balloting. Apparently, City of Madison officials facilitated the events, and they were promoted by Biden radio advertisements. The ballots in this category account for just over 17,000 of the nearly 21,000 Trump needed to close the gap with Biden.

When the Wisconsin Supreme Court addressed Trump's four challenges for the 2020 election, it was not a complete ruling against Trump, as many media sources may have suggested. So why did we hear otherwise in the news? The Court ruled that Trump's challenge to voters claiming to be indefinitely confined was baseless and dismissed it. The other three challenges, in a 4-3 decision, the Court said this case was filed too late and as a result, it was too late to change the results. According to Justice Hagedon writing for the majority, the Trump legal team was "not entitled to the relief it seeks." Even though the votes had been certified by the state at this point, the electors had not yet been sent to DC. This says to me that the Trump team did indeed have a case on three of the four challenges, but the Wisconsin Supreme Court decided they were not going to do anything about it.

We've gone over more detail now on our three main states, without that even being all of it. Let's continue looking at the other three states and see if the pattern continues.

16. Elections

Arizona

Arizona was called almost immediately for Joe Biden after the polls closed, with only a fraction of the state reporting at the time, as opposed to other states like Ohio, Florida and Texas where Trump held a commanding lead most of election night, and carried the states by a significant majority, with the "fair and balanced" media outlet, Fox news leading that claim before other networks.

Arizona had mail-in ballots cast on or before the postmark date. Votes arriving on or before the postmark date, while suspicious, may be a simple error at the post office. They may have simply grabbed the wrong stamp to indicate date on the envelopes. If this was only a handful of votes, it could be easily overlooked as a simple mistake. However, since the same thing happened on two different days to the tune of almost 23,000 votes in numerous Post Offices, well within the margin of victory, it raises serious concerns whether or not this was a simple error or a coup by postal workers (whose organization had endorsed Joe Biden) in an effort to help alter the outcome of the state's election. How hard is it really to check the postmark date before you stamp anything at the post office? You look at the envelope after the first stamp, and if the postmark is incorrect, you change it. It is not that difficult to do or remember.

One unique data anomaly, which is listed in "The Navarro Report" and whose numbers match up with election data analyst Matt Brainard, is the number of people who voted with an absentee ballot in Arizona from an address where they no longer legally reside. To ensure the data stands, Mr. Brainard used authoritative data the state provides and has documentation on, such as absentee ballot requests. After the election, these names and numbers were taken and compared with phone numbers, the national change of address database maintained by the postal service, as well as the Social Security death index and the master death file to see what ballots were invalid. In other words, the ballots were checked using name, phone number, address, and Social Security number for verification. The number that matches up to both reports is 19,997 ballots of people who had moved out of the state. This was close to double the victory margin for Joe Biden in the presidential election. Mr. Brainard had numbers for this as well in the states of Georgia and Wisconsin but were not included in "The Navarro Report." Was it an oversight by Peter Navarro and the Trump legal team? Did Mr. Brainard's numbers not add up in those states, or did something change between when "The Navarro Report" was written and when Mr. Brainard released his numbers? It should be noted that Mr. Brainard's numbers greatly exceed the margin of victory for Biden in both Georgia and Wisconsin, which if accurate, would have denied Biden the necessary 270 electoral college votes for the win, when including all three states. The data is out there and documented with redundancies in place to verify the right people were being looked at. So why did politicians and most of the media ignore investigating this aspect, instead of simply looking into it and reporting their findings no matter what the results? Did they not want to run the risk it would overturn the results of the presidential election for their preferred candidate?

16. Elections

The last single area that is claimed to have potentially cost Trump the state of Arizona is non-citizens voting, which was estimated in excess of 36,000 votes. Is this possible? Yes, it is. Is there a paper trail to know for sure? Yes, there is. Arizona state law requires proof of citizenship to be shown to vote, but the Federal National Voter Registration Act of 1993 requires states to accept federal voter registration forms, which don't have a proof-of-citizenship requirement. The U.S. Supreme Court ruled in 2013 that Arizona cannot reject these forms despite the disparity between state and federal law.

Let's get this straight. With widespread mail-in ballots on an extraordinarily large scale in play across the country, proof of citizenship cannot be asked for on the federal level in accepting federal voter registration forms. I have one simple question. Why? If U.S. citizenship is required to vote, why not have citizenship as a requirement to accept federal voter registration forms as one of the redundancies in tamping down potential voter fraud?

Consider the following scenario. A person is in the country illegally and has a preferred candidate they want to vote for. They can easily have their voter registration form accepted, getting by one check right there. What about other checks in areas more on the local level that traditionally favor a particular party, and absentee ballots normally favor that party as well? Wouldn't it be more likely for illegitimate votes to get through, especially in these areas, where there is nothing demanding proof of citizenship when voting? Could this be part of the reason why Maricopa County was fighting against allowing the state to thoroughly inspect the ballots and the machines? I am well aware of the laws surrounding the reasons given, but Article I, section IV of the United States Constitution trumps those laws.

Now a more detailed, forensic audit was held in Maricopa County. It revealed seven different types of irregularities on several fronts, not counting the issue with the voting machines which was unable to be collected and examined because of stonewalling. Maricopa County officials attributed the reasons for all of these irregularities to various explanations. Many of them seem plausible on the surface, which is why it is important to dig deeper to learn how many can actually be attributed to the reasons they gave, and if this detailed audit came up short.

Nevada

Nevada's largest amount of voting irregularities appear to stem from potential signature-matching errors from the use of Agilis signature-matching machines, which is listed at 130,000. From my research, it apparently is a direct violation of Nevada State law to use machines instead of people for signature match verification. This alone should have invalidated enough ballots by nearly four times, as the margin of victory for Biden was 33,596 votes, unless an in person visual signature verification was done as well by both sides. To my knowledge that has not happened.

There have also been allegations that the Agilis machines were improperly used for Election Day in 2020. The Agilis machines to my understanding have images on file they use to compare signatures on the outside of mail-in ballots. The allegations of improper use are that these machines were adjusted to a lower setting of recognition than manufacturer's recommendations. This system could potentially allow for a large percentage of fraudulent ballots to be counted. It also allows for partisan election officials in charge of these machines to manipulate the vote if your preferred candidate is expected to have more mail-in ballots, and the other candidate have more in person ballots, or vice-versa. Concerns of voter fraud in Nevada could have been much more easily alleviated, if a visual signature match had been conducted, at the start, but as we have seen plenty of other times, practices were enacted that raise concerns about the legitimacy of certain ballots.

The final individual allegation to overcome the victory margin in Nevada is double voting in the state. Double voting could occur if a mail-in ballot is accepted, along with an in-person ballot for the same person. This number is listed at over 42,000 and was ascertained by reviewing the list of voters and comparing name, address and date of birth. Without being able to conclusively prove who legitimately voted for who on what ballot, the number must be subtracted from the margin of victory; this leaves Nevada a toss-up as well.

Michigan

Michigan is the unique state with the fewest types of errors of the six swing states. Aside from the alleged voting machine irregularities where spikes occurred in the early morning hours, there is the lack of corresponding voter registration numbers to corresponding precincts.

Of the four members from the Wayne County Board of Canvassers tasked with certifying the votes in Wayne County, which includes Detroit and is the most populous county in Michigan, there were two from the Republican party and two from the Democrat party. The two Republicans initially blocked the certification in Wayne County citing discrepancies in the poll books in certain precincts in Detroit. The response from Democrats and the media was not to say: Let's look closer at everything, to alleviate the concerns of everyone and to ensure a free and fair election. Instead, these two representatives were ridiculed online by voters and other leaders from the Democrat Party, even going so far as to call the move racist. After three hours, they relented, and the vote was certified. When they tried to take it back afterwards, the state of Michigan refused to allow it.

Why? What harm would it have done to take a few days to address the discrepancies to alleviate the concerns? People from both major parties go over the discrepancies at the same time to ensure it was done fairly and then go from there. It was not a small number of irregularities found in that county either; from what I understand, it was around 75 percent of the vote.

If this wasn't true, what would be the harm in agreeing to further scrutiny? If true on such a large scale, for such a large county, there are only three possible reasons I can think of that the Democrats did not object as well. The first is shear laziness. They didn't want to be bothered doing a thorough job. This is a possible, but not a likely reason as the objective of any election campaign is to win.

16. Elections

The second reason is partisan politics. They saw something wrong but were not willing to risk their preferred candidate losing the state's electoral votes for President, as well as the Senate race. The third reason is the electoral process there is already seen as corrupt, and it was part of their job to ensure problems were not looked at so closely that corruption be brought into the light of day. Only they know for sure.

The Endgame

"The accumulation of all powers, Legislative, Executive and Judiciary, in the same hands... may justly be pronounced the very definition of tyranny."
– James Madison

The question of "Isn't it possible?" has been asked and answered, which leads us to the final question. What will happen if we don't enact and follow through on more serious measures to ensure ballot integrity? You only need to look at what actions were taken shortly after the new elected officials were sworn in following the 2020 elections.

The "For the People Act," was brought forth almost immediately in the House of Representatives to be voted on after the new Congress and Joe Biden were sworn in, and it is one of the most telling things regarding how Democrats look to conduct elections. The proposal passed in the House of Representatives and was stopped in the Senate. This piece of legislation is specifically designed to modify election laws. Does it reduce the potential for fraudulent votes at all? Let me go into some of the more interesting details, courtesy of the Heritage Foundation. H.R. 1 would:

- *Force states to implement automatic voter registration, same-day voter registration, and online voter registration.*

So, the goal is to massively expand voter registration. First the automatic voter registration. Everyone in a government database on the local level, whether it be DMV or welfare office, Social Security office, whatever, would automatically be registered. Why do that if a portion of these people aren't voting or even in the country legally in some cases, unless it is the plan to use them for fraudulent votes if necessary? After all, those extra people won't be making the complaint; they weren't the ones who voted; and the government knows who votes, and who doesn't and how often. The rest of the registration requirements seem to be designed to pick up the stragglers that automatic voter registration may leave behind.

The harm in same day voter registration, is the lack of time to verify the accuracy of information pertaining to those registering to vote. This is especially true if you have no idea how many people will show up to register the same day, with people scrambling to verify the voter registration and count the vote. How likely is it that a fair amount of invalid or fraudulent votes could slip through the cracks?

Online voter registration? That is an open invitation for hackers to commit voter fraud because the online registration would not be tied to a state record. Looking at everything here, the goal appears to ensure the registration of as many names as possible with practically no security behind it to verify names and faces. Remember this is a push to force states on a national level to adopt these measures.

- *Force states to require early voting and no-fault absentee balloting.*

Early voting? The purpose of an election is for an informed electorate to vote on election day after all the facts are presented. If someone wants to vote early, that is first the call of the state they reside in, and then the individual if it is allowed in that state. Why the need to make it mandatory unless you are afraid of information coming out that will change the voters mind regarding the candidates?

Forced no-fault absentee balloting in the states, means anyone can vote by mail early for any reason. There would be no need to give a reason, such as being handicapped, being ill, etc. Now stop and consider everything mentioned so far before we continue. What is being proposed here is flooding the system with voter registration that was not requested by the individual, and then allow absentee ballots to be accepted with no reason whatsoever given. Where are the checks and balances to ensure election integrity? Moving on.

- *Mandate states to count ballots cast by voters outside of their prescribed precincts.*

The main reason we have these precincts, is to help maintain the integrity of the vote. What is to stop anyone from voting multiple times in other precincts, as either themselves or someone else? Wouldn't the checks and balances of voter ID, and signatures counter such practices? It could, but there are numerous problems with that. The biggest being, once fraudulent ballot(s) are cast at a different precinct, there is no way to prove which specific ballot(s) are the fraudulent ones, and what the specific votes are, even if poll workers or election officials actually go back and check to discover them. We saw reluctance to do so in 2020 where the allegation was made.

- *States would be prevented from having election officials check the eligibility and qualifications of voters, and as a result keep states from removing ineligible voters.*

This includes prevention or severe restrictions on using tools like the Postal systems, the national change-of-address system to verify people that are still registered to vote in the state, and possibly the Social Security death index to ensure that names of dead people are removed from the index. Even people who haven't voted in a long time will be forced to stay on the roles. What is the purpose of this requirement unless you have less than honorable intentions?

- *States would be required to allow felons to vote.*

This would be effective the day these people are released from prison. Never mind that Section 2 of the Fourteenth Amendment of the United States Constitution, gives states the constitutional authority to decide when felons may again vote in their state. As this measure seems very important to the left, in March of 2021, Joe Biden signed an executive order, to force states to allow felons to vote. This of course is a blatant violation of the United States Constitution under Article 1, Section 4, which if you will remember gives that power only to Congress and the State Legislators. Joe Biden falls into neither category.

- *Allow individuals without a state voter ID to vote.*

Rather than prove who you are with a state voter ID when you vote, you just sign a piece of paper saying you are who you say you are. How reliable would this be? Anyone would be able to alter their signature if they were trying to vote as someone else, and what is to stop them from succeeding if they do this outside of the prescribed precinct?

This is just a portion of this bill that is concerning. It goes back to the biggest question of fraud. *Isn't it possible?* Clearly it would have been very possible if this bill had been made law. Rather than address the concerns of a rigged election, the winners seemed to want to expand on a number of the things that raised questions with the election to begin with, as well as making it mandatory for all states to adopt and comply with those measures. All but one Democrat voted to pass this bill in the House of Representatives.

From their perspective I can understand why they would feel confident passing such a shady bill. In looking at the 2020 election, most courts refused to hold an evidentiary hearing when these issues were brought before them. Even the Supreme Court refused to hear these cases after the fact in a 6-3 decision. The mainstream media kept repeating the claim that the allegations were baseless from the beginning, raises questions of how much investigating they did into the matter. Social networking sites kept shutting down those who raised questions on the integrity of the 2020 presidential election. Assuming that intentional voter fraud swayed the election, is it any wonder these politicians would have felt emboldened to make those measures federal law?

While the "For the People Act" was defeated, that was not the end of it. In October 2021, Senator Chuck Schumer, brought up S.2747, also known as the "Freedom to Vote Act" for a cloture vote in the Senate, which is said to be a compromise of the "For the People Act" to gain Senator Joe Manchin's support. This bill would have still overridden State voter I.D. requirements, eliminated many election integrity measures for absentee voting, and make it more difficult for states to maintain accurate and up to date voter registration rolls.

One thing about these bills that should terrify anyone who cares about elections being free and fair. It is the fact that enacting such measures can easily make the voters irrelevant. If the officials don't like the projected result of the vote, they can alter it either with mysteriously discovered ballots if they are losing, or by adding as many ballots as they think are needed to the tally if they think it will be close. At that point they can do whatever they want because the majority of voters is no longer needed. The ability to steal any election and get away with it will be secured.

Without any kind of voter ID requirements, a chain of custody strictly followed, coupled with automatically registering everyone to vote, the needed ballots can be filled out to get their desired result using anyone's name, without any way to prove otherwise. After all, without any form of voter identification, how can you prove who actually voted and if they voted under their own name? How can you prove whether or not illegitimate votes were added without a strict and unbroken chain of custody? Remember the voter registry shows who votes and how often, so this is information the election officials already know. Do you honestly think they wouldn't know who has never voted before if either of these bills were made law? Couldn't ballots have been filled out in advance for non-voters or people who rarely vote to ensure victory? Such a law will ensure the will of the political elite will determine who our elected representatives are from here on and not the American voters. Think this sounds a like a farfetched conspiracy theory? Just answer the earlier question of why dictators are simply not just voted out of office in other countries? The simple answer is the vote is controlled to keep them in office. That is exactly what I described.

I barely scratched the surface in this chapter with the concerns of the 2020 Presidential election, as I didn't even describe in detail the allegations and other circumstances surrounding the Dominion voting machines, or the details of some of the more notable claims of the thousands of sworn affidavits. While the last paragraph would have been a good place to end the chapter, there is one final question we should ask about the results of the 2020 Presidential election. At the time I write this the 2024 primaries just ended. If Trump can be impeached in record time for supposedly inciting an insurrection, why after well over three years of Biden in the White House, have no charges we know of been pursued against any of these people who signed a sworn affidavit saying there were election shenanigans? Assuming insurrection was the goal of all people questioning the results of the 2020 election, are they not just as guilty as Trump? Surely among thousands of sworn affidavits, we can find at least a few where the charges of perjury would stick, where they would be forced to serve five years in prison. Yet we hear nothing on that front. Just like we hear nothing of any of the January 6th protestor actually being charged with insurrection. It appears government officials have no evidence that any of these people lied under oath. While probably true, I am sure they more likely fear that such investigations may uncover more solid evidence that these people crying 'voter fraud' were right all along. Best to let that sleeping dog lie.

17. Gun Control: Controlling the Ability to Fight

With freedom comes the need to protect it, not only from a potentially tyrannical government, but from those who seek to infringe on the life, liberty and property of others. Thus, there is the need for self-defense. Here we enter the gun control debate.

There are normally three types of people when it comes to this debate. The pro-gun crowd, the neutral crowd, and the gun-control crowd. Many times, the more emotional crowd supports the gun control crowd when a tragedy occurs where a gun was used. Whenever there is a school shooting for example, the gun control crowd tries to focus the emotions of the neutral crowd toward what they want blamed for the tragedy, which is of course the guns. If we just got rid of the guns or had stricter laws, this wouldn't have happened.

Are they correct though? Would even stricter gun control measures save the lives of more people as well as their freedom? Let's look at the arguments in the major aspects of gun control and see where that leads us on the Freedom Scale, starting with the Second Amendment to the United States Constitution.

> ***"A well- regulated Militia being necessary to the security of a free state, the right of the people to keep and bear arms shall not be infringed."***
> *– Second Amendment, United States Constitution*

There are numerous points of view concerning the Second Amendment. Some believe it only applies to the National Guard, seeing them as the militia. Others believe it is an individual right.

Here is a bit of a history lesson. The National Guard's birth date is set as December 13, 1636, as this is when the oldest American militia regiment met for the first time in Salem, Massachusetts. These were ordinary people with their own firearms, who could come and go as they pleased. Organizing them into military-style regiments increased efficiency in the defense of their communities, but the militia was not part of the government. In 1916, the term militia was done away with, and the term National Guard was adopted. Service was obligated at this time for as long as was deemed necessary, and the state each National Guard Unit represented was supplied with the needed equipment and firearms. In other words, the militia as it used to be known is now fully dependent on the individual state government it represents in each of the fifty states. Was this a sly 'power grab' over time? Who knows? The National Guard is good for state emergencies or during wartime in the event of invasion.

Many scholars have argued that the language of the Second Amendment makes it clear it was written for the militia and not for individual citizens. Looking at it as a regular, everyday blue collar American, I have to disagree. The first part makes a claim.

17. Gun Control

A well-regulated militia is indeed necessary to the security of a free state. A state, however, is defined as a nation or territory considered as an organized political community under one government. This definition applies to individual states as well as the United States as a whole. A well-regulated militia is necessary for the security of a free state on both the federal and state levels to protect itself against enemies, both foreign and domestic when threatened. However, what happens when both the state and federal governments are corrupted or the state is corrupted, and the federal government is indifferent to the corruption? What happens if the federal government becomes tyrannical, and the state governments becomes complaisant regarding that tyranny? When this happens, who watches the watchers? The founding fathers already knew.

This brings us to the second half of the Second Amendment. The right of the people to keep and bear arms shall not be infringed. Look closely at the words. It doesn't say the right of the militia. It doesn't say the right of the National Guard. It expressly says the right of the people. The Founders already knew any government on any level could be corrupted, and the last line of defense would fall on the people themselves. Broadly defined it is *all the people*. Shall not be infringed is self-explanatory as the government not hindering, restricting, or forbidding in any way a United States citizen from owning a firearm or other weapon.

The first half of the Second Amendment describes the need and reason for the Second Amendment. The second half describes how it is accomplished.

Does this mean every legal U.S. citizen can possess a firearm? Not quite. Everyone agrees that we don't want convicted violent criminals to possess firearms, whether in prison or out on the streets. *But wouldn't that violate "shall not be infringed"?* Every citizen of the United States starts with a clean slate, able to legally purchase a firearm assuming they are of legal age. If an individual unlawfully violates the life, liberty or property of someone through violence or the threat thereof, they forfeit that right and others. Should it be for the rest of their lives or for a set amount of time? That is a debate for another time.

There is no way that individuals with guns alone could beat the military in modern times, so there is no need for guns to defend against a tyrannical government. Can a group of people armed only with rifles and handguns prevail against the military in combat today? Highly unlikely. However, the military in question would not be without significant losses. That in itself is one hell of a deterrent.

Take Switzerland for example. In 1912, they had an army of 281,000 and an auxiliary troop count of 200,000 that could be called on. All of them to my understanding were proficient with firearms. In that same year Kaiser Wilhelm II of Germany visited Switzerland and met with Swiss President Ludwig Forrer who reportedly told Wilhelm of their resolve to defend themselves and their land while observing Swiss military maneuvers.

Depicted on a contemporary postcard, Wilhelm asked what the quarter of a million Swiss army would do if faced with invasion of half a million Germans. The answer was "shoot twice." Is this true or just a clever postcard? I am not 100 percent sure how accurate it is, but I am inclined to believe there is at least some

17. Gun Control

truth to it for one simple reason.

Switzerland remained neutral during both World War I and World War II, despite being in a strategic location. There was no invasion from either side in either war. There was not even an attempt by either side to march through and launch an attack on their enemy. The most likely reason is conquering or provoking Switzerland would have come at too high a price militarily. You don't invade a country where not only their military has guns, but their citizenry own guns, and expert shooters are among both groups. The invading army would never know when they could be shot or by whom.

It is expected about 40 percent of U.S. households are gun owners, most of whom are peaceful and law-abiding. That is several tens of millions of people scattered across the entire country. If it eventually came to the military going door to door to collect guns, how many would die on both sides? How many lawful gun owners would have the attitude of Charlton Heston, ". . . from my cold dead hands"? Probably many more than most would think. Surrendering firearms is openly surrendering your willingness to fight for your freedom when all other measures have failed. Many who value freedom would likely choose to live adhering to the adage, "It is better to die on your feet than live on your knees".

> *"I prefer liberty with danger than peace with slavery."*
> *– Jean-Jacques Rousseau*

We don't want to outlaw guns. We just want common sense gun control measures to curb gun violence. The gun-control

The Freedom Scale

crowd goes from this to advocating that certain firearm like the AR-15 be banned. With the claims of numerous gun control advocates constantly flip-flopping on what they want, it is hard to take them at their word. Let's discuss some of those common-sense gun control measures and then take a look at gun violence in the United States.

Assault Weapons Bans: Before discussing assault weapons bans, we must define 'assault weapons' in general as the definition differs from state to state. According to Wikipedia, "Drawing from federal and state law definitions, the term assault weapon refers primarily to semi-automatic rifles, pistols and shotguns that are able to accept detachable magazines and possess one or more other features."

Time to break down the wording. First the term "primarily," meaning *mainly* but not *limited to*. Next, we go to the term "semiautomatic." This simply means one pull of the trigger equals one round fired, and another round is automatically chambered and ready to fire with the next pull of the trigger. Finally, "able to accept detachable magazines *and* posses one or more other features." These features can be changed out and are not part of the normal firing mechanism that can include but is not limited to folding stocks, pistol grips, barrel shrouds, forward grips, and flash suppressors.

For clarity in this section, the focus will primarily be on the AR-15 as it receives the most attention when talking about assault weapons.

Many in the gun control crowd despise the AR-15 and focus

17. Gun Control

much of their attention on eliminating it from being able to be sold to the public, claiming weapons of war have no business on our streets. However, it is not a weapon of war, as it is not used by the military. That would be the M16, which is fully automatic meaning it fires multiple rounds with one squeeze of the trigger and is practically identical in appearance to the AR-15 which is semi-automatic. Modifying an AR-15 to be fully automatic is already illegal.

Many gun control advocates will say you don't need an AR-15. Many people don't need a lot of things. But having freedom isn't about having only what others feel you need. It is about choosing for yourself what you want and deciding for yourself what best fits your specific needs.

But why is this gun specifically targeted as opposed to other guns? We already established that it is not a weapon of war, as it is not fully automatic. Is it the damage the .223 round typically does when fired at someone? Not a chance. .223 caliber rounds can be very lethal but won't put a hole in someone the size of a grapefruit in one shot, nor easily go through good body armor if at all. There are many more powerful weapons out there to choose from.

AR-15s can be fired at a rapid rate. So can a very large range of other firearms, not all of them being semiautomatic. All it takes with some guns is practice. Speed shooters do it all the time. How fast are they? In 1999 Jerry Miculek, using a Smith and Wesson performance center built 8 shot revolver; shot 8 rounds off into 1 target in 1 second and then 8 rounds into 4 different targets in 1.06 seconds. Finally, again in another revolver, he shot 6 rounds, emptied the cylinder, reloaded and fired six more shots all in under 3 seconds.

Is it the ability for an AR-15 to carry a 30-round magazine? Again no. Many kinds of rifles can carry 30 round magazines, and they are not targeted. A prime example is the Ruger Mini 14. It uses .223 ammunition the same as an AR-15. It has readily available 30 round magazines, the same as an AR-15. One is just as capable as the other in nearly every noticeable regard. What is the difference? Primarily aesthetics. The Ruger mini 14 looks like a standard hunting rifle with little ability to be customized, such as the stock or a forward grip (hence not meeting the definition of assault weapon stated earlier), while the AR-15 looks like a military rifle and can be easily customized to the owner's preferences, and as a result is among the most popular firearms available for purchase in the United States. Why the call to ban one and not the other? If it is about keeping people safe, why are the customizable options such a big deal? Options such as a forward grip, a collapsible stock or pistol grip does not make the firearm itself more lethal. It makes use of the firearm easier and/or more comfortable for the user. Would such luxuries be a deterrent for someone intent on committing a mass shooting if they couldn't have them?

There are many reasons the AR-15 is so popular. Aside from it being easily customizable in a wide variety of ways to best fit individual tastes, it has very low recoil, making it easy for most people to shoot accurately. Many rounds can be fired off in succession at a rapid pace by most anyone. As stated earlier, while the rounds may not be the most powerful, such a characteristic

17. Gun Control

helps ensure anyone threatening you or your loved ones, will have much less chance of carrying out that threat if the first shot is missed. It is easier to clean and easier to repair compared to many other guns. In essence, it is the perfect rifle for self-defense or practice shooting.

Ban magazines that carry more than 10 rounds: We touched on this earlier with the 30-round magazine argument with AR-15s. The argument is limiting the rounds allowed in a magazine will decrease the ability of mass shooters to inflict mass amounts of damage. I already mentioned Jerry Miculek and his speed shooting abilities. This wasn't an isolated attempt at breaking a world record. Speed shooting competitions do exist. Shooters compete to see who can most accurately shoot the fastest, reload, and continue shooting. Anyone can train to do it, and anyone can get quite good at it with enough practice.

For the moment, forget about speed shooting in a controlled environment such as the range or a competition. Imagine someone has broken into your house. You confront them in your house, and they turn and start shooting at you. You have an AR-15 in hand, with one 10-round magazine, which is all you could get before confronting the intruder. No matter how good a shot you are, adrenaline is racing at this point, and you may not be as accurate as you are at the range. This isn't fun anymore. This is a real life and death situation where your life and the life of your family may hang in the balance. You may blow through those ten rounds in 3 seconds as a result missing with every shot or just wounding the intruder. If you are cut off from getting another magazine, you may be as good as dead since

The Freedom Scale

you do not know what the intruder has or how many rounds he may have. It is also possible the intruder would hightail it, not knowing what else you may have. Personally, I would want the best chance for survival and that includes having the option of a 30-round magazine. I know I will be responsible for every round I fire and accept responsibility for my actions. Like most others I would rather be judged by 12 than carried by 6 after such a confrontation.

Close the gun show loophole: Everyone who buys a gun at a gun show from a federal firearms licensed dealer, must go through the following steps:

1. *Present a government issued photo ID.*
2. *Complete a questionnaire for the background check.*
3. *Process the application through the National Instant Background Check System (NICS) which takes anywhere from a few minutes to over an hour.*

Buying a gun online is a thorough process as well. You can buy a gun online, but it won't be shipped directly to you. It will be shipped to another FFL (Federal Firearms Licensee) dealer who will make you fill out the questionnaire, show your ID, and run your name through the NICS system the same as at a gun show.

The main problem talked about in the gun show loophole, though, is private sellers, who do not have to perform a background check to sell a gun; nor does a buyer even have to show ID to purchase a gun. So how bad is the gun show loophole relative to criminals being able to get firearms illegally? Does

17. Gun Control

the gun show loophole warrant such attention from lawmakers? According to a 2019 survey from the Department of Justice, only 0.8 percent purchased the gun they used to commit a crime at a gun show. They do not tell how many had a criminal record beforehand. That criminal record would have disqualified them to begin with.

Why refer to it as the 'gun show loophole' when only 0.8 percent of criminals get their guns from a gun show? Controlling who-you-can-sell-your-property-to loophole has a negative, anti-freedom connotation. Overall, at 0.8 percent, it appears people at gun shows have a good track record overall when it comes to avoiding selling to criminals. If anything, it tells me individuals (not dealers) who sell their personal firearms at gun shows are some of the most discriminating sellers. Are they simply good judges of character? Possibly. But I think a fair amount of it has to do with the fact that most any gun shop with a booth at a gun show selling firearms, will likely run the NICS background check for a fee even if you are not buying a gun from them. The fee is normally insignificant compared to the cost of the gun, and the vast majority of lawful gun owners wouldn't sell to a stranger if asking for a background check would be a deal breaker. Lawful gun owners overwhelmingly want to be sure they are selling to lawful citizens.

Also keep in mind that both parties in the private sale of a firearm are taking a chance. Although highly unlikely, a criminal may be selling a gun used in an armed robbery, where someone was killed. If the person who buys it ever uses that gun for self-defense, that bystander will have some explaining to do if bal-

The Freedom Scale

listics match that gun to an earlier crime. Both parties get piece of mind with this background check.

In all honesty, I can see the reason for limiting anonymous sales of your personal firearms at gun shows, by having everyone go through NICS, the same as the licensed dealers do. However, it is doubtful common sense would be applied to distinguish between strangers and people you know and trust, or the circumstances or even keeping new regulations exclusive to gun shows. How far would restrictions go and how broad would the language be? Could you be penalized for loaning a gun to a friend for target practice, or giving one to a family member for protection? What about letting them shoot your gun at the range in your company?

It is still illegal to sell a firearm to someone knowing they cannot legally own a firearm because of being convicted of criminal activity. Of the guns I own, one I bought from a friend of my dad, whom I never met. It was not at a gun show. Despite not knowing the man personally, I trusted my dad in this regard, as he would not buy guns from potential criminals or lead me to buy a gun from someone he did not trust. Another gun I inherited from my paternal grandfather, a police officer, when he died. In both circumstances, neither I, nor they asked for permission regarding what we were allowed to do with our respective properties. It was our choice.

What I do with my guns is my business and nobody else's, so long as I do not infringe on someone's life, liberty or property. If I loan my gun to a friend to go to the range and shoot, it is my business. Is it possible that criminals may buy guns through private, anonymous sales at gun shows and use one to shoot someone? Yes, it is. But elaborating on that leads us into the next gun control argument.

Universal background checks: The idea of universal background checks says that every sale of a firearm whether private or public, through a licensed vendor must go through an intensive background check to be legal. The reasoning is that it will eliminate or decrease the ability of violent criminals to obtain a deadly weapon. Sounds reasonable enough right? This would expand on the background check already done when buying a gun at a gun store. The problem with universal background checks, is that they are not enforceable without a national gun registry. The government would have to know every firearm that every individual owns, which would be a useful tool for the government, should confiscation of privately owned firearms ever come to be.

Before considering such measures, we must ask: Will universal background checks prevent violent criminals from getting firearms? To some degree, yes, but not near as much as you might think. We have already seen the insignificant number of crimes committed with guns acquired at gun shows. It is already illegal for anyone convicted of a violent crime to possess a firearm or for anyone to sell or give a firearm to someone they know has a violent criminal record. The statistics, strongly suggest that restrictions would do little to prevent violent criminals from acquiring a firearm. Let's look at a 2019 survey conducted by the Department of Justice for clarification. It found that:

The Freedom Scale

- 43 percent of criminals bought their firearms on the black market.
- 6 percent of criminals stole the firearms.
- 11 percent of criminals acquired their firearms through a straw purchase. (They had someone else buy the gun for them.)
- 10 percent of criminals made a retail purchase, with 0.8 percent of them making a purchase at a gun show.
- 15 percent of criminals got their gun from a friend or relative.
- 12 percent of weapons found at crime scenes had been brought there by someone else.

Let's look at this more closely. The first three statistics listed are already illegal on every measure and make up 60 percent of guns used in crimes. Do gang members get oozies from gun shows or licensed firearms distributers? Of course not. Acquiring a fully automatic weapon legally requires much more paperwork, money, and effort. The black market is a different story. The people selling guns there don't ask questions because they obtained their guns by illegal means.

Those who make a retail purchase, either slipped through the system, or have not yet committed a crime. Hard to catch them when a crime has not happened yet. Remember there is always a first time for everything done by everyone. Two important questions to ask: What percentage of these people had a criminal record at the time of their purchase that would disqualify them from purchasing and did they lie when filling out the paperwork

17. Gun Control

for their background check? Submitting false information on the form for a background check is a federal felony, with punishment of up to ten years in prison and a fine of $250,000. I have gone through this process numerous times in purchasing guns, and the person submitting the form has always checked my answers before submitting the paperwork because their business is on the line if the sale goes through. If the seller didn't screw up, it means someone at the FBI got lazy in running the check.

Getting a gun from a friend or family member? It is best to know the background of that friend or family member and be sure that they can legally possess a firearm. If you knew the person could not legally possess a firearm, you are an accessory, and that friend or family member can easily point the finger at you for a reduced sentence. The question here is: Does the 15 percent who got their gun from a friend or relative include those who stole the gun from a friend or relative? I cannot say with 100 percent certainty, but it is possible.

Guns found at a crime scene can include any of the prior examples. It can also include the victim losing control of their weapon to a perpetrator, or someone with a concealed carry permit using it to stop a crime. Keep in mind, such actions are investigated as a crime pending the final outcome.

What percentage of gun-related crimes would be stopped by universal background checks? It wouldn't have stopped the black-market acquisitions. Various drugs like cocaine and heroin are illegal and still found everywhere on the black market. Stealing the guns? You don't ask for a background check to rob someone. Universal background checks would do nothing to stop crime from firearm straw purchases as the final owner is not having his background checked, and it is already a crime to knowingly give, sell, or loan a gun to someone who has a criminal record and is forbidden from owning a gun.

The retail scenario might be helped, but again we have to know the percentage that had no red flags against them before the purchase. We also have to look at those that made the purchase under a false identity. How would a universal background check help those situations? Getting a gun from a friend or relative is our last stop. For that, go back and reread the straw purchase argument.

Banning the online sale of guns and ammunition: Part of Joe Biden's run for the White House in 2020 included a proposal to ban all online sales of guns and ammunition. Is it something needed to curb gun violence, or a power grab?

As I write this, neither state nor federal law prohibits the online sale of ammunition or purchase of ammunition. Some online companies post criteria the purchaser must meet in order to buy ammunition, such as the age of the buyer. If you meet the criteria, your purchase is completed, and you receive your order.

We already discussed online firearm sales and that process, so why ban the online sale of guns and ammunition, if you go through the exact same procedure as buying a gun locally? It amounts to a power grab by elected officials. This type of proposal relies on the ignorance of people who support it and believe a gun is shipped directly to you, when the exact opposite is true.

17. Gun Control

Think about it more closely now. Why do people buy anything from Amazon, when they can go to Walmart to fill their needs? The reason is that Walmart may not have everything we are looking for at a price we want to pay. The internet allows us to better search for what we want at a price we are willing to pay. Say someone collects antique guns and is looking for something in particular. Odds are they will not find it at a regular gun shop that deals with more modern firearms. Pawn shops and gun show are hit or miss at best, so it leaves only the internet.

It isn't only antique firearms. Some modern firearms are in high demand and difficult to keep in stock. If you don't want to wait until it is in inventory, you can look online and decide if you want to pay what an online seller is asking. Would this ban on buying guns online extend to FFL dealers? Biden doesn't say. After all, some people are not tech savvy on a computer or may want their local gun shop to do the leg work and find what they want. After all, employees at the local gun shop may know the right people to help get you what you want.

In essence, banning the online sale of guns and ammunition is nothing more than outlawing guns and ammo by a specific type of retailer. If you think criminals are going this route, think a little harder. Buying a gun online has extra steps. More digital fingerprints are online, and criminals will prefer minimal evidence against them if they get caught. It would be foolish for a criminal to try to get a gun online.

Holding gun manufacturers liable for the actions of criminals: In every industry, there are examples of manufacturers being liable for harm caused by their product. This liability, however,

The Freedom Scale

only applies if there is a defect. If you hit someone with your car, you are liable—not the car manufacturer—because the car was operating as it was supposed to. If you are driving, and the airbag suddenly deploys because of a defect and you crash, that liability is on the manufacturer. Normally in this case, there would be a recall to replace the defective airbag. If you ignore the recall, the liability switches back to you.

The above examples illustrate how liability works. The manufacturer does what it can to correct faults in its product but accepts no responsibility for misuse by the operator. However, some individuals who want gun control want to change that standard. In their view, the gun manufacturer can be held civilly liable if a gun they made is used to commit a crime.

When you look at a gun in its most basic sense, its design is not for killing, though it can be used for that purpose, the same as a car. It is designed to fire a projectile (bullet) out of a cylindrical tube (barrel) at a highly accelerated speed. What is aimed at depends on the operator, not the manufacturer. This is why many gun owners refer to guns as tools. How they are handled is important.

To hold the manufacturer responsible would set a dangerous precedent. Such a law for guns could be applied to other tools when incorrectly used. No businesses would be left because they would all be sued at the earliest opportunity. Of course, those pushing these measures already know that, and figure it can be limited to guns. The mentality is a simple one. If they can't outlaw what they want banned, just backdoor freedom by cutting off the supply.

17. Gun Control

Mandatory buybacks: I always found this argument amusing. It is the train of thought that if a specific gun or type of gun is made illegal, owners of said gun, will have X amount of time 'to sell it back' to the government. First of all, the term buyback is a blatant lie to everyone's face. People can buy guns from many retailers and manufacturers, but government—at least in the United States—is not one of them. They are buying back nothing, having never sold you the gun to begin with, but instead are forcing you to hand over your firearm for compensation that they deem is appropriate.

Never mind that you may see those you turn your guns into as unfit and untrustworthy; they don't pass your own personal background check as it were. You are not given a choice. The main question here is: Who turns in the firearms in question in these buybacks? Would a convicted felon who is already forbidden from owning a firearm to begin with turn in his guns? Highly doubtful. That would be the equivalent of confessing to a crime that would likely send them right back to prison for a number of years. Only law-abiding citizens would do something like that and only out of fear of being labeled a criminal if they are caught for refusing to hand it over. There are also law-abiding people for whom that would be the final straw.

Take down the NRA: The National Rifle Association was founded in 1871 by union veterans Colonel William Church and General George Wingate. According to an article written by Church in an August 1871 issue of the *Army and Navy Journal*, he wanted to "promote and encourage rifle shooting on a scientific basis" in New York City. It later grew into what is today considered by many the largest and most effective means of protecting gun rights along with the Second Amendment. Yet today it is the gun organization most demonized by gun control advocates. Why? It strongly opposes what the gun control people call "common sense gun laws." A number of those laws were just discussed. Look at the NRA more closely though. It strongly advocates teaching gun safety to children, with the Eddie Eagle program as the means for teaching it. It is a strong advocate of teaching safe and effective operation of firearms for everyone, including teaching firearms instructor courses.

The NRA argues that the best way to bring down gun violence is 'a good guy with a gun.' They support concealed carry and encourage the use of firearms for self-defense. Their monthly magazines have stories of regular, everyday people who use firearms in defense of their lives and the lives of others. The stories don't always end with the bad guy dying. Sometimes the bad guy is wounded and arrested. Sometimes the bad guy is scared off.

Most importantly, the NRA does not oppose gun control legislation that specifically targets convicted felons from owning a firearm. The worst it can be accused of is supporting certain convicted felons regaining their right to own a firearm after X amount of time following their release. The NRA opposes gun control legislation that targets law abiding Americans. The reason is the law-abiding citizen has done nothing to warrant an infringement on their liberties in regard to guns. The punishment comes after the crime, not before. We are not living in the movie, *The Minority Report*, where the crime can be seen before it happens.

17. Gun Control

"If violent crime is to be curbed, it is only the intended victim that can do it. The felon does not fear the police, and he fears neither judge or jury. Therefore, what he must be taught to fear is his victim."
– Lieutenant Colonel Jeff Cooper, U.S.M.C.

What can everyone agree on? Violent, convicted criminals forfeit their right to legally own a firearm. There should be harsher penalties in the justice system for those who use a firearm in the commission of a crime. Yet most efforts from the gun control crowd appear to be involve making more and more laws, with little emphasis on enforcing the ones already on the books.

With that said, when looking at the gun control argument, it is important to ask one very important question in each piece of proposed legislation. Who is it designed to restrict? Everyone or just the criminals? It is already a no brainer that criminals do not follow the law; hence the term *criminal*. A criminal will not change his mind about using a gun to rob or kill someone just because there is a gun control measure against it. Killing and stealing is already illegal and has harsher sentences, so violating a gun control law is a slap on the wrist at best compared to the time most would be facing. What will new gun control laws do except restrict the freedom of law-abiding people?

What would warrant such need for gun control that the NRA must be vilified for reluctance to support new gun control measures? I assume it would be in the interest of saving lives, right? To answer that, let's first look at gun death statistics from the CDC. In 2017 there were 39,773-gun related fatalities. Of that number:

- 60 percent were suicides (23,854).
- 37 percent were homicides (14,542).
- 3 percent other (unintentional (486), involved law enforcement (553), undetermined (338).

Gun control is unlikely to sway suicides. Anyone truly intent on killing themselves will do so with or without a gun. I also highly doubt anyone would refrain from suicide because they couldn't use an assault weapon.

In 2017, the population of the United States was 325.1 million people. As the percentage of the population killed by homicide is so small, we have to break it down to number of murders for X amount of the population per year. The number comes to just under 4.5 murders with a gun, per 100,000 people.

Quite a small percentage considering the size of the U.S. population, but how many Americans lawfully own guns? This is impossible to tell as there is no national registry, but as stated earlier the number is estimated to be several tens of millions. The United States alone makes up a large percentage of all private gun owners in the world. With numbers like this, it is hard to argue the U.S. population in general is unlawful or reckless with firearms considering the large amount of gun ownership throughout the country. It reinforces that the issue isn't the law-abiding gun owners or the guns they own, but the criminals who use them. With that being the case, rather than pushing for more gun control that would primarily affect law abiding citizens, wouldn't it be wiser to push for deterrents and measures to primarily affect and punish criminals, or make them more fearful? Those would be the true common sense gun control measures.

17. Gun Control

Similar to the Castle Doctrine, which allows you to defend your home if broken into instead of retreating, Florida's Stand Your Ground Law was passed in 2005. It allows people who feel a reasonable threat of death or bodily injury to meet force with force instead of running away. Yet many gun control advocates oppose such measures. Why? There is nothing to discourage criminals when the potential negative consequences for their actions are diminished. At least in the stand your ground scenarios, it is likely that at least some criminals will think twice before taking an action that could end your life. Stand Your Ground does not mean someone has a right to pick a fight and attack someone under the guise of standing their ground. It means when confronted with a dangerous situation, the threatened individual is not forced to run to protect themself.

Mass shootings: At least once a year, we hear about a mass shooting in a school, a church, or wherever. Often mass shootings occur at soft targets—places where guns are not allowed by private citizens.

The media will carry the story of a mass shooting for days on end, and gun control groups along with their supporting politicians will push for more gun control if it fits the narrative of demonizing a certain race, political party and involves a gun like the AR-15. One story of particular interest fizzled out rather quickly as it defied the gun control narrative.

That story is the Sutherland Springs Church shooting from November 5, 2017. On this day, Devin Patrick Kelly fatally shot twenty-six people and wounded twenty others at the Sutherland Springs Church in Sutherland Springs Texas. Kelly used an AR-

556 (a type of Ar-15) and is estimated to have shot approximately 700 rounds during the estimated 11-minute shooting. At that time a nearby resident named Stephen Willieford was running toward the church and yelling which he claims drew Kelly out. Kelly then apparently shot at Willieford hitting a neighbor's truck. Willieford, however, was armed with an AR-15 and was a former NRA firearms instructor. After Kelly was hit in the body armor, he attempted to flee while Willieford continued to fire. As Kelly sped off, Willieford flagged down a car and they chased him while calling the police. When the police arrived on the scene where Kelly was stopped, he had committed suicide.

A few questions need to be asked here. Could Kelly legally purchase the Ar-556 he used to commit this horrible crime? The answer is *no*, but because the Air Force failed to submit Kelly's criminal history despite being required to do so by Pentagon rules, he was able to make the purchase. This was a massive failure by a part of the government. Yet we are told to trust that same government whose failure cost those twenty-six people their lives. What gun control measures would have stopped Kelly's massacre? Some say an assault weapons ban. Someone could argue that he could have gotten it, or something comparable on the black market, through a straw purchase or any of the other examples previously listed. Finally, how many lives did Willieford save by engaging Kelly? It is impossible to know for certain, but it is likely his actions did save some people. There is no doubt that had Willieford arrived a few minutes sooner, some of those twenty-six people Kelly shot, would likely be alive or unharmed considering the way the situation played out. How

17. Gun Control

many more could Kelly have killed more if he had gotten away or if he had not been interrupted inside the church?

Despite the heroics of Willieford, this story was buried in record time because it did not fit the narrative of pushing gun control. A good guy with a gun, with ties to the NRA, who was not a policeman stopped senseless bloodshed.

My own personal opinion in regard to stopping mass shootings is two-fold. First; quit giving them so much media attention. At least a portion of these shooters are looking for their fifteen minutes of fame. Deny them that, and that portion will have to seek attention another way. One way of accomplishing this is for the media to withhold the shooter's identity in every way. Ask the media to identify the shooter as a statistical number. Second, quit fighting concealed carry and start allowing teachers with firearms training to be armed in school. This sends the message to would be mass shooters: You will not get your fifteen minutes of fame, and you could be gunned down before trying. As we learned about Mr. Kelly, he became quite the coward when confronted with someone who could shoot back.

Final Thoughts on Gun Control

When all is said and done, no country will ever eliminate gun crimes, no matter how many laws are passed, even if all guns are illegal or if everyone is not only allowed but encouraged to 'conceal carry.' We have to find what will likely keep gun crime to a minimum. The gun control side argues that good guys with a gun don't really prevent much gun crime from a bad guy. At a press conference in 2022, as part of a response to a

The Freedom Scale

Supreme Court Ruling about New York conceal carry, New York Governor, Kathy Hochul attempted to argue this point by casting a broad net that can be easily used to mislead people.

She mentioned how New York State has the fifth lowest gun-related death rate of any state at 5.3 firearm related deaths per 100,000. She also gave the number of gun-related deaths of other states annually that have concealed carry.

- Mississippi - 28 deaths by firearm per 100,000 people.
- Louisiana - 26 deaths by firearm per 100,000 people.
- Wyoming - 25 deaths by firearm per 100,000 people.
- Missouri - 24 deaths by firearm per 100,000 people.
- Alabama - 23 deaths by firearm per 100,000 people.

Like with everything else, more questions must be asked to get the clearest picture. What percentage of New York's 5.3 deaths by firearm per 100,000, are suicides, homicides, self-defense, accidental, law enforcement, and undetermined? What are the statistics when breaking down the states by cities, towns, parishes, counties, etc.? Is the average number of suicides across New York by all methods less than these other states' by all methods? Where does New York rank in comparison to these other states' violent crime rates with and without firearms and firearms related injuries that don't result in death? If you are going to try to dispel the good-guy-with-a-gun argument, you need to compare apples to apples directly and not include oranges, pears, and bananas in your comparison. Without the necessary context and relevant facts, it becomes another deliberate spin to achieve the desired narrative.

17. Gun Control

As stated earlier, the NRA publishes multiple stories in their magazines each month about such events. Sometimes brandishing a gun at a home intruder or a mugger with a knife is enough to scare them off. Holding a gun on a home intruder until the police arrive also stops them and ensures that you and your family are safe from that threat. Without a gun, at a home invasion, a person's only option is to hope the invader isn't better armed and hope the police arrive in time. Some instances are never reported to police, and some are misfiled. The result is lack of complete information, so we do not know how many criminals are stopped or deterred nationally by the threat or potential threat of an armed target. Imagine yourself as a criminal looking for a victim. Would you likely break into a home at midnight where gun ownership and concealed carry rates are high? Personally, I would be packing up to move to a new town if I were the criminal. I would go after softer targets.

Your safety is your responsibility first and foremost. It is your responsibility for the safe operation of the firearm(s) you use, and you must suffer the consequences of your decisions with those firearms whether intentional or accidental. If you choose not to own a gun, that is your choice, but don't complain when you must rely on someone else to protect you, like the police. If you are not using your firearm to infringe on the life, liberty, or property of someone else, enjoy whatever firearm you can afford, but be ready to surrender them upon conviction if you unjustly violate the freedom of others. A gun operates when an operator controls it. Gun ownership involves one of the biggest choices and responsibilities of any individual, and one of the

The Freedom Scale

greatest checks and balances against a tyrannical government. That is the stance on the Freedom Scale.

Before moving on, I will state the most important question to ask the gun control advocates. Ask the ones that say they aren't looking to take your guns away. Few are asked, and we never get a straight answer. What is the endgame in pushing gun control? When is it enough? What specific laws are enough to say, "Ok we passed sufficient gun control laws; we aren't going to need to pass any more? Many on the pro-gun side would argue that their goal is confiscation of all guns owned by law abiding citizens—regardless of what the gun control groups say? This is definitely a reasonable conclusion based on the words and actions of the gun control advocates. After all, that is the farthest they can take gun control.

Owning guns, whether it is an eighteenth-century musket or an AR-15 with a bunch of accessories, does not in and of itself infringe on the life, liberty, or property of another individual through force. Try to infringe on a gun owner's life, liberty, or property though force, and like millions of other gun owners, they will defend it with all reasonable force at their disposal.

18. Healthcare: Controlling Medical Needs

*"Every human being is the author of
his own health or disease."*
– Buddha

There has been much discussion and claims over the years that healthcare is a right, and that everyone should be entitled to healthcare. How does the issue of healthcare as a human right figure into the Freedom Scale? Let's start by looking at the basics we can agree on. What we mean when we are talking about healthcare. We can agree that receiving healthcare is the treatment of any physical malady through medical means. In practically every case, healthcare is the coordinated effort of numerous people, at a medical facility, utilizing their expertise as well as the supplies and equipment in the facility in treating each patient.

So why shouldn't it be a right? Look at the difference between healthcare, and all other rights such as freedom of speech or Second Amendment rights. With freedom of speech or Second Amendment rights, nobody else is legally required to provide you with anything if they choose not to. They don't have to provide you with a platform to speak from, or a gun to defend yourself with. Those responsibilities are yours. Healthcare as a right, on the other hand, has to come at the expense of someone else.

Think about it. The equipment and supplies that are used

to treat patients are bought and paid for by the hospital or the organization they are a part of. If you say healthcare is a right, you are saying you are entitled to the supplies and equipment someone else has bought and paid for. You are saying you are entitled to what they own at least in part. For those 'owners' to refuse to provide any of those supplies and equipment is to deny your right to healthcare. What about their right to their privately owned property? It doesn't end there though.

Moving on to the labor aspect, you are saying you are entitled to a portion of the life of everyone involved in providing your healthcare. What do you call someone being forced to do specific work against their will for the soul benefit of someone else? Are you entitled to the time of the doctors, nurses, techs, and everyone involved in the care you need?

A proponent for universal healthcare might say, *"Quit tripping. Healthcare workers would still be paid, so they wouldn't be slaves as you are alluding to."* No? Suppose everyone at nearby hospitals decided to quit immediately. That would deny you your right to healthcare. What happens then? Should they be forced to report to work and provide treatment until suitable replacements are found? What about their right to quit? Should they be forced to accommodate your right to healthcare by applying their medical skills? Where is *their* individual choice? How much or even whether they are paid isn't the issue. It is the *choice* of the individual. This is why healthcare is a provided service and not a right. Rights do not require the labor of others.

But does that mean hospitals can turn people away and refuse lifesaving treatment on a whim? We wouldn't be much of a society if we did that. Because hospitals are in the business of saving lives, nobody is turned away because of an inability to pay for their services. Deal with the medical situation now and worry about payment later. Hospital employees do their part to help save lives. If those employees got picky about who they would help, they would be out of a job.

There are certain exceptions to the healthcare rule. If the condition of a patient requires unavailable options—greater expertise, a specialty, sophisticated equipment—that are not available at the facility, the patient is transferred to a facility that can meet those needs. There are also personal aspects that sometimes has to be considered. If you are a hospital employee, for example, and your mother comes in for life-saving surgery, you can be relieved from working on that case because of the emotional circumstances involved.

In all instances, though, the healthcare worker has a choice. Follow the hospital guidelines or work somewhere else. When there is enough of an imbalance at a specific facility, travelers are hired until permanent staff is hired and trained.

People with preexisting medical conditions need to be taken care of, and it is our job to help look out for those people as they cannot look out for themselves. Even if it goes against freedom, it is part of living in a civilized society.

Now we are getting into territory that is subjective, but I believe there is a need for discussion in this area. Let's delve into the issue that made Obamacare such a big issue: preexisting conditions. What specific preexisting conditions are we talking about? Yes, that does matter. People who can help themselves with preexisting conditions are less likely to garner sympathy from the public who will be forced to pay for their treatment under universal healthcare. That is probably why politicians who support universal healthcare discuss preexisting conditions as if there is no distinction between a condition that is self inflicted and a condition that is not the individual's fault. Appeal to one group of people while minimizing the alarms raised with other people. Back to the question.

Are we talking about congenital conditions that a person is born with? Something that can start at various ages and become more pronounced as a person gets older through no fault of their own? Or are we talking about a condition that is the result of the person's chosen lifestyle?

Let's look at some examples. Epilepsy is a neurological condition that makes a person prone to seizures. Someone can be born with it, or it can start at any age. Keeping it controlled requires specific and often expensive medication. Sometimes the medications have to be switched because the current medication can become less effective. This is a permanent, severe medical condition that when properly managed, can allow people afflicted with it to lead relatively normal lives.

Now look at epilepsy and other conditions that afflict people through no fault of their own. From a personal responsibility aspect, a child clearly cannot be held responsible for their medical conditions. They are also probably unable to get affordable medical insurance in the future because of their condition. We can't hold the child responsible for the possible careless decisions of the parents who did not provide health insurance. The

18. Healthcare

child requires medication. So what is to be done?

This can be debated, but I believe an answer is a form of taxpayer funded system, but not one run by the government. The proposed system would be paid to insurance companies to cover children into adulthood to help offset the extra cost. We already have something similar in Medicaid, but the proposed system could be used by anyone for children who have special medical needs. My wife is a pediatric vent trache nurse and believe me there is no shortage of potential clients.

While it would be collected as taxes to be paid to insurance companies, think of it as a form of insurance for those specific conditions and only those specific conditions. If you don't need the services for you or your child, count your blessings, but know that it is available for anyone if it becomes necessary. This is something I doubt most taxpayers would mind paying into. After all, such people are in this situation through no fault of their own. More details would need to be worked out, but it is a start.

On the flipside, regarding lifestyle people bring many conditions on themselves. Working in the operating room, the one that stands out the most for me is type II diabetes.

In the O.R., this is normally seen in morbidly obese people. The treatment is usually a healthy diet, exercise, and various medications. Following this regimen is often enough to get rid of type II diabetes, but some people choose not to help themselves, and severe medical issues result.

The potential complications from untreated type II diabetes are numerous, costly, and severe. Such conditions include heart disease, stroke, and kidney damage, resulting in the need for dialysis. The condition I see most often is an amputation which happens because the disease can lead to peripheral artery disease, narrowing and reducing the blood flow to your legs and feet. Combine that with peripheral neuropathy in your lower extremities, another potential complication, and it almost guarantees amputation. It happens because peripheral neuropathy can prevent you from feeling pain.

Without that pain, you may not realize you have a wound or ulcer on your foot, causing increasing damage as you put pressure on it, likely leading to infection. It normally starts with an incision and drainage of the area; then toe amputations, followed by foot amputation and finally leg amputation. The severity of what needs to be done between the incision and drainage of the area and the leg amputation depends upon whether the patient takes personal responsibility for their health.

The primary question is asked by someone who takes responsibility for their own health. Why should a person be forced to be pay for the poor health decisions of others under universal healthcare? A large part of medical expenses involves people who refuse to take proper care of themselves. And why should they take care of themselves when their medical bills are already taken care of?

Would enacting universal healthcare encourage or discourage healthy living? Refusing to take personal responsibility would likely encourage an unhealthy lifestyle leading to using medical resources that could be better utilized elsewhere. Would people decide to go to the emergency room 'just to be safe' under universal healthcare more often? I would say yes without hesitation,

18. Healthcare

to get reassurance from doctors and nurses. And why not? We're talking about 'free' healthcare, right?

What few people think of in going to the E.R. to get that reassurance, is that they make it more likely that someone else with a severe condition will be overlooked or misdiagnosed, because E.R. doctors and nurses are overwhelmed due to 'free' healthcare. Personally, I wouldn't like the odds for the patient with a serious condition.

Here is one question to consider in the push for universal healthcare. Would people be willing to agree to no longer hold medical professionals and institutions civilly liable for negligence or major errors as the U.S. military does? Here is a prime example. Before a total joint surgery is performed, it is thoroughly documented, a time-out is performed while the patient is still awake and lucid describing the procedure where everyone, including the patient, agrees on what specific procedure is about to be done. The surgeon even initials the location of the surgery on the patient's skin. Before going into the medical field, I heard of an Army surgeon who did a total knee replacement on the wrong knee. I heard the surgeon lost his license, among other disciplinary measures, but could not be sued, as he performed the surgery as a military surgeon. All the patient got was an expedited bump in the schedule to replace the correct knee by a different surgeon.

Assuming more serious mistakes would be made because of the medical system being overwhelmed, how long would any medical institution or professional last with an increase of heavy lawsuits? In the civilian world, the total knee screw up, would be a successful multimillion dollar lawsuit. Both doctors and medical facilities already pay a fortune in malpractice insurance. How long before the cost of the insurance becomes too high for them to continue in their profession? Where will we go then?

What about an individual mandate on individuals that require insurance companies to take people with preexisting conditions as we saw with the Affordable Care Act?

The main argument for an individual mandate in the Affordable Care Act was that health insurance was a necessity for all people. Actually, it isn't. A wealthy person can easily pay out of pocket and disregard getting health insurance. This clearly shows that health insurance isn't a necessity for everyone. Why should people be forced to pay into a they don't need or even want?

I just argued for something similar for children leading into adulthood. I admit it and I do see the hypocrisy. How is what I proposed different from the individual mandate under Obamacare? The difference is how specific what I proposed is as well as the influence and power of the government. The government footprint is as minimal as it gets. Only people with conditions through no fault of their own would only be covered as far as would allow them to pay what everyone else pays for insurance. There is also charity to look at. Whichever method you prefer, both approaches allow respectful discussion in regards to freedom.

As the Affordable Care Act showed, a large number of people had insurance they liked, but they were forced to give it up as a consequence of the Affordable Care Act, and they were required to sign up for the insurance offered by this bill. In many

18. Healthcare

of these cases, this new insurance people were forced to get was substandard, and more costly with fewer benefits. For some, it was too expensive, forcing them to pay the federal government a fine (tax).

So why was the cost so outrageous that everyone was forced to get health insurance or pay a fine? There are many reasons, but the primary reason is the aforementioned pre-existing conditions. They are expensive to treat. If an insurance company already knows they have to dole out a fair amount of money for someone's health condition, they need a way to recoup that money.

Imagine how expensive it is to treat people who refuse to take personal responsibility for their health. That amount of money becomes excessive. If covered by the ACA, they are taking out far more than they are putting in. Why take care of themselves if treatment is free? To be healthy you may say, so they don't have to deal with medical complications in their day-to-day life. This will work for some but not the majority depending on the condition.

I have been a part of too many surgeries to know it won't work on a large number of people who are morbidly obese for example. I have seen and participated in hundreds of diabetic amputations of the lower extremities on people who don't take care of themselves. Sometimes it was the same person coming back for another amputation. This was working at a small community hospital for eleven years, before moving to a much busier trauma center hospital.

Let's look at some of the costs involved in a surgical case at a hospital to get an idea of how much time and resources can be wasted.

The Freedom Scale

- The cost of the staff involved from beginning to end, which likely involves two dozen people at least. Count admission, pre-op, peri-op, post-op, etc. Keep in mind the overwhelming majority of the staff have expensive degrees that demand high cost for staff.
- The cost of supplies from medical venders, most of which are very expensive because they require sterilization. If specialty supplies are required, the cost goes up. The cost of one significant supply for a surgical case can run from a few hundred to several thousand dollars each. The cheapest sterile surgical supplies you would find are sponges, (which from my experience the patient is not charged for) and sutures (which I believe start at around $30 each depending on the suture). Usually, implants are the most expensive.
- The cost of drugs. Never have I seen a surgical case without drugs. You can imagine the price tag there, especially for anesthesia.
- The cost of equipment. Start with surgical instruments. Most are specially designed and made specifically for surgery. Instruments included in disposable case packs are not surgical grade and thus are disposable. Occasionally, the surgical grade instruments break and need to be repaired or replaced. These instrument sets are also washed, reassembled, and sterilized by even more staff after each use, so the machines are running almost constantly and require maintenance, which is expensive.

18. Healthcare

Different surgical procedures require different surgical tables, such as fracture tables for fixing certain hip and femur fractures, and specialized tables for cysto procedures.

- The costs of medical tests. This would include taking cultures for analysis in the lab. Possible x-rays, computed tomography (CT scans), etc. All equipment used for this is expensive and needs constant maintenance.
- The cost of follow-up care. It isn't just removing the foot and applying dressing. Numerous follow-ups are needed to ensure there are no further issues and to ensure proper healing.
- The cost of prosthetics, and everyone involved in that aspect of their medical care.

These are by no means all the costs. Taxes, the cost of following regulations, utilities, stationary, computers, laundry, housekeeping, insurance and a large number of other expenses have to be factored into the cost. Every patient's fair share is factored in. Add that up, and the cost is tens of thousands to hundreds of thousands of dollars. Will all of these be used by someone needing surgical treatment? No. However, the expenses listed will be used in other types of surgical cases, which include people needing surgical treatment because they neglected their health.

We cannot afford such an increase to the cost of our medical care under a universal healthcare system, nor can freedom survive under such a system.

But Nordic countries such as Sweden have universal healthcare, and they manage to make it work. Implementation of single payer health care as it stands now would likely mirror what we see in Venezuela rather than Sweden. How can I be so sure? Look at the three main states that tried to implement universal healthcare over the years: Massachusetts, Vermont, and Colorado. All three found the increased cost through taxation would be too high for it to be implemented, despite trying. Politicians there didn't want to risk their political careers because taxes would be raised to such a high level. Unlike federal politicians, state politicians are actually held to a degree of fiscal responsibility.

More than that, they and current politicians don't want to enact the measures that countries like Sweden use. The first is a very high tax on everyone, rich and poor alike. In addition to high income taxes, a 25 percent value added tax (VAT) is applied on goods and services for everyone. There is more though. The medical industry in the United States represents 1/6 of the national economy, and is by far the most regulated industry in the nation. Sweden and other Nordic countries have far fewer regulations and interference from the government, and are privately owned. This allows them to operate more efficiently. For example, a doctor can go about the best way they see fit in diagnosing and treating patients rather than go through the government checklist doctors in the U.S. have to follow.

Sweden and other Nordic countries also have private insurance for people to shorten wait times and get into better facilities. While it is not unanimous among those wanting universal healthcare enacted in the U.S., there are those that have talked about doing away with a private insurance option. Why do that if you want the health system to be more like theirs? Shouldn't we

18. Healthcare

follow the same path they did?

Nowadays in many states, it is near impossible for many new healthcare facilities to emerge or for smaller ones to stay in business as most are bought out by big name healthcare providers. Many doctors no longer have private offices, but are employees of those big healthcare providers. I have seen and heard firsthand of this happening because the hospital where I used to work started as a small, independent, community hospital, that got bought out after incurring millions in debt. This happened not long after the Affordable Care Act became law. I have also heard of similar buyouts of small independent hospitals and physician practices in the country at approximately the same time. Could this have been the first goal of the politicians with the ACA, to give large medical providers an advantage over smaller ones in the area as they are better equipped to absorb the extra costs? After all, if you get rid of the competition, or the political class makes it too expensive or difficult for them to start up a business, your potential patients have little choice of whom to see for medical needs. I am not saying that is what happened here, but it makes one wonder.

When was the last time you heard of a United States politician in support of universal healthcare, advocate for reducing regulations in the medical field to make it more affordable? When was the last time you even heard of one publicly saying they are going to follow the exact same playbook for implementing universal healthcare as Nordic countries? Politicians like Bernie Sanders say we will have healthcare like the Nordic countries, but his proposals on how to proceed are more in line

The Freedom Scale

with how Venezuela or Cuba run their healthcare. Those proposals involve a strong central government overseeing the details of every aspect, which leads me to my main question: Politicians in the U.S. who advocate for universal healthcare, have shown no indication I can see they want to enact any proposal to lower costs and make healthcare more efficient that takes power away from them. All of their proposals give them or other government agencies more power over you.

Are there proposals to reduce costs without sacrificing quality or giving more control to the government? That is necessary to begin with, but let's go through a number of ideas. First: Healthcare in this country is too focused on insurance. Even when going to a small clinic for something minor, you will first be asked about your insurance. We need to get away from that. Create a price list for minor, every day services. This fuels competition for these clinics to provide the best quality care at the lowest cost possible because then their prices are advertised. It also gives people an incentive to be more responsible for their own health. The more visits a person makes, the more money comes out of their own pocket.

The benefits get even better though. Fewer resources are used at hospitals and their ERs with more people going to the clinics for more minor ailments, and only when they feel they need to. The less insurance companies are forced to cover, the cheaper they can offer insurance, making it more affordable for everyone. This would also create a resurgence in private practice physicians because the same non-insurance policies regarding seeing and treating patients can be applied to their medical specialties.

18. Healthcare

Buying insurance across state lines is another option. Many in the media have dismissed this for various reasons, but let us look at it plainly. While in the Navy I was stationed at a base on the Maryland/Virginia border. This was in the early 2000s when cigarette prices started to spike in some states because of taxes. While there were caps on the amount of cigarettes that out-of-state visitors could buy, the retailers on the Maryland side who now had a significantly higher tax placed on this product saw far fewer sales.

The same principle applies here, but you aren't driving across state lines and picking up a physical product. Different states have different rules and regulations that impact the cost of health insurance and operating costs on medical facilities. If you can get the same policy from the same company for $200 less a month in a different state, you would do so if it was convenient. That puts the states with high-cost health insurance in an awkward position. If medical treatment doesn't occur in the state a person resides in, the state cannot collect taxes for services rendered, leading to a revenue shortfall. If people could buy health insurance across state lines, it would force the states to revisit the policies that may be driving up the cost of health insurance, so they can be more competitive. Of course, this would reduce political power; therefore, no buying health insurance across state lines.

When it comes to drugs, you have the brand name and the generic. The brand name is what was initially developed and required roughly a billion dollars, and years of development. The generic drug is the 'knock' off that was created after the patent has expired allowing other drug companies to produce it. A drug company that cannot recoup its costs in developing new drugs, would not develop new drugs; therefore, the reason for a patent for a certain amount of time.

Now suppose these pharmaceutical companies get together and decide to raise the cost of certain necessary generic drugs. Rather than using government force and capping the price of certain drugs like insulin, give them a choice, that involves no arm twisting.

As we saw with the corona virus vaccine, President Trump cut through a lot of bureaucratic red tape allowing a treatment to be developed faster than expected. The choice would be to eliminate the high amount of red tape regulations for pharmaceutical companies and eliminate what was excessive and unneeded, allowing them to create new drugs faster and cheaper without cutting corners. This would apply only to pharmaceutical companies that put a cap on the profit margin of all the drugs they sell. These drug companies then get to save a great deal of time and money on the drugs they are developing, probably more than they would make from price gouging. Insurance companies aren't paying as much for generic drugs, so they are saving money allowing them to lower the cost of insurance. Everybody wins.

Individual or family health savings accounts are another way to help better manage the cost of health insurance. As many of you know, the lower the deductible on insurance, the less you pay out of pocket if something happens. For someone worried about out-of-pocket expenses while living on a limited income, this can be a game changer. It is like a piggy bank, saving X

18. Healthcare

amount of dollars every time you get paid. Then when you need medical care, it is there to help cover the out-of-pocket cost. The longer you go without using it, the more you save. The more you put into it, the less you pay out of pocket when you use it.

While there are many ways to cut medical costs while maintaining quality, I will discuss only one more. While I work in the medical community, like most people I am not an expert on the logistics. One of the last areas I will cover is *waste*. A fair amount—though not all—can be eliminated by getting rid of unnecessary, burdensome regulations as I said above. Some waste is unavoidable, and some is accidental. There are plenty of examples of that in the operating room. A surgeon may request ten sutures opened, and only use six. A supply may be opened, but it may slide onto the floor and become contaminated, making it useless because it can no longer be used. Perhaps a surgical case was canceled at the last minute, so all the items opened were not used. A disposable sterile item may be past its expiration date, making it unusable. You get the point.

Like other companies, hospitals have a pie chart of all of their expenses which must be matched with income. At some surgery centers, primarily for elective surgeries, there is profit sharing with the O.R. staff. For disposable sterile supplies, the surgery center looks at the pie chart and says we spend X amount of dollars on these supplies a year. If less is spent, some of the difference is split with the O.R. staff. Keep in mind the amount spent for post operative surgical infections is factored in as well, so contaminated supplies are not used to merely help ensure the bonus.

The Freedom Scale

How could all of this help the surgical patient? Imagine if healthcare facilities did something like this. I have seen supplies run out and we had to do without. Occasionally there is such a high demand, that the item is on backorder for months. Working harder to reduce waste reduces the likelihood of backorder issues and ensures we have what we need. Surgeons use the bare minimum instead of demanding supplies be opened on a whim that they may not need. There are many more possibilities in other hospital departments.

Moving on from costs, let us finally look at medical treatments. Ask yourself something. If you had a terminal illness, do you believe you have the right to try any experimental treatment? What about if you were told you must take full responsibility? If it doesn't work, the person providing the treatment cannot be sued. At the present time, people can participate only in approved medical treatments. Your body, your choice, right? So why does the government restrict people in this manner. They looked to do so with the COVID-19 vaccines, looking to disallow the use of repurposed drugs.

It is not about what is best for the public. In describing those supporting universal health care, it is about power for the political elite over the people. Nearly everyone will need access to quality medical care at some point in their lifetime. If left with what the government provides, people lose their freedom to choose. The government would decide who gets what treatment and when. Suppose under a universal healthcare system, 90 percent of people over the age of 80 don't support the party in power. What is to stop the government from upping wait times

18. Healthcare

for treatment or denying certain treatment for those people?

You know what? Let us look at something simpler, heading into what could be considered 'conspiracy theory' territory. What is to stop politicians whose party is in the majority from delaying treatment to people opposed to their political agenda? Those unfortunate people could be put on a wait list through voter registration, for example, so their politicians' supporters get preference in regard to medical treatment. Think that sounds too farfetched? In socialist dictatorships, whom do you think gets the fastest and best medical care available? Only the politicians and the most devout party loyalists. Whether you think it is likely to happen or not is irrelevant. It is possible. Do you really want to take that chance with your life or the lives of your loved ones? If you do, good for you. I and millions of other freedom loving Americans are not.

19. Education: How to Think vs. What to Think

K-12

"Who controls the past controls the future. Who controls the present controls the past."
– Winston Smith, 1984

Education is highly important for getting by in this world. Few would argue this, as you can't do much of anything without being able to read, write, or do simple math. Education is one of the things tax dollars are necessary for. How it is carried out is something that has been debated for many years. It is especially important because the power of teaching—in the wrong hands—is one of the greatest dangers to freedom, especially in the subjects of political science and history. My best teachers challenged me to think, and look at different perspectives, even if it challenged their viewpoint. It is the key difference between education and indoctrination. The indoctrinator has a viewpoint of history that may very well contain facts, but with a spin that is anything but dispassionate. Facts that cast a negative light on the desired narrative of these people are seldom, if ever, presented. Indoctrinators prefer having as many educators attuned to their way of thinking as possible. We need educators who will present unbiased facts instead.

19. Education

Presently, we pay taxes to have our children educated from kindergarten through twelfth grade. After those children have reached adulthood, they can move in many different directions, whether it be college, trade school, the military, etc. Now numerous options are available to educate children, such as public schools, private schools, charter schools, or even home schooling. The main problem is that while some charter schools are available in some areas, there is only one option for those who are not wealthy, and that is public schools. For the most part, they are the ones getting tax dollars for education. They are unionized, opposing attempts to allow competition that is taxpayer funded; thus, they have a monopoly. In most public schools, it is near impossible to get rid of bad teachers, thanks to the teachers' unions.

What is the main difference between public schools and charter schools that are funded by taxpayer dollars? Charter schools are held to a higher standard. They do not deal with the politics of being unionized. They are held accountable to the parents of the students they are teaching. To put it simply, if they don't deliver adequately, they lose their funding.

Are charter schools better than public schools? From the sound of it, being held accountable is a big plus for the charter schools, but let us look at some of the facts in more detail, starting with schools in New York state, from economist Thomas Sowell's book *Charter Schools and their Enemies*. Sometimes the charter school students and public-school students attend classes in the same school building. They are given the same tests in math and English every year. What are the differences in academic performances of each group in the same school?

On average, 14 percent of public-school classes achieve a level defined as "proficient" in English for their grade level, by the New York Department of education. For the charter school counterparts, the number is 65 percent. In math, the numbers are 10 percent for public schools and 68 percent for charter schools. Pretty large gap between the two, adding a big plus for charter schools.

We hear the argument that nationwide charter schools are no better than public schools. Looking on the surface, this is true. There are, however, specific facts left out and questions that must be asked. Apparently, the majority of public-school students nationwide are made up of white and Asian students, while the majority of charter schools nationwide are made up of black and Hispanic students. Statistically, whites and Asians perform higher in school on average than black and Hispanic students. No, I am not saying whites and Asians are naturally smarter. But to get a real picture on how effective charter schools are, we have to compare apples to apples, by asking specific questions. What is the difference in numbers between mostly black and Hispanic charter schools and public schools? What is the difference in numbers between mostly white and Asian charter schools and public schools? What is the difference in comparing these schools when comparing low-income area charter schools and public schools? What is the difference in grades between all four groups in charter schools compared to the grades in all four groups of nearby public schools?

In numerous places charter schools have an extensive waiting list while others determine student admission through a lottery process. Where the lottery exists, it destroys the argument of charter schools stealing the best and the brightest. Some places give even less money for charter schools than public schools, and a number of charter schools still survive. Do some charter schools fail because they are 'not good'? Of course. That, however, is a grim possibility for anyone who has run a business. If you don't deliver, the business will fail.

So, let's go take a look at the pros vs. cons.

- Charter schools must deliver results or go out of business. Public schools do not.
- Charter schools are not unionized and thus are less expensive
- It is easier to fire bad teachers in charter schools as opposed to public schools.
- A student's learning at charter school could be disrupted if it goes out of business. Such a worry does not exist for public schools.

Looking at this comparison, the charter school is the way I would want to go for my child. Consider the following comparison. Would you voluntarily go to a restaurant again, where the staff was rude and constantly got your order wrong, and overcharged you? The owners and management would not stand for that kind of behavior from their employees, as they would soon be out of business if they allowed it to continue. Would that be the attitude of the managers and owners if you and others were forced to be patrons of that restaurant because you couldn't afford to pay more elsewhere and were required to go out to eat? It is highly unlikely. In that scenario, the restaurant has nothing to lose, and you have no option but to be their customer.

This is just charter schools. What about parents who want to send their kids to a private school? Even if the parents are willing to make up the difference in cost from public school, they are not given that option. So why such a huge fight against anything that threatens the monopoly of public schools. As with many things, it is all about money. Teachers and their union representatives don't want money for education going elsewhere.

There is a saying that healthcare providers live by. *Aeger Primo*. It is Latin for 'patient first', making the care of the patient the primary concern. Shouldn't educators have a similar standard, where the education of students is the primary concern? There are of course a number of fine public-school teachers who live up to those standards. I am by no means suggesting otherwise. My daughter's elementary school teachers in Texas are the perfect example.

There are, however, a large number of teachers and teachers' union officials who put themselves and their self-interests above that of the minds they are charged with teaching. The most notable example detailing this would have to be former teachers' union official Albert Shanker, who is quoted as saying, "I'll put it this way: I'll start representing schoolchildren, when schoolchildren start paying union dues." Imagine if healthcare professionals took this attitude about being patient advocates. How well do you suppose patients in medical facilities would

19. Education

fare if that were the attitude portrayed by the people taking care of them? Why should the education of our offspring be any less important?

Why do our elected officials allow such actions? First, most of our elected officials decide to pay the bill for private schools. They can afford it. Without their children in public schools, they lack incentive to ensure the best education is received from public schools. More importantly is what appears to be an unspoken agreement between public schools and politicians.

What appears to concern the politicians (primarily Democrat) about the issue of public schools is the political agenda they want driven in the schools. It has been shown that supporters of these politicians will not question the agenda, and public-school teachers are all too happy to provide it in their classrooms, so long as they and their unions get what they want. Whether it is having kids writing letters to members of congress over global warming; having kids sing, "Yes we can" celebrating Barrack Obama; or banning clothing such as MAGA hats because they deemed them hateful. Each is a means to an end. The narrative supporting what big government politicians want is taught in public school, and teachers unions are rewarded with taxpayer dollars, while their competition is distanced. Coincidence?

Certain subjects taught in K-12 focus entirely on facts, such as math, science, and English. Some people, however, are attempting to change that. George Orwell's classic book *1984*, shows the attempt to convince someone that 2+2=5. We see attempts in areas such as biology where it is said that gender is a 'social construct,' or we see it in environmental sciences when discussing climate change. We will discuss that another time though. For now, we will be discussing history; more specifically American history, starting with Howards Zimm's book, *A History of the United States*. Throughout world history, something that is almost a constant is the presence of one form of oppression or another. Whether it is slaves building the pyramids in ancient Egypt or the gladiator games in the Coliseum in Rome during the days of the Roman Empire, oppression can be found in numerous places.

While the United States has a fair share of ugly history, a negative history is the focus in Zimm's book to a level of great exaggeration, spin and personal bias. Dinesh D'Souza does an adequate job of addressing this and adding a balance in his documentary *America: Imagine a World Without Her*, but it does not change the fact that Zimm's book is used to teach millions of school children a blatantly biased version of American history.

That is part of the main problem. While history has never known a truly dispassionate perspective, the facts of both the good and bad of history must be presented without prejudice as much as possible. This includes neglecting to address present-day facts that do not fit with a specific narrative. History must be presented as the unaltered school picture, which shows the stray hairs, the zits and the scars, instead of only showing us what we want to see or what others want us to see.

Most everyone wants the best education for their children, making the lack of choice in where their children go to school a rotten deal for those living in areas with rampant crime. The proposed solution to most of the problems with bad schools is to throw more money at it, and it will work out. That approach has failed decade after decade; yet the same solution is still promoted. Why not try something different and break the monopoly of the teachers' unions, expanding beyond the public-school classroom? Those with the power to shape the young minds of today, have the power to shape the destiny of tomorrow's world, and those who would threaten freedom want the young indoctrinated into their way of thinking. The best way of doing that is controlling their education. It is easier to program a child to think a certain way, than it is to change the thinking of an adult. By the time these children reach college age, those controlling what is taught already have many of these children blindly accepting the narratives they were taught.

College years

"Beware of false knowledge; it is more
dangerous than ignorance."
– George Bernard Shaw

Looking back at the Middle Ages, the public was taught unwavering loyalty to the church. Those who questioned this narrative had accusations lobbed at them, including witchcraft. The questioning normally ended with the death of those doing the questioning.

Fast forward to the twentieth century and we revisit Nazi Germany and the practice of *gleichschaltung*, which was one of their main ways of controlling the public through education. It was meant to draw the public in line with the will of the authoritarian state. Books that did not conform with Nazi ideology were burned in public gatherings. The educators that taught outside that ideology, as well as those who believed differently than the Nazis were intimidated, threatened, and physically assaulted. These assaults eventually cost some people their lives. First this happened under the Nazi brownshirts who intimidated people to be in line with their way of thinking. Later when the Nazi party had full and total control of the government, certain brownshirt leaders like Rudolph Hess were done away with, and the state started charging and executing certain people—even if they weren't Jewish—for speaking out against Hitler or the Nazi platform. Sophie Scholl is a prime example. She was executed by the Nazi government after having been caught distributing anti-Nazi material that was critical of the Nazi Party and Adolf Hitler.

Today on major college campuses, the woke, politically correct students are not much different than the brownshirts before the deadly assaults. They look to shut down opposing viewpoints on campus. Extra security is often ordered whenever a conservative is invited to be a speaker because of how unhinged many get in their response to hearing such a person was even invited.

I asked these questions earlier, but they warrant being asked again. Why? If the viewpoint they oppose is so hateful, why not let them speak and prove it to everyone? I'm willing to bet it is because they have been conditioned on what to think instead of listening and critically think for themselves, as I highly doubt most of these students have ever heard what these speakers have said or read their work. Odds are they rely on what they were

19. Education

told by their professors or others who dislike them.

I believe the professors and administrators end up being a contributing factor to this behavior, as the views expressed by many of these outspoken students, mirror their professors and the school administration. From what I can see, they aren't taught to confront and examine different viewpoints, but to conform, making rational discussion much more difficult. What do you expect from facilities that offer safe spaces instead of requiring the students to deal with their discomfort? In the real world, life will chew you up and spit you out before even hinting at a safe space.

> *"If everyone looks different but thinks the same, that is conformity, not diversity."*
> *– Charlie Kirk*

Sometimes students' grades depend on their sharing the professor's view. Many administrators at these universities praise diversity but shun the diversity that matters most in centers of higher learning, and that is diversity of thought. Good luck to anyone who openly expresses differing political views when applying for a job at one of these prestigious institutions of higher learning. It appears to be a big disqualifier for applicants when you look at the numbers. Why is that? Are they afraid the students will not share their views if viewpoints other than theirs are taught, or do they just not want to take the chance? Having conservative professors won't automatically convert students to their way of thinking and vice versa.

The Freedom Scale

Thomas Sowell as a prime example. He is a world-renowned economist, former columnist, a former teacher, and has written numerous books, delving into a wide variety of topics. He further helped inspire me to ask the important, relevant questions in writing this book as he looks at every possible angle and statistic in forming his opinions. Today, while highly regarded by conservatives, he started off as a Marxist and was still a Marxist after taking a course taught by Milton Friedman who was also highly regarded by conservatives.

What changed Thomas Sowell's Marxist thinking? It was a summer as an intern working for the U.S. federal government. There he questioned everything, using all the empirical data to form his opinions. He had looked at the policy of minimum wage and weighed the pros and cons. At the Labor Department, he tried to discuss it with them and came up with a test showing how beneficial his solution would be. But according to Sowell, they were stunned and wanted no part of it, refusing the test. You have to ask what harm could it have done to carry out the test, when it could have provided insight on improving the system? The bureaucrats seemed to care more about maintaining their narrative than making things better. You can't make things better when maintaining the narrative is the most important thing.

Instead of using their positions to try and promote tolerance and understanding of differing viewpoints and encouraging widespread civil debates to expand minds, the big college administrations and professors continue to treat these young adults like children that need to be protected and told what to think. Safe spaces are set up, designed to keep students isolated from

19. Education

whatever may offend them. The thinking must remain 'politically correct.' Instead of being threatened with administrative action for violent behavior, these students are coddled and not held responsible for their actions, much like spoiled brats getting what they want from their parent when they throw a tantrum.

How often are these students held responsible for massive protests or for providing the money to cover the extra security needed as because of the uproar? Why not make them pay the bill for the extra security? How about threatening criminal charges and expelling those who partake in violent action or directly promote violence against those they disagree with? High resolution cameras set up around campus would result in easily identifying them.

That is one of the main differences between the big-league colleges and the military. Those who join the military are taught discipline and taught to carry on with what needs to be done despite their personal feelings. They are expected to behave in a professional manner that is respectful of superiors and coworkers. Actions have consequences. The real world does not bow down to you and conform to what you want. You must adapt to what the world throws at you, or it will kick your ass. If discipline and personal responsibility were enforced on college campuses, it is likely we would have fewer problems with protests and riots.

The lack of personal responsibility starts at home, not with the officials at colleges. It is merely supposed to be reinforced at the college level. If more parents were focused on such things today, it wouldn't be such an issue. Let me share an example involving my niece, Margaret. My niece's circumstances changed

The Freedom Scale

when she was a couple of years into her studies at a prestigious and expensive college. Her parents started off paying for it and eventually put the burden on her when she refused to accept their conditions. Something popped up on the feed for one of my social media platforms when Margaret commented on a post on a pro Bernie Sanders page that asked what tuition-free and debt-free higher education would mean for you and your family.

Margaret answered the question like someone who has not thought things out. She said it would mean that she wouldn't be paying off college debt for the rest of her life and would allow her to live a happier and fuller life.

In response, I asked her what about those who are forced to pay that college debt for a degree she chose to pursue so she can live a happier and more fulfilling life without worrying? She didn't realize, even in her response, that especially with the career she chose to pursue, she would be taxed excessively to pay for not only her education, but everyone else's higher education leaving her right back where she started, or even worse off.

Instead of answering my question and telling me why it would be fair to force others to pay for an educational path she chose so she could live that life, she pointed out that I was in the military and had my education paid for by those same taxpayers. It showed her ignorance in the matter, but let's explore that argument.

When I joined the Navy in 1996, my pay as an E-1 was approximately $810 a month. My food, housing and medical care was already paid for by the military on their terms. I was given the option to sign up for the G.I. Bill, which was not free of

19. Education

charge, but had conditions. I had to first serve four years and receive an honorable discharge. That first year with E-1 pay, I also had to pay $100 a month for my first full year into the G.I. Bill, nearly 1/8th of what I made. To get what I wanted, I as an individual had to give the military even more on their terms. Such an arrangement is no different than a hospital giving the opportunity for a technologist to become a registered nurse on the hospital's dime in exchange for a few years of service to the hospital in that capacity after graduation. If the new RN leaves the employment at the hospital before the obligated service time is up, they have to pay the hospital the costs for the school they graduated from as agreed upon.

In the Navy, my service and the service of everyone else utilizing the GI Bill had to come first. If we got kicked out, we lost that benefit, even if we already paid our $1200 into it.

Margaret could have followed a similar path, but chose to let her parents pay her way until they decided not to because of her need to have her own way, and she decided it should be everyone else's problem. When I was that age, my parents offered to send me to college, which would have been culinary school at that time. I declined for two simple reasons. I didn't want to be in anyone's debt, but to succeed on my own for starters. More importantly though, I did not want the fact that my parents paid for me to go to college to be held over my head. That same entitlement mentality that I refused to adopt, has taken over far too many of today's youth.

College Costs and the Responsibility

As I stated earlier in the book, I did not attend college until I was in my thirties. Being married at the time and planning to move and start a family, I looked at the local community college and what they offered. Three questions helped me decide what to major in aside from what I thought I might enjoy because it was up to me to pay my way, and my wife was depending on me. Failure was not an option.

1. How much will this degree cost me?
2. What is the pay scale for a job with this degree?
3. How readily available are jobs with this degree?

One person in favor of government paying for college actually said these were deep questions needing a four-year college degree to be able to answer. It is nowhere near that complicated. It is the same as buying any commercial good or service with a slight twist. You first ask how much it will cost, like you would if you were buying anything else. Unlike a car loan, where you already know what you are making at your job, you must look at what you will be earning after getting the degree to determine if it is worth it. That is where question three come into play. It does no good to get everything needed for a specific high paying job, if that job is hard to come by.

Unfortunately, at the present time, most young people do not ask such questions; nor do a lot of parents who pay the bill. These kids look at what is socially acceptable, what classes are easiest to pass, what institutions have the best recreation equipment available, and their parents just look at them getting into college. Some of the kids have no idea what they want to major in, and they may drift through college, figuring any degree will be enough.

A coworker once told me that her son wanted to be a forest ranger. It requires a specific degree, though I don't remember what, and the degree would cost around $100,000. She was willing to help pay for that degree until the other two questions were answered. Jobs as a forest ranger are very hard to come by because so many people want that job; far more than are available. As a result, the pay is quite low, being only around $20,000 a year from what she said he told her. Considering these facts, she told him if this was what he wanted, he could pay for it out of his own pocket, as she didn't think it was worth it. He chose to pursue a career elsewhere.

The cost of college tuition has increased over 3,000 percent the past few decades, most of it since 2010, so it is no wonder my niece and many other kids nowadays have adopted the mentality of free college when their parents said, "no more." Why such a sharp increase? It is conspiracy theory time, some of you may think, as I am about to link the reason for the belief systems on college campuses and the cost of student loans. It is just my opinion, but it is far from an outlandish theory, especially since the solution Democrats offer is taxpayer funded college for everyone.

The Federal Family Education Loan program (FFEL) was established in 1965 and has helped more than 60 million students pay for college education. The program used government loan guarantees to make college affordable for low-income students who did not have sufficient credit. The FFEL was later expanded to include every American. Banks would make the loans, and the federal government would back the loans in case of default. Because banks were the 'go to' for the loans, colleges avoided raising the costs too much for a while. However, the government couldn't leave well enough alone. Despite the success of the FFEL, the program's loan subsidies, were steadily reduced over time, as Pell grants and other educational programs were created.

The FFEL was abruptly made unprofitable in mid-2008 because of a combination of higher credit costs resulting from the financial crisis, and deep subsidy cuts. Banks would not make student loans at this time. Short term measures were put in place, until in 2010, the Healthcare and Education Reconciliation Act of 2010 (HCERA) was passed, and put the federal government in charge of student lending.

This made the government the provider of 80 percent of student loans, up from 20 percent. What was the result? Student loan debt went from 154.9 billion dollars in 2009 to approximately 1.75 trillion dollars in 2022. Many blamed the greedy banks for making predatory loans even in 2022, but that is no longer the case. Congresswoman Maxine Waters attempted to grill major bank CEOs on the student loan issues, before getting egg on her face when she was reminded by them, they no longer deal with student loans.

If it is not the banks, what is causing the outrageous increase in the cost of student loans? A number of factors I can think of. First up would be lack of accountability by the government. Many schools see the government as picking up the tab, now so they can charge a good amount more, even for degrees that are either useless (gender studies) or not worth it (degree to be a forest ranger mentioned earlier). After all, banks wouldn't make such loans for such degrees. They would lose money and go out of business. The federal government doesn't worry about that though with all of their reckless spending elsewhere. They are the ones primarily agreeing to outrageous loans and having outrageous interest rates. It isn't a big leap to assume the rules and regulations governing the HCERA are not written very well and leave plenty of room for abuse from both borrowers and the government.

Here comes the conspiracy theory part of what I think is going on. I find it reasonable to believe there is quid pro quo between the federal government and colleges/universities across the country, much like with teachers' unions in public schools, but on a grander scale. Colleges teach in the manner certain politicians want, namely Democrat politics. In return colleges get to raise the cost of tuition to ridiculous levels and the government continues to agree to back it. The government then moves to agree to pay for everyone to attend college, and enrollment in college goes through the roof at inflated prices from the college that will likely continue to go up at a rapid pace. This creates a dependency on the government to provide, and with the personal politics of most of the staff, provides an atmosphere of indoctrination. The large interest rates present in student loans now in the HCERA are a steppingstone to acquiring complete dependency. Whether or not you believe this is the intent, it is the end result.

Many people would argue in response to this that college would still be much more affordable with the federal government paying for student loans as the interest would be done away with, so why not go ahead and do it?

First; doing so would go against freedom. It takes away individual responsibility for your decisions and forces everyone to be responsible through tax dollars, not to mention the dependency issue I just mentioned. Second: Going this route focuses on treating the symptom as opposed to the disease which is the cause. The disease in this case is outrageous tuition costs. In earlier days, you worked a summer job or a part-time job and made enough to pay for college. Now, even interest free, most people can't do that, and the goal in a freedom-loving society is to lower the cost of higher education through freedom, not to pass that cost on to everyone else. Finally: The student loans have not been made interest free.

If a person is afflicted with cancer, they do more than take over the counter medicine to take care of the symptoms. When you say, just have the government pay for everyone's college, it is the same thing. It only addresses the symptom, when the cause of the problem needs to be addressed. Why am I so sure colleges would raise prices even more, besides the fact they have already? Imagine everyone was entitled to a new car. You wouldn't care what it would cost because someone else would pay. Do you think the dealership would keep the prices the same, or would they see it as an opportunity to jack the prices up astronomically for a nice windfall? Apply the same logic to college. Do you think it would be any different?

Now imagine if nothing was done by the federal government when banks withdrew from offering student loans under FFEL. Would there have been a huge increase in unemployment because people had no way to go to college? That may have been the case in the short term, but only the short term. Why? Colleges are businesses looking to make money. If they don't make money, they close their doors for good. When a business needs to make up for a revenue shortfall, they need to be creative to stay in business. What could colleges have done? Lower tuition rates, lower cost of textbooks, expand class sizes, expand online classes, with at least some being prerecorded, so people could take those online classes at their leisure. A combination of all of these would make colleges much more affordable, although the colleges would have had to work harder for their money.

Many were up in arms about Biden canceling student loan debt in 2022 shortly before the midterm elections. Those people said, "These kids took out the loans. It is their responsibility to pay it back." That is consistent with freedom. If you are not held responsible for your actions, someone else must be.

In discussing this Biden student loan forgiveness, I have one question that nobody else seems to have asked. It is a negative on Biden however it is answered. Was it principle or interest being canceled in his student loan forgiveness? If it is principle, then taxpayers are forced to subsidize a portion of the debt others willfully took on, although the students are still stuck making interest payments. If it is the interest, there is nothing lost as the interest is just extra taxes owed and will continue to accumulate interest. This will have done little for the college student in debt at tremendous cost to the taxpayers. At most, it will give the illusion Biden and his party care and are trying to help when they were the ones who created a huge problem in the first place.

Despite looking at all of this, some still say those trying to make the individuals responsible for the debt they voluntarily took on—is wanting to make these children suffer because *we* suffered. Our college expense was affordable they say. College costs are so high now that students can't be expected to pay the debt, so the taxpayers must fund it.

Thus, their solution remains to force the taxpayer to pay for the schooling of others rather than look to reduce the college cost. While political stakes are at risk, it sounds more like laziness with a false quick fix, more than anything else. But we must ask ourselves if their college education isn't worth it to pay for themselves, why should it be important enough for the rest of us to pay for it? Even more important is if the college education these kids today are getting is so great, why is government funded college the best solution they can come up. I guess it is one more argument for Charlie Kirk to add to his list of why he believes college for the most part is a scam.

I have a better solution, and all I have is a simple associates degree from a community college. The solution not only involves reducing current student loan debt since 2010 but reducing it in the future. The answer is quite simple. We'll start with those moving forward. First make high schools do their jobs. It is their job to help students prepare for life after high school. If high

19. Education

school graduates are too stupid after graduation and before college to ask the simple questions I mentioned earlier, the high school isn't doing their job along with the parents.

The most important thing that can be done is eliminating much of the federal Influence. This is done in four ways.

1. *Eliminate subsidies colleges receive from the federal government.*
2. *Prohibit the federal government from granting student loans.*
3. *Prohibit the federal government from backing student loans.*
4. *Simplify the process of removing the red tape by allowing new colleges and universities to open and become accredited.*

We addressed earlier why this would work. The colleges either adapt or they go under. Nothing inspires creativity more than necessity.

In dealing with students who are drowning in debt from 2010 and on, there is a solution that is beneficial to most everyone. Lower the interest owed to the government for operating cost to oversee student government loans. Whatever the government spends outside of the principle will be divided among those with the loans to pay for bare minimum operating costs, depending on tuition cost; how long they have been paying back; and what amount they have been paying back, not to exceed X amount paid. Once that amount is paid, there is no more interest. The government doesn't get to profit. It just breaks even with tax dollars. The least amount will be the individual's fair share of the interest in operating the HCERA annually. The federal government will have to get very transparent with their spending in this area. Politicians can campaign on education reform. They are pushing to reduce wasteful spending in this manner for the HCERA to lower interest on college education.

Diversity on Campus

I mentioned earlier how colleges are obsessed with diversity. This is diversity based on race, gender, sexual orientation, those kinds of things. How much good does it do not only for these students, but the rest of the country as well? While governor of California, it was brought to Ronald Reagan's attention that admitting students to Berkeley based solely on individual performance could mean that the student body of the school might be Asian American. His response was "So what?" That statement cut right to the heart of the matter.

Now should college admissions have race-based preference in addition to other such preferences in place of academic performance? No. On the same level colleges have the right to do so if they are entirely privately funded institutions, and if they so choose. Allowing politicians to influence that decision say with tax dollars is where the line must be drawn. The government's main function should be making sure the academic standard is upheld to ensure the school is teaching skills adequately.

As far as diversity goes, I think it is safe to say the overwhelming majority of people care far more about the skills of a surgeon

19. Education

performing delicate surgery on them or the skills of an architect building the bridge they cross every day than any other personal detail. What does it say about the school's administration, when their admittance policy has irrelevant standards unrelated to the academic record of the applicant? To me it says to them diversity is more important to the college than whether they are capable of the academic work or not; hence the need to enforce the academic standard. Competing under the same standard is the only way for students to truly prove themselves. If you are part of a marginalized group, then you have the opportunity to prove yourself.

★ ★ ★

IV. Deciding Where You Stand

*"The secret of happiness is freedom.
The secret of freedom is courage."
– Carrie Jones*

20. Republicans or Democrats in Pursuit of Freedom?

"Liberty is not a means to higher political end. It is itself the highest political end."
– Lord Acton

Assuming anyone on the left bought this book, let alone read this far, they probably assume I am a hack spilling Republican propaganda. Many of those people would have one burning question. Why support Republicans over Democrats? After all we know that Democrats support minorities, gay rights, abortion rights and aren't looking to ban books. I'm not going to go tit for tat on Republican vs. Democrat. Neither side is perfect. The simple answer concerns where they stand on controlling freedoms. Democrats go after the controlling freedoms far more aggressively than Republicans. Too many Republicans lack a backbone when it comes to standing up for freedom. More often than not, enough Republicans decide to compromise by constantly agreeing to some form of Big Government expansion, instead of the other side agreeing on a compromise of how much to shrink government.

Think I don't know what I'm talking about in regard to the main political parties and freedom? Let's recap the controlling freedoms with our first round of big questions. Answer Republican or Democrat.

20. Republicans or Democrats in Pursuit of Freedom?

1. *Which party focuses more on increasing taxes, saying it costs the government money when taxes are cut as though the money belongs to them?* **(Most of us would that neither party focuses on fiscal responsibility.)**
2. *Which party is against allowing individual choice in Social Security, insisting the government must provide for everyone?*
3. *Which party most promotes dependence on government programs, in essence bribing voters with the programs to help keep their politicians in office?*
4. *Which party promotes an economic model that increases power and dependence on the political class (socialism) over one that more largely promotes individual freedom and prosperity (capitalism)?*
5. *Which political ideology actively tries to ban free speech on college campuses under the justification that it is hate speech?*
6. *Which party has actively opposed making elections as free from fraud as possible in the name of making it easy to vote as possible?*
7. *Which party screams about tyranny of the other side, but actively promotes disarming citizens to prevent them from standing against tyranny?*
8. *Which party looks to actively control every aspect of how individuals can get healthcare?*
9. *Which party opposes school choice for its citizen's children?*

The Freedom Scale

10. Which party promotes taxpayers paying for higher education?

11. Which party has and is actively pursuing measures to eliminate the two-party system on the federal level?

All eleven questions directly address the controlling freedoms addressed earlier with the answer to each question being Democrat. It has gotten to the point where Democrats in office don't even try to hide their position anymore on the above questions, and for any freedom-loving American, that should be scary.

When asked about freedom, and how Democrats support it, it comes down to a number of issues where many don't bother to look below the surface. From my experience, most rely on talking points to respond on these issues, instead of debating pure facts. That is usually a dead giveaway that people aren't thinking for themselves. Look at the main examples from those talking points.

There is the issue of abortion, where the personal responsibility aspect of two mutually informed adults having consensual sex is generally ignored, and the most extreme and rare cases are brought up in every discussion to argue in favor of it. We have the issue of gay rights, which became such a non-issue for most that transgenderism and drag shows for children took center stage. Next is the modern feminist movement, whose arguments are so strong, the average modern feminist cannot tell us what rights men have that women don't, and often the argument is shut down by using the term *mansplaining*. Finally: Calling selective choice of what books are appropriate for what age in

20. Republicans or Democrats in Pursuit of Freedom?

what libraries book bans when no books have been banned from being sold, bought or read by those on the right to any adult by any government in the United States.

I have heard few substantiated facts from Democrats who accuse Republicans of planning to radically subvert individual freedom, let alone control freedoms. Most are from radically religious politicians, who have nowhere near the support that Democrats would have us believe. They have made ridiculous claims on a variety of issues such as voter suppression which was discussed earlier. My opinion is that they are projecting in childish ways. Sometimes they say, "Yeah but Republicans do this" as justification, or they project and make a pathetic case of, "I know you are, but what am I?"

That is the best I have seen Democrats come up with, and I have been looking for years, reading their arguments and trying to find common ground, not to mention logical debate. That is one great thing about the internet. You are able to get people's true feelings because they feel emboldened addressing strangers while feeling secure hiding in their home behind the keyboard. The sad fact is many don't value freedom as much as they value what makes them feel good and righteous. It doesn't matter if they proceed from false assumption or even outright lies. In their mind they and their elected officials know what is best for us.

More important than those issues, assuming for a moment Democrats are advocating individual freedom in all of those ways they claim to champion, we still have one burning question. How important are those issues in comparison to the controlling freedoms?

The Freedom Scale

What good is equal pay for equal work, if more than half of one's income is taken away in taxes to feed the reckless spending desires of the political beast? What good is freedom of speech if nobody thinks to question or dares to speak out against the narrative because of the consequences or because they have only been conditioned to think a certain way? What good are elections if we can't get the reassurance that everything is 100 percent legitimate because one side looks to obstruct all attempts at conclusively proving the results? What good is standing up to tyranny if we are unable to fight it with the necessary tools because the tools are made illegal? How free can a nation be if the government can leverage what its citizens need in exchange for compliance?

As much as I try, I cannot see why the issues of abortion and book bans from school libraries for example, rank so high in importance to many voters on the left as they both have flawed arguments in supporting them on the Freedom Scale. Both issues seem insignificant to the logical freedom lover in comparison to the controlling freedoms. The less significant freedoms are where power-hungry politicians of any party want the attention of the people. Keep them focused on the insignificant, or what makes them feel good about themselves, and they don't pay attention to the most significant freedoms being stripped away.

Now let's move beyond political parties. The issue is individual freedoms and not party politics. Forget looking at yourself as a Republican, Democrat, Independent or whatever. It is time to be completely party neutral and focus on individual liberty with the final two rounds of questions. Here, your critical thinking

20. Republicans or Democrats in Pursuit of Freedom?

will be challenged on many fronts, and you will finally answer the ultimate question. How much . . .

21. ...Do You Support Real Freedom?

Proposals/Positions/Legislation Questions

In asking about real freedom, I am asking how much you truly value freedom for yourself and for every other American. The following questions cut to the point for every political issue, and will be uncomfortable for everyone, depending on the specific issue. This will be especially true if you ended up reevaluating any of your positions on the issues as you read this book. Here is where we can move beyond the controlling freedoms and examine things in a much broader sense.

Do you support proposals/positions/legislation of any elected officials in general that does at least one of the following:

1. Eliminates individual choices of the American people?
2. Provides for one group of people at the forced expense of another?
3. Discourages personal responsibility?
4. 4. Encourages or creates dependency on government?
5. Gives the political class more power over the American people at the expense of their individual freedom?

6. *Promotes government-led and government-funded solutions instead of individual solutions to problems in society?*
7. *Overrides a parent's choice regarding what and how their underage children are taught?*
8. *Allows permanent infringement on the natural development of children under 18.*

Power-hungry politicians, promote at least one of the above in the legislation they support as all eight follow a model for big government. To them government is the answer. The elected officials who have at least some proposals/positions/legislation that don't to do any of the above are the ones we need to look to in a free society, as all of these questions address the foundational needs of freedom discussed at the beginning of the book. Individual Choice, Personal Responsibility, and Privately Owned Property. I have asked these specific questions multiple times on social media of people on both sides of the aisle, with only one response directly given by a Democrat, and even that one failed to meet the criteria. Whatever party you support, compare these questions to the policies they support, and it will show their real thoughts on freedom. Even more so, the answers to those questions are the standard for making a test of the Freedom Scale. More on that in moment.

First, consider the fact that many fail and/or refuse to look closely at our freedoms being surrendered. The power-hungry politicians are winning, and constantly achieving their goal with the public. But why is that? There is a long list, but the primary reason can be summed up easily. It is the entitlement mindset;

dependency on government continues to become the new norm. Those people don't want the independence of freedom and figuring things out for themselves. They want the government to fix their problems in a way that makes them feel good about themselves. Even if their problems aren't fixed, it doesn't matter. Failure can always be blamed on the other side.

A specific movie quotation sums up that government dependence best.

> *"You have to understand, most of these people are not ready to be unplugged. And many of them are so inured, so hopelessly dependent on the system, that they will fight to protect it."*
> *– Morpheus, The Matrix*

Why do you think we see so many career politicians when most people on both sides agree that many politicians are scum? Too many people today are far more interested in how their favored candidates are going to make their life easier with a new government program; or how much they hate the candidate of the opposing party instead of asking how either candidate plans to protect or restore our individual freedom. This may be why we saw practically no mention of freedom in a serious and lasting manner, until around 2020. Even then, in many cases we saw a blatantly hypocritical view of freedom that continues to this day. It isn't a top issue. When it is, it often involves matters that are not controlling freedoms.

For me, controlling freedoms are always the top issue, and are the types of questions I look at when deciding whom to vote for. Is it always the candidate who checks off the most boxes related to freedom? If it is between Republicans or Democrats, then *yes*. If it is between one of those two and a third-party candidate, then *no*. Looking practically at elections, it is almost always between Republicans or Democrats as to who will be the victor, so if the Republican is not much better than the Democrat in supporting freedom or vice versa, I hold my nose and vote for the lesser of two evils. If both are just as bad, I either don't vote or vote for the third-party candidate that best supports freedom. That is one reason why voting in the primaries is so important.

This doesn't change my mind regarding what I hold dear or makes me a hypocrite. I see it as buying time to save freedom when I choose the lesser of two evils, the same way a tourniquet helps buy time to save the life of someone bleeding to death. Once the lesser of two evils is in, especially if that person's views are more in line with freedom, you must push back on them if they step out of line. Hold them accountable. If you don't address what is unacceptable with your party and deal with it, opting instead to make excuses, then you are the problem.

Let's say in our hemorrhaging analogy that the freedom in our nation is the body, and the main political parties are the limbs. The tourniquet gives you time to save your party. This is addressing the wound and fixing it. Remove the tourniquet without addressing the wound, is refusing to see anything wrong with your party until the body will dies. Another option is to keep the tourniquet on and ignore the wound. Eventually, that limb stops working for the body and turns gangrenous. This string of events equates to your party turning into something that can't be saved

The Freedom Scale

and kills the body in the process. Either way the result is the same with freedom dying unless the issues are addressed.

If you ignore the problem on your preferred limbs, because of the other party, it is the same as keeping the tourniquet on for your side indefinitely. Standing up to your preferred party, sends a message to those politicians about what their constituents find acceptable and what they don't. This is one of the main reasons why it is so important for politicians to control what we think. They don't want that kind of pushback. Pushing back may take more time with the party and may not happen with specific candidates, but it will happen. That is another reason why primary elections are so important, and it does work. Just ask Liz Cheney who was the incumbent for the House of Representatives in Wyoming. She lost her primary reelection bid by double digits for 2022 because her constituents pushed back because of her actions.

I could end this chapter here, but I have a gift every one of you, I hope you all will utilize it to some degree in the future. I want to give a way and rate yourself on the Freedom Scale, to see where your values truly lie. If this book helped give you a better appreciation for freedom, let it be a way to look past the smooth talking of politicians if they start to draw you back in.

This is where the following sample quiz comes in. Remember the eight proposals/positions/legislation questions from earlier in the chapter? Ask yourself those eight questions again after **each** of the *Issues* questions to verify where you stand, especially if your answer depends on other factors.

- If the answer to an *Issues* question is a yes, it is a point toward the slavery.
- If the answer to an *Issues* question is a no, and the answer is no to all eight *proposals/positions/legislation* questions, it is a point towards liberty.
- If the answer to an *Issues* question is no, and the answer is yes to any of the *proposals/positions/legislation* questions, it is a point towards slavery as hypocrisy is exposed.

All of the *Issues* questions are simple yes or no and they are off of the top of my head for each chapter, with no deep digging. To rate your performance on the Freedom Scale, start in the middle of the scale. For each question answered, move it one spot in the appropriate direction, and see what happens. I highly recommend reading each of the following questions carefully. You will soon see why.

The Issues Questions

Do you support:

1. Being taxed in a manner that is dictated, and you must pay with no choice?
2. A specific wage mandate that must be paid to an employee based on what certain people believe is acceptable with the employer given no say in the matter?
3. Unions for government agencies or departments, where union members can vote for elected officials?

The Freedom Scale

4. Union dues being contributed to politicians and political parties with the individual union member having no say?
5. Taxpayer subsidies for businesses?
6. Excessive and complex regulations for businesses over minimal and simple regulations?
7. Being able to freely opt out of Social Security in favor of a retirement plan of your choice with the individual taking full responsibility for this decision?
8. The government being allowed to silence speech in any way that does not specifically and directly incite or call for violence or panic?
9. The government or any extension of it being able to silence any speech they deem is misinformation?
10. Measures making it easier to vote when the measures may sacrifice election integrity beyond a reasonable doubt.
11. Having to accept the results of an election, without a fully detailed, bipartisan forensic audit of the vote when the result is highly questioned regardless of the party who is questioning it?
12. The government limiting the kind of small arms that are legal for law abiding citizens based on any public opinion or the personal opinions of elected officials?
13. The government being able to hold any manufacturer responsible for deaths caused by the use of their products, which are not malfunctions, but are due to the actions of individuals?

...Do You Support Real Freedom?

14. Politicians from any political party controlling healthcare and requiring the citizens to participate?
15. Healthcare as a human right as opposed to a service?
16. School or government officials having the final say about what their children are taught in public schools regardless of the opinions of the majority of parents?
17. Requiring taxpayer funded public schools over some kind of school choice program for grades K-12?
18. No-strings-attached-taxpayer funded college tuition?
19. Taxpayer funded subsidies for colleges?
20. Any amount of government regulations?
21. Any form of government taxation?

How did you rate in supporting freedom based on these questions? I must confess this is a much simpler format than I originally intended. The goal is to get people to think. The question format does not need to be overly complicated to get people to think and to get direct answers. Complicated surveys often annoy people and take away their willingness to participate. Politicians, when writing bills often use too many words. It would make sense if that were done to conceal the specifics.

The grading scale for this quiz, I made extra easy. Every question answered yes is a vote against freedom. In fact, the last two questions were added with an answer of no needed to prevent slipping into anarchy. Anyone scoring a 19 is at maximum sustainable freedom. Congratulations if this is you. Scoring in the middle is literally straddling the fence on whether freedom or slavery is preferred. I don't consider that a position to be proud

The Freedom Scale

of. These 21 questions were a sample test. I encourage other individuals to write more questions using the same format and start questioning others. I don't care who does this or on what platform although I would love to see a standardized freedom test that must be answered by everyone running for office, and then used in debates. Write the questions on one issue or spread them out over a wide variety of issues as I did here. The objective is making freedom a central topic of discussion again, which is long overdue. Let politicians defend their positions approached from the angle of freedom where there is a final tally of where they rank on the Freedom Scale. Let their past positions on the issues back them up. The more questions, the better. Ask the questions in a manner that allows people little wiggle room to dance around questions. Keep it yes or no answers. Doing otherwise allows people to more easily lie to themselves and to others.

22. The Resolve for Freedom

"Our future is not cast in stone. It does not have to be this way. It does not have to be that the greatest American generation is behind us. It does not have to be that our children will have a lower standard of living. It will be that way if we choose to believe that. I choose not to believe that."
– Glenn Beck, Conservative Political Action Committee 2010

I have written things in this book that amount to observations, and I have asked many questions that have never been considered in a conscience manner by many. I have also written a number of solutions for how we as individuals and as a country can better embrace freedom. Some people will look at what I wrote and roll their eyes.

Others will look at what I wrote and may agree with a large percentage of it, but figure any significant change needed is far-fetched and has no chance of succeeding, so what is the point of pushing all this? You may be right. I don't have all the answers. I am a simple, blue-collar man. As knowledgeable as I am in politics, I am by no means a great political genius with political science and economic PhDs behind my name.

I am however smart enough to know two important things. The way back to more freedom isn't through more power and influence for the political class. A method back to more freedom that doesn't follow the Freedom Scale in a fair and consistent manner, will be doomed to fail. Smart politicians will say otherwise, as they can always make the excuse for one more exception, and believe me, they will. Keeping or slightly adding government influence that violates the Freedom Scale because you feel you and others may benefit from it, highlights hypocrisy. Whether or not you think it was well intended is irrelevant. We know what the road to Hell is paved with. I think most people prefer favorable *results* and *accountability* from our elected officials. That is the great thing about personal responsibility being part of the foundation of true individual freedom. If politicians are held accountable for the consequences of their policies passed into law, we would likely get more workable results and a lot less interference in our lives. If those politicians left us to our own devices while ensuring individual freedom, their hands could be clean.

Many still think that it is impossible or too difficult in this day and age to retake lost liberties. They believe we will never regain the freedom we have lost or stop politicians from grabbing more, so we might as well settle for the lesser of two evils at every turn, as all we can do is slow the power grab. No, it is not all we can do. This is the importance of resolve. I am willing to bet despite a roughly 50/50 split in this country of the two main parties, far more Americans prefer freedom, but they don't act on it for a variety of reasons. It could be they are politically uninterested and take freedom for granted. Maybe they are convinced the ends justify the means. Maybe they have not thought to ask the right questions or believe everything they are told by certain people.

The Resolve for Freedom

Whatever the reason, if you truly love freedom, keep something important in mind. If you remember nothing else from this book, remember this. Those who prefer that the state control much of our lives and take our freedom for "the greater good" need us freedom lovers, and more importantly they need our compliance. We don't need them. Their way of running things relies on force or the threat of force in some form. Their way involves us being responsible for the lives of others. Their way involves giving to some at the forced expense of others. They are about equity in the outcome of our lives, instead of equality in individual freedom, so they become bigger hypocrites, the higher up the ladder they go.

The way I propose—and the way of those who cherish freedom—involves voluntary cooperation without force or the threat of force. This way involves being responsible for ourselves, our actions, our decisions and our families. Nobody else. This way is receiving only what is mutually agreed upon by all parties based upon informed decisions. This way is about equality under the law. This way gives us opportunity and fairness that is impartial and unbiased. And what can be fairer than succeeding or failing as the master of your own destiny?

Those on the side of tyranny already have too much control of entertainment, the media, and institutions of higher education. With the bullying and fear tactics exercised by the side of tyranny, they count on pushing people who don't agree with them, into a go-along-to-get-along attitude. That is usually enough to get people into submission, as life is already hard enough.

When this happens, freedom is in the most danger. For those

who don't go along, the bullying and intimidation can turn to violence, with that violence eventually escalating to the point where lives are lost. Those people who won't be silenced become enemies of the state and can be beaten, jailed, or even killed. I already gave examples of what Nazi Germany did to those who spoke against the state or even questioned officials in a manner they did not like. Try looking up what other authoritarian nations did.

Most people would lose hope at the point they are jailed for speaking against or questioning their government. While the cause of the underdog is usually seen as lost at this point, it is not always the case. One of the best underdog stories in this country's history turned around when things were at their bleakest.

In the latter half of 1776, the colonials' desire for freedom when fighting the British for independence could have easily been lost. In August of that year, General George Washington had lost New York City to the British. A total of 11,000 colonial volunteers quit the fight between September and December of that year because morale was at an all-time low. If too many more chose to return home when their contracts expired at the end of December, the American Revolution would have ended.

Washington would secure a major victory when crossing the Delaware River, surprising the British that December, but a big morale booster was needed before then. On December 19, 1776, Thomas Paine published The *American Crisis* which would reignite the desire for American independence and freedom.

The Resolve for Freedom

"These are the times that try men's souls. The summer soldier and the sunshine patriot will, in this crisis, shrink from the service of their country, but he that stands it now, deserves the love and thanks of man and woman. Tyranny, like hell, is not easily conquered; yet we have this consolation with us, that the harder the conflict, the more glorious the triumph. What we obtain too cheap, we esteem too lightly: it is dearness only that gives everything its value. Heaven knows how to put a proper price upon it's goods; and it would be strange indeed if so celestial an article as FREEDOM should not be highly rated."
– Thomas Paine, The American Crisis

Paine inspired the colonial army to believe they could succeed against what many considered at the time to be a lost cause as they fought the strongest army in the world. And succeed they did, gaining independence and freedom for themselves, their families and every American citizen today. The cause of the underdog is not always a lost cause. History has shown this time and again.

The United States has not always been perfect in implementing freedom for all, but it has always strived to be better in that regard, from the Civil War to the Civil Rights Act in the 1960s. It is up to us to keep that desire going. Are you the summer soldier/sunshine patriot who will only stand for freedom when it is easy, popular, and guaranteed? Or will you stand unwavering in support of freedom despite the odds against it or in spite of what that stance may cost you?

The first major test for me, was the attempt at forcing the CO-

The Freedom Scale

VID-19 'vaccines' on the American public. I was part of a lawful and peaceful protest outside of one of the hospitals owned by the 'parent' company to my hospital. I helped establish a line of communication with these protestors and people at my hospital. We were unwilling to get the injection. It was made clear to everyone we could possibly lose our jobs as a result of not complying. We held firm, and both the government and our employer backed down. That was after close to half the reluctant people at our employer's hospitals had given in and gotten the jab.

I am proud of that stance I took and would do it again. As a society, we need the resolve to stand up to government. Freedom cannot be achieved by the efforts of one individual; nor is the participation of every individual required. But enough of us must be willing to stand firm, no matter the personal cost, to regain and keep our liberty.

> *"I know I'm asking a lot. The price of freedom is high. It always has been. And it's a price I'm willing to pay. And if I'm the only one, so be it. But I'm willing to bet I'm not."*
> *– Steve Rodgers, Captain America: The Winter Soldier*

This is not a call to violence. We have not reached that point yet, though we are fast approaching it. Until then, follow the example of Rosa Parks and refuse to follow the established norm in a passive manner when it goes against freedom. Act with the ballot box. Go to town hall meetings, and ask the tough questions of your elected officials, especially if you already support them. I can't imagine anything more terrifying for a politician than having their feet held to the fire by loyal constituents instead of their political opponents. That means holding them accountable when they try to steal power at the expense of its citizens' liberty or enrich themselves through their position at our expense. Instead of making excuses for them, vote then out. Don't let partisan politics decide for you; otherwise, that will become their shield. Let freedom be your deciding factor. This is our country, and it's about time for us to take it back to rebuild freedom from the ground up.

We can once again set the example for the rest of the world and hold freedom in the highest regard; to once again be the shining city on the hill that everyone wants to emulate. I want that kind of country back more than ever, not only for my child, but for all of our children and grandchildren. It won't be easy. It will be an arduous road, and like Moses leading the Israelites out of Egypt to the promised land, I may not see the end of that road in my lifetime. But when I look into the face of my little girl, I refuse to let the difficulty ahead deter me from pursuing that road back to freedom. Those that fight for and achieve that goal will be the next greatest American generation, as they will have delivered us from the jaws of tyranny. Will you be a part of that movement? In the words of radio talk show host Larry Elder, "We've got a country to save."